# CRIME ON DEADLINE

D1530999

# CRIME ON DEADLINE

edited by
*Lisa Beth Pulitzer*

BOULEVARD BOOKS, NEW YORK

CRIME ON DEADLINE

A Boulevard Book/published by arrangement with
Lisa Beth Pulitzer

PRINTING HISTORY
Boulevard edition/December 1996

The Putnam Berkley World Wide Web site address is
http://www.berkley.com/berkley

ISBN: 1-57297-175-4

BOULEVARD
Boulevard Books are published by The Berkley Publishing Group,
200 Madison Avenue, New York, New York 10016.
BOULEVARD and its logo are trademarks
belonging to Berkley Publishing Corporation.

PRINTED IN THE UNITED STATES OF AMERICA

10  9  8  7  6  5  4  3  2  1

The eleven stories you are about to read were written by the police reporters who covered them. The named newspaper appearing at the beginning of each chapter is the publication for which the reporter wrote the original news story. The facts of those original stories form the basis for the pieces in this book.

# Acknowledgments

I am deeply grateful to all the people who helped bring *Crime on Deadline* to completion.

Bill, Scott, Diana, Jon, Lynn, Nick, Melvin, Paula, Susan and Yolanda, without your hard work and unwaning enthusiasm this book could never be as wonderful as it is!

To my literary agent, Denise Stinson, who gave me the idea for this book, "Thanks, you're the greatest!"

To Elizabeth Beier, senior editor at Berkley Books, "Thanks for believing in this exciting project!"

And to the great Edna Buchanan, I know I speak for all the reporters involved in the writing of this book when I say, "Thank you. Your participation means everything to us!"

*In Loving Memory of*
*Frances Siegal*

# Contents

# Introduction
## EDNA BUCHANAN

You are about to meet headless corpses, courageous children and stone cold killers. This book was written by the police reporters who know them all.

One of the authors, S. K. Bardwell, a well-educated and intelligent young woman, invited a serial murder suspect to dinner. The thirty year old unsolved murder of a little girl in a choir loft became the haunting obsession of another, former education writer J. D. Mullane. When high school principal Bill Hermann, a former English teacher, changed careers in mid-life, he never dreamed he would soon find himself wandering a dark and desolate Arizona desert in search of a severed head. Or that hours later, he would stumble into a fatal shootout.

They, and the eight others who present their stories here are heroes in the world of journalism. Men and women who witness as much blood, heartbreak and combat on America's streets as war correspondents do at the front. They report from the trenches, from the front on the war we seem to be losing.

The police beat can be messy, stomach-churning and dangerous, but the job has its joys. What pursuit is more noble than seeking the truth and informing the public? Every day is an adventure.

Police reporters listen to the pulsebeat of the community and are the first to know when a plane crashes, a building collapses or a devastating tornado touches down. The adrenaline rush is like no other. It is easy to become hooked on the excitement.

Their beat is a window on the world, a front-row seat on life. It has it all: sex and violence, comedy and tragedy, heroes and villains. Shakespeare would have loved it.

It takes a certain talent to read between the lines of a police report, to decipher police jargon, to approach the bereaved and to do right by the victims. Good police reporters must be sensitive of spirit, tough-skinned and possess survivalist instincts. They visit the morgues, climb the stairs and ride the midnight shift with the cops. A good reporter's consciousness is raised by the plight of the little guy wronged by the system. They know that the ultimate wrong is premature death—at any age. So they blunder into the cross fire; they smell the blood; they gaze, unblinking, into a killer's colorless eyes and listen without flinching.

The best have an eye for detail and a rare gift of being in the right place at the right moment, with the right question. Their secret is timing. They are tireless, they keep their promises and, most of all, they ask "Why?"

Their job is not easy. Nobody loves a police reporter. Many would rather kill the messenger, like the jealous husband who murdered the mailman who delivered another man's love letters to his wife.

Police reporters endure threats, obscene phone calls and

subpoenas, surly editors and stonewalling cops. They duck rocks and bottles and, sometimes, gunfire. They know how to use the phones and scale the barricades. Nobody issues them bullet-proof vests or hazard pay. Armed with only pencils and notebooks, they canvass neighborhoods where even cops fear to tread, capturing for readers the moments that change lives, people and communities forever. They try to piece together what human beings do to themselves and each other, as though that next elusive answer might be the one to finally make sense of it all.

In the process, they survive on coffee, action and vending machine cuisine and suffer from numbing overload, shell shock and post-traumatic stress. Should you doubt for a moment their sense of humanity, read Diana K. Sugg's chapter for rare insight into a brave heart that will never become callused.

These reporters could be interviewing celebrities or safely covering county commission meetings, or write sports or gardening columns instead. But they are not, because what they do is too important, because putting it in the newspaper does work. It can even be a matter of life or death. Read Lynn Bartels, whose stories aroused the public, sounding a clarion call that saved innocent lives. When police reporting works, nothing can diminish the high.

When people ask, "How can you work the police beat?" these writers answer, "How could you not?" In a frustrating world full of useless bureaucrats, traffic jams, voice mail and social agencies that fail us, journalists are among the last people on the planet whose work can make things happen. Nowhere is that power more important than on the police beat. Do the story right and laws can be changed, criminals can be jailed, the innocent freed. A reporter may even be a catalyst for that rarest and most elusive prize of all: justice. Putting it in the newspaper does work.

It is not surprising that a police reporter often feels like Superman or Wonder Woman. He or she can be the public's best friend, because if the press does not inform us, who will? Not the chamber of commerce, not the police and certainly not our politicians.

The authors you are about to read are the men and women who listen to victims, knowing all the while that these unfortunates will probably be victimized again, by the system. They share a passion for trying to right wrongs. They are among the few who can.

Stout-hearted and resourceful, wrapped in cloaks of invincibility, they are on a mission, and they are fearless, mindful only of deadlines. They know that the stories are what counts. Here they are.

# ONE

—m—

# The Execution

## SCOTT BOWLES

### The Hot Springs Sentinel-Record

The day Ronald Gene Simmons stopped killing, a horse was raped in its barn near Hot Springs, Arkansas. I was covering the latter.

As the newest reporter at the *Hot Springs Sentinel-Record,* I was assigned to find out why a transient broke into the barn and, equipped with harnesses and a rope, scaled the animal and violated it. An elderly woman heard the commotion, discovered the assault on her livestock and, against the advice of prosecutors, decided to press charges. The charge made it a public record, a veterinarian report confirmed vaginal burns, and I was on one of my worst stories.

At the last minute, my editors decided the article might be too offensive for our elderly readers and winnowed it to a brief. This was fortunate for two reasons. One, the story itself scared the hell out of me. I had recently left the University of Michigan to take this job, sight unseen, in the heart of Arkansas. If they do this to horses, how do they treat Yankees? While I was born in South Carolina, I was raised a Detroit boy. My knowledge of the deep South was based loosely on the film *Deliverance.*

Second, it spared my name from being attached to the story, which would have been fodder for endless newsroom kidding. My non-drawl and rookie sheen already made me a marked man among the old hands at the paper, and a scoop on a horse's ass wouldn't have helped.

It also gave me time to sit and read the wire reports coming out of the town of Russellville about Ronald Gene Simmons. At the time I had no idea I would meet him, much less watch him die.

The deaths happened this way.

On December 28, 1987, with the Christmas holiday over and the work week under way, Kathy Kendrick was sitting behind the reception desk at the Peel and Eddy law firm in Russellville. She had been at work for about an hour when Ronald Gene Simmons came through the door at 10:17 A.M.

Kendrick, 24, knew Simmons. She had worked with him at Woodline Motor Freight in 1986 before joining the law firm. At Woodline, Simmons made several passes at her, although he was married and had seven children. She spurned him and reported his advances to her superiors.

Embittered with Kathy and work, he had walked off the job after telling his supervisor, Joyce Butts, to "take this job and shove it."

He had then walked into Kendrick's office while she was on the phone. He pressed the hold button.

"I hope you're happy now," he told her and walked off. She didn't see Simmons again until he walked up to her desk at the law firm on December 28.

"May I help you?" she asked.

Simmons, wearing a white cowboy hat, blue jeans and a blue-jean jacket, said nothing. He pulled a .22-caliber pistol from inside his jacket and shot her four times in the head. She died a few minutes after she was rushed to St. Mary's Regional Medical Center in Russellville.

Police had just arrived at the law firm when another call came to the dispatcher, this one from Taylor Oil Company. The time was 10:27; Taylor Oil was twenty blocks from the scene of the shooting.

Arriving at the oil company, officers found the body of J. D. Chaffin on the loading dock. Chaffin, 33, a Russellville firefighter who worked part-time at the oil company, was dead, a single bullet fired point-blank into his eye.

Inside the building, the police found Rusty Taylor lying wounded from a gunshot to the upper chest. Taylor, 38, had been Simmons's boss at Taylor Oil. Chaffin apparently never knew Simmons and was simply in the wrong place at the wrong time.

At 10:39 A.M., police got a report of a third shooting, this one at the Sinclair Mini-Mart, down the highway from Taylor Oil.

Inside the Mini-Mart, police found David Salyer shot in the head and Roberta Woolery shot in the jaw. Both were former coworkers of Simmons. Both survived.

After shooting Butts, Simmons barricaded himself in Woodline's computer room. There he discovered another former coworker, Vicki Jackson, covering on the floor.

"Vicki, get up, I'm not going to hurt you," Simmons said.

Vicki stood up.

"Gene, please don't shoot me."

"I'm not going to hurt you," he said. "But why haven't you come down to Sinclair and seen me before? Why haven't you been to see me?"

"Oh, Gene, I've been down before," she said, trying to calm him. "You just wasn't in there when I've been there."

"Well, you know I just work on weekends," he said.

"I've been in there. You just haven't been there."

"Well, I'm not going to hurt you," he said. "I just want you to call the police. Call an ambulance for Joyce and call the police. I'm going to turn myself in to you. I want to turn myself in to you because you've never done anything to me."

"Gene, what is going on?"

"Nothing," he said. "It's all over now. I just want to turn myself in. Call the police." He tried to hand Jackson his pistol.

"Gene, I don't want to touch it," she said. "Just lay it on the desk there."

"Do you want your cigarettes?" he asked.

"Yes."

He went into her office and brought back the pack.

"Gene, what is going on?"

"Nothing now," he responded. "Everything is all over with. I just wanted to kill Joyce. I just wanted to kill Joyce. I don't want to hurt nobody else. Just call an officer."

When dozens of them arrived, Simmons came out peacefully and silently. Before they knew what had happened at Simmons's secluded farmhouse, officers speculated that they were dealing with a fired employee gone berserk.

But Simmons was different from the outset. He was so unresponsive to their initial queries that detectives thought he was deaf. He stared at his jail cell wall for hours, refusing to discuss the shootings with investigators or even his own attorneys.

He also wouldn't talk about his family or even if he had one. Detectives noticed that whenever they brought up the subject, his eyes became furtive. His lips trembled.

As they bore in on the line of questioning, an increasingly nervous-looking Simmons was making detectives edgy.

Finally, officers descended on Simmons's home in Ward, Arkansas, a double-trailer pauper's castle, surrounded by cinder block and barbed wire and overlooking thirteen acres of land.

The spread was a dump. Two rotting outhouses flanked the trailer. Garbage, toys and old furniture were scattered in the yard. The thirteen acres of land were wild, the grass and leaves around the home unkempt.

That is, except for a carefully raked plot of dirt, about 150 feet from the trailer. It was covered by a piece of tin and was centered over a four-foot square crisscross of barbed wire. The smell from the seven decomposing bodies hit officers hard when they removed the metal and began to dig into the earthen grave.

Inside the house were five more corpses. Two bodies—infants—in a car trunk.

In all, authorities learned, Simmons had killed every member of his immediate family, as well as their husbands, wives and children, over the Christmas holiday. Fourteen in all. He added two more to the body count when he drove into Russellville.

When the victims were finally identified, it was official: Simmons had committed the country's deadliest family massacre ever recorded.

As details of the crimes and pending trial unfolded, the case against Ronald Gene Simmons made him the O. J. of the Ozarks. No event went unreported, no relative, friend, or associate left unharrassed. Problem was, there still weren't many people to interview. Simmons had killed everyone who knew him well and shunned neighbors who had the chance to know him. The former air force sergeant spent his early life on various military bases and moved his family just as often when he became a civilian.

Still, there was no shortage of macabre tidbits. Reports circulated that Simmons raped his youngest daughter and had a child by her, that he shot the adults and strangled the babies, dunking them in barrels of water to ensure they were dead.

The details mesmerized me. Not only because of the horrific nature of the story, but because I was unwittingly being trained to be a police reporter, thanks to an eccentric medical examiner named Dr. William Mashburn.

I joined the paper as a criminal courts reporter, so technically my duties were to focus on crimes after the bodies had been found, after police had made an arrest.

But no one does one thing at a newspaper, especially one as small as the *Sentinel-Record*. While it had a circulation of more than 16,000—formidable in Arkansas—the staff was paper-thin. In addition to courts reporting, I wrote obituaries, covered high school basketball, shot pictures, laid out pages, and was weekend news editor, a job prestigious in title only. Weekend news editor is journalese for one who sits in an empty newsroom trying to understand the police scanner.

And late at night, or perhaps before dawn, I was a police reporter, depending on when Mashburn rousted me from bed.

He rarely identified himself first or said hello. His calls typically began, "There's a body you might want to see."

That often was not the case. Mashburn felt it important that I see any corpse that had exposed internal organs or was missing vital body parts, like a face. Many times he assured me that he was going to make me "the best damn police reporter this city has seen in years," despite my reminders that I was supposed to be a court reporter.

Still, the training was invaluable. My first corpse was a derelict woman who had wandered into the woods and simply lay down to die. Her body was found days after she passed away, and the smell and discoloration of her skin remain disturbingly clear to me. "See the maggots?" Mashburn asked, pointing to her face with a pencil. "It can give you some idea how long she's been out here."

Then: "Put your hand on his rear end," Mashburn instructed me.

"Excuse me?" It was still early in the morning, and I was hoping he had said, "Your lamb is on the mend."

"His ass, son. Touch his back pocket. He's dead. He ain't gonna slap it off."

I reached down, my eyes locked on the small red hole in the small of his back, barely coloring his T-shirt. I felt a wallet.

"That means the killer wasn't looking for money," Mashburn said. "He just wanted to kill him, or maybe he wanted the guy's car or wife. But he didn't need money. A body can tell you a lot, even if it can't say anything." Sure enough, police found the killer the next day on a Tennessee highway, driving the man's van.

And so it went. Mashburn was nothing short of Hot Springs' Quincy, a staple at every crime scene, sliding past police tape to corpses and cops, as involved as any investigator. I never failed to see him at a suspicious death and never saw him get frazzled, frustrated, or shaken by what he had seen.

But a couple of days after the Simmons slaughter, as we talked about a local killing, Mashburn drifted for a moment, the conversation turning to the deaths and the work that lay ahead for his counterpart in Russellville.

"All those bodies, all those kids," Mashburn said. "That's gotta be a terrible sight."

\*　　\*　　\*

After a year at the *Sentinel-Record,* I got what I considered the call to the big leagues: the *Arkansas Gazette.* The Gray Lady—as it was once known for its somber, print-laden appearance—was the largest paper in the state and the authoritative voice in the news, winning the Pulitzer prize in the 1950s for its editorials on school segregation.

Power and prestige were in jeopardy in 1988, though. The tiny *Arkansas Democrat,* owned by local media magnate Walter Hussman, had grown exponentially in the 1980s and was rivaling the *Gazette* in size and influence. It did so by being aggressive, conservative, and at times simply nasty. The paper touted itself as homegrown and ridiculed the *Gazette,* which was owned by the Gannett Corporation, as a soft-feature paper run by out-of-town, out-of-touch news executives.

And they were killing us on the Ronald Gene Simmons story. This was through no fault of our reporting staff. It had more to do with our reporters on the story being male.

Simmons had become a prolific letter writer from his prison cell, sending long, rambling missives to distant survivors of his victims and to certain members of the media—all of them female—promising that he might soon talk about the death of his family.

To the dismay of my editors, Simmons had sent several letters to the *Democrat,* namely, a female reporter there who used the correspondence to turn Simmons into a minibeat, and an effective one. And while Simmons's letters never revealed much about the man, my bosses worried that they soon might.

I was working as a general assignment reporter at the *Gazette,* handling a few crime stories but setting my sights on covering the upcoming governor's race between Bill Clinton and a handful of hopefuls. I had been placed on the campaign team in February 1990 and had finished a profile piece when a telephone call from my sister turned me into a police reporter.

Midway through the evening conversation, Caroline asked me about the man who killed his family, if he had been convicted, if he would be executed. I found myself recounting a number of dramatic events—that he had been convicted and once punched his attorney in the face and tried to escape. That he had said he wanted to die and asked that the execution be carried through as swiftly as possible.

As we spoke, I realized that our newspaper had covered the entire event piecemeal, in episodic stories that updated the reader but had done little to put the massacre in perspective. The next day, after sketching a rough story outline, I asked managing editor John Hanchette to free me for the next three months to cover Simmons's life in one comprehensive article, to run the day before his execution. After a day of consideration he approved the story.

I had just been handed the biggest story in the state and had no idea how the hell to do it.

It was bad enough that Simmons's life would be monumentally difficult to retrace. His house was damned hard to find.

I had no idea where else to start. In retrospect, I could have headed to court, copied transcripts of his trial, gotten names and addresses of witnesses.

But more than anything I wanted to have a feel for where Simmons kept his family under wraps; where the children walked to catch the bus; where Becky Simmons, his wife, tended to chores, the only work Simmons ever permitted her.

Ward, Arkansas, was mainly farm country, a good fifty miles from Little Rock. And like many of the rural paths that corduroy the hillsides there, Broomfield Road had no signs anywhere. Finally, I stopped at a farmhouse where a man was wrestling with a tractor lawn mower.

"Excuse me, can you tell me where Broomfield Road is?"

"You're standing on it."

"Oh. That's good. I'm looking for Ronald Gene Simmons's house. You know where that might be?"

Wrong question. The man laid his wrench on his tractor and pushed back the bill of his cap to get a good look at the pain in the ass before him. The tie must have clinched it.

"Who are you? With the TV? I tell you, since we had all of this happen, we've had people coming here, asking where his home is, if I knew him, what he was like."

Scratch my first three questions.

"Why don't you leave this place alone?" he continued. "You're just looking for gossip. Leave this alone, and it will pass after a while. After a while, you'll find some other bad news."

This is one of the two hardest elements of police reporting: explaining why you want to delve into someone's personal tragedy and chronicle it for thousands of strangers to read. To this day I don't understand why grief-stricken people will talk to a reporter. Perhaps it's cathartic to talk it out with a stranger.

This farmer, however, had had his fill of catharsis—and gravy, for that matter. He was easily as large as his tractor and in no mood for either of us.

I proceeded cautiously, joining him in a damning indictment of television reporters and explaining that I was with the PRINT media. He explained that he found news coverage by the print and electronic media troublingly similar. Actually, he said he didn't give a good goddamn who I was doing the story for, his name wasn't going on the goddamn TV for his goddamn neighbors to see.

I backpedaled, asked if I could simply ask him some questions about Ward. How were neighbors holding up? How long have you been here? What do you do for a living? Eventually, we soft shoed into Simmons, and he began to open up.

This is where I have been luckiest. I'd like to believe interviewees speak to me because of my obvious integrity and insightful questions, but I think it has more to do with looking fifteen. People pity me, assume I will lose my internship if I don't come back with a story and grant me interviews.

Whatever the reason, the farmer told me what little he knew about Simmons and the few discussions he'd had with the man. He went inside to get the names of some neighbors who might know him better. I took off the tie, swearing I'd not wear it again for the duration of the story.

He offered me some iced tea, gave me a handwritten list of neighbors' numbers and pointed out Simmons's land, only a quarter-mile down the road. I told him I couldn't see his trailer, although it was supposed to be massive.

"That's cause we burnt it down two months ago," he said. "People were looting from it, taking stuff as souvenirs. Ain't that the sickest thing? But go down there, and you'll find it. You gotta get a lot closer than this to see."

\*　　\*　　\*

One look at the rubble that was left of Simmons's home and I understood how angry his neighbors must have become, not only at the grisly deaths in their midst, but the media invasion that had followed. They left virtually nothing standing, except for a blackened chimney overlooking the debris. The deep hole where seven bodies were discovered also remained. Ward had once been a town where few neighbors were strangers. Now, few strangers were welcome.

As I walked through the remains, I tried to get an image of the house when it stood. Were the adults running out the door when they were shot or moving to protect the children? It seemed fitting that for all the fury that had been let loose here, everything was charred and broken.

A thirteen-year-old girl came up the gravel driveway and startled me when she spoke. "What are you looking for?" Angie Laymon asked.

I explained that I was doing a story on what happened, and Angie said she went to school with two of Simmons's girls, Loretta and Marianne.

This was too easy, I thought. I had a farmer who provided me a contact list and a girl who sat on the bus with his daughters my first day out. But as Angie spoke, I understood why Simmons was a mystery to police and even neighbors. Everyone feared him.

Angie spoke just like the farmer, as if she had seen Simmons from afar and was afraid of getting too close. I had seen pictures of Simmons and understood this. He had let a beard grow untamed while he was in prison, and his vacant blue eyes were often the only feature truly distinguishable. One witness to the downtown shooting described his "ghostlike grin" as he opened fire. Even Simmons's children seemed to speak of their father in distant terms.

"Loretta was the first girl I knew who was afraid to be around her dad," Angie said. When the topic of family came up, Loretta usually changed the subject to school activities of boys.

Once, on a school bus, Loretta confided that "her mom was much softer than Mr. Simmons was," Angie said. Angie explained that she never got to find out what that meant because Loretta mentioned it before stepping off the bus to begin the Christmas holiday, her last.

For the next several weeks, I was living in paper. There were Freedom of Information requests with the army and the air force, requesting Simmons's military records; his birth records from Chicago; our own stories of the slayings; transcripts from Simmons's trial that would fill phone books. I also sent letter after letter to Simmons himself, promising him the chance to tell the world his story. He never wrote back.

Short of an interview, what I really wanted was a look at the investigative files of the Ward County Sheriff's Department, the agency that arrested Simmons and found the bodies.

But seeing the files meant overcoming the other most difficult obstacle in police reporting: getting a cop to give you the time of day.

This is tough if you have been working the beat for a year. I considered it wishful thinking that I could get to the files in ten weeks. Although Simmons had been convicted and sentenced to death for the murder of the two people in Russellville, he was never tried for his family's murders. While there was nothing illegal in showing me the file on a closed case, police detested the media circus and vigorously guarded the case file.

The gatekeeper was a toughened sheriff named James Bolin, a lumbering man with thinning hair, thick accent, and painfully tight handshake. There was one way to connect to a man who could have been cut out of a Marlboro ad, I decided. I begged daily to see the file.

Bolin was having none of it. He told me that once Simmons was executed, I could have my own personal copy of the file, but not before. He did, however, tell me to pay close attention to the files in court, which were open to the public and might hold more answers than I thought. Especially the names, he said.

So I went back to my personal Simmons file, which had become a fire hazard on my desk, and created a checklist of witnesses and distant relatives interviewed by police. I would interview everyone I could find, I decided, though there were well over fifty names on my legal pad. Somewhere in the middle was Edith Nesby.

Edith must have done these interviews a hundred times. When I first reached her at her Colorado home, she was patient but pat with me. The answers sounded, if not rehearsed, regurgitated. She stated her anger at Simmons, the failure of the system for not investigating reports of abuse and chasing Simmons across the country when he fled incest charges.

I hung up that night more distressed than when I called. I had a few weeks left before the June 26 execution and enough to do a passable story with information gleaned from the court files and interviews with those who knew him peripherally.

But nothing in my notes said much about Simmons— what his childhood was like, how he met his wife, how the relationship turned oppressive. Most importantly, nothing that explained exactly what happened in that house and why.

I called Edith back the next morning and told her that we had to have a real talk. Not about her emotions or the upcoming execution, but about her sister. I asked her if she would take a day to jot down notes, look over photo albums, talk to other relatives—anything that would refresh her memory of Becky and young Gene Simmons.

Edith was understandably hesitant but finally agreed. The next night, as she chain-smoked cigarettes and ignored the television sitcoms blaring in the background, Edith began a three-and-a-half-hour oral history of her family, her sister and the young soldier who swept her off her feet.

For the first time, I felt I was beginning to grasp the story internally. If the court files and police reports had put the bones of the story together, Edith was putting flesh on it, a soul. No doubt about it, though, it was a dark soul.

Becky had met Gene at a USO dance, Edith said, where they had challenged one another in a back room to see who could type the fastest. A quick courtship and marriage followed, as did a child.

But the letters from Becky to Edith illustrated a slow evolution within the growing family. Gene, Becky wrote, was much more possessive a husband than he was a suitor. He exercised more and more control over his wife until, in 1963, three years after they wed, Becky had lost virtually all freedom.

He wouldn't let Becky get a driver's license. There was a telephone in their house, but Gene refused to connect it. Becky could contact her family only by mail. Later he stopped letting her buy stamps or mail letters, so she had to secretly slip letters to others to mail for her. To allow him to read and censor his family's mail Gene kept Post Office boxes in nearby communities—but never close to the family's home.

When he was sent to Vietnam in 1967, Gene sent Becky $15 a month, even though the family now had three children. Becky survived off her parents for food and transportation.

Still, Becky did not complain. She expected hardship in marriage and respected Gene's decisions because he was the breadwinner—even when those decisions dictated her existence.

"You have to understand," Edith told me. "Becky was not stupid by any means, but she was insecure. Ronald had made her believe that things were her fault, that she deserved what she got."

By the end of the evening, my fingers ached from trying to type as quickly as Edith spoke. As we wrapped up the conversation, she went to answer the door. I scrolled through screen after screen of notes. I finally had a picture of Simmons as a young adult, a man whose demons seemed to be surfacing.

But the letters Becky sent seemed to spend little time on Gene as a youth, and months before she died, she was forbidden to speak to Edith at all. Still nothing on the beginning and end of his life. When Edith returned, I asked her about both.

"I don't think I can help you," she said. "She never talked about him being a little boy. I have a hard time believing he ever was one. But did you know Gene had a younger brother? Maybe he could help."

A kid brother. When Edith told me, I was simultaneously angry and elated. If I had checked social services records in Chicago, files might have mentioned Pete, perhaps even contained tidbits about Simmons's family life. But I was two weeks from deadline and had no time to start another paper swap with a bureaucrat.

Edith didn't have Pete's number but said she thought he lived in Los Angeles or San Diego. His last name, which will remain confidential here was somewhat unusual, though there were eight in Los Angeles, three in San Diego.

Pete's name didn't show up in any stories in the *Gazette* or *Democrat,* so either no one knew about him, or he never came forward. I assumed both and decided in the heat of deadline that deceit would be the best way to get Pete to talk to me. I called these strange men, greeting them by their first name, explaining I needed to talk to them about Gene. Deceit got me a few hang-ups, a few dumbfounded responses, and one man who talked about Jean, an aunt who did not massacre her family.

The second listing in San Diego was my man.

"Hello, Pete?"

"Yes"

"This is Scott Bowles. I'm a reporter with the *Arkansas Gazette,* and I'd like to talk with you for a minute about Gene."

"What do you want to know?"

I suddenly realized I hadn't prepared beyond finding Pete. I stammered, rambled a little about the story I was doing and lost him. He said he didn't want to have his neighbors know who his brother was or that he even had a brother, and he was sorry but he wasn't going to help on the story.

I hung up desperate, considering having a more experienced reporter call or perhaps pose as a police detective needing information. As a police reporter, I have often wished my parents had given me the first name Sergeant.

Finally I decided to play hardball, hardly my forte. I phoned Pete back and explained that I was doing a biography of Gene, and his younger brother was a part of that. I said I understood that he didn't want to be associated with the story, but it would be incorrect to say Gene had no siblings.

I offered him a deal. If he would speak to me, I would agree not to identify him except in a laundry list of family members. I would quote him as a family member only. If this wasn't acceptable, I said, I would be forced to write that his brother, Pete, was reached at his San Diego home but refused to comment.

"Let me think about it," Pete said. "Can you call back tomorrow night?"

I called back the next afternoon, the next evening, and finally reached him at night. He said he would speak to me but that I could never fully identify him or even tell my editors his last name or where he lived. "If Gene gets out and gets you, I don't want them sending another reporter after me," he said. He knew the business better than he realized.

And so another chapter of Gene's life unfolded. Pete's description of his older brother was textbook stuff; the loss of his biological father, abuse of animals, the progression to violence against smaller children. It didn't explain what happened December 28 but put it in some perspective.

I was almost ready to write but wanted to take a final stab at interviewing Simmons himself.

Throughout the course of the trial and subsequent sentencing, Simmons made himself available to the press for news conferences with his attorneys. He loved the attention. Nothing substantial ever came from the events, except Simmons's stated readiness to die. He criticized authorities for taking too long to prosecute, too long to punish.

I attended what would be his final press conference, held in the office of his attorney, Irwin Allen.

Same drill: questions why, answers around. He acknowledged some of the female reporters by first name, having corresponded with them. He answered my only question with visible disdain.

As the circus ended and his lawyers motioned for him to be escorted back to their offices, I sidled up as close as I could get, behind two guards, within a crush of microphones and cameras.

"Mr. Simmons, I'm doing a story on you," I blurted.

"Who isn't?" he said. I deserved that.

"No, a story chronicling your life. Would you be willing to sit down and talk with me?"

He never paused, never stopped to acknowledge the voice behind him. "There's nothing you can do for me." And was gone.

He was right, of course. In the ten weeks I had worked on this story, I hadn't done much for anybody except to dredge up the worst moment of their life. I had made at least a half dozen people weep at recalling their loss. I enraged them by having them reread letters from Simmons, as he taunted them, holding out the chance he might explain why he slaughtered sixteen people. I dreaded putting it all in print.

I stopped by Sheriff Bolin's office. Over the weeks we had become not friends, but at least allies in the case. He had discovered seven of the bodies and had confided that he still had nightmares from the discovery. I had acknowledged that this was my first real police story and that I had winged much of it.

He asked me what Mr. Simmons had to say today. Again, I told him, Simmons was in a teasing mood. Nothing about why or how.

I don't recall sounding sullen or looking defeated. I still had enough new facts to write a good story. But something cracked Bolin's shell.

"Come here," he said, standing up. I followed him to a squad room, where several detectives pecked at typewriters. He told me to have a seat at an empty table.

Moments later, two thick manila envelopes landed in front of me. Simmons's name was on both. "Give 'em back when you're done" was all he said before leaving the room.

I whipped through the papers, trying to see everything before they were whisked away. Why hadn't I taken a speed-reading course? I scribbled notes frantically on my pad but moved at what seemed a snail's pace. It was already late afternoon, and I doubted they would let me take the files home.

Finally, I grabbed my tape recorder from my bag, prayed the batteries were fresh and began reading aloud. It took both sides of an hour tape, but on it I had the final piece. Through autopsies and interviews, the details of what investigators believed happened on Broomfield Road were spelled out.

Gene began plotting the murders at least two months before they occurred, when he learned that his wife had had enough and planned to leave him. He had intercepted at least one letter from his wife to her daughter Sheila, who had married and moved out.

"I've been a prisoner long enough," she wrote. "He has mistreated us all long enough, so I don't feel any pity for him and being alone is what he deserves. All this will take time but I don't want to continue this life with Fatso."

Not long after, Gene ordered his youngest children to dig a deep pit outside, telling them it would be used for another outhouse.

On the morning of December 22, Simmons's school-aged children left for the last day of classes before the Christmas break. Becky was sleeping in one room of the mobile home.

His son, Gene, Jr., 26, and Gene Jr.'s daughter, Barbara, 3, had visited for the holiday and were asleep in another bedroom. Little Gene had driven from his home in San Antonio, Texas, to pick up his daughter, who had been staying with her grandparents before the holidays.

Simmons attacked his wife first, hitting her with a crowbar, killing her or rendering her unconscious.

Little Gene may have awakened. Evidence indicated that he had started to get up from the bed when his father hit him in the neck and head with the crowbar, splattering blood on the wall and ceiling.

Only injured, he struggled with his father for the crowbar, but Simmons pulled out his .22-caliber pistol and shot his son four times in the head and once in the stomach.

Simmons strangled his granddaughter with an electrical cord, then returned to his wife's bedroom and shot her twice in the head.

Next he waited for the schoolchildren to come home.

When they arrived, police believed, Simmons told them to wait outside. Then he brought them in one by one and strangled them with an electrical cord.

Simmons then carried the seven bodies to the grave and dropped them in. He soaked them with kerosene to mask the odor of decaying flesh and covered the grave with barbed wire to keep animals out.

For the next four days, he waited around the house for more relatives.

On December 26, his son Bill Simmons, his wife, Renata, and their son, Trae, 20 months old, arrived. Simmons apparently shot the adults as they sat at the dining room table. He strangled Trae with the electrical cord and dunked the body in a barrel of water to make sure he was dead.

Later that day, his daughter Sheila and her husband, Dennis, arrived with their children, Sylvia, 6, and Michael, 21 months. Sheila and children apparently came in first, and Simmons shot her six times in the head. Police believed Dennis ran inside when he heard the shots. His father-in-law shot him once in the head.

Sylvia fled into a bedroom and covered herself with blankets. Simmons followed her, pinned her arms with his legs and strangled her with the cord. He then picked Michael up off the floor and, for reasons authorities do not know, used fishing wire to strangle him before dunking him in water.

He put the two babies' bodies in trash bags before placing them in the car trunks. He left the other bodies in the house where they fell, covering them with coats and blankets so that he wouldn't have to look at them.

That night, he drove to the Sears store in Russellville, picking up Christmas gifts that had been ordered through the catalog.

Then he waited out the weekend, driving into Russellville on Monday.

I brought the files back and thanked Bolin. Again. And again. He told me not to get his ass in a sling. I think I grunted an assurance.

The drive to Little Rock took forever. I was ready to write. I knew I had the details I needed for the story, which I outlined in my head, recounting the interviews, the files, the brief exchange with Simmons. And for the first time, I realized that perhaps I had too many details. I wanted Gene Simmons to die.

I had done only a handful of police stories, but I knew that my feelings had blatantly crossed the line of objective reporting. I had become too involved with some surviving relatives, whom I occasionally called simply to update them with news of the execution. Their fear had become my fear: that Simmons, who had never asked for an appeal, would do so on the execution table, sending the execution into a tailspin of appeals, allowing him more letters, more news conferences, more Simmons.

I couldn't write that night. I left all my notes at the paper and decided to skip work on Friday, taking the weekend to consider my options. I could tell my editors, who had given me unprecedented freedom to pursue the story, that I failed and there wasn't an epic story after all. I could drastically cut the space they offered me, keeping it a bare-facts retelling of the deaths before his execution.

Over the weekend, I kept my fears to myself but bounced the events of the story off my best friend and photographer at the paper, Spencer Tirey. Finally, I conceded that I might be in too deep to see the story objectively.

He shrugged off the concern with a wave. A Texas country boy, Spencer's advice was usually simple, nearly always right. Better to be too deep in a story, he said, than too far away from it.

I started the story on Monday, worked through the night and finished three days later. With only a few changes to the text, we ran a 250-inch story Sunday, June 25, the day before Ronald Gene Simmons was to die by lethal injection.

When I look back on the story now, the style seems a little crude, with many sentences wordier than they need to be. There is some shock within it; it reeks of a police reporter covering one of his first big stories, still a little unnerved by the violence he's covering. It is the best story I have written.

We sent a team of reporters to the Arkansas state penitentiary to cover Simmons's execution. I was among them, still exhausted from the opus that ran Sunday.

When I walked into the press room, I was greeted with handshakes and congratulations from reporters I had never met. Some asked where I got the information, interested in follow-up articles, but most realized the story would die when he did.

The plan was to station a reporter at every center of activity at the prison: outside the entrance, where death-penalty protesters had lined up; in the press room, to interview execution witnesses; and with key players in the death . . . attorneys, prison officials, relatives.

I was to write the main story, collecting reports. I sat at a press table, jotting notes as members of the media voted on who would witness the execution.

At Arkansas executions, two members of the media are allowed to witness and then return to the press pool to brief the other reporters. Tradition has it that one member of the Associated Press is voted in, along with a reporter from the town where the crime occurred. I assumed that a reporter from Russellville or Ward would be allowed in.

But when I heard a reporter from the rival *Arkansas Democrat* moan, I looked up and saw our managing editor, Max Brantley, walking toward me. He pointed, grinned and said, "You're in."

I became cold. This was not going to be like the bodies

William Mashburn showed me in Hot Springs, I assumed.
I didn't know what it was going to be like.

The reporters and editors huddled and restructured our
coverage. I was to write a first-person account of the execution, so it was essential, Brantley told me, that I make
notes on everything that happened in the death chamber,
no matter how innocuous. That was assuming the feeling
had returned to my extremities.

Bill Simmons—no relation—the veteran bureau chief
of the AP, set me down at a table before we were escorted
away. He was a wonderful, calming presence, having witnessed these deaths before, and he told me what to expect.

I forgot every word when we filed into the death chamber and a guard handed me a vomit bag.

We were seated in two rows of seven chairs on a hard
ceramic floor, facing a long glass blocked by a black curtain. I wrote down the names of everyone there, including
myself. Every motion, every noise went down in my notebook. That night I saw I had written that someone burped.
I still don't know who.

After a few comments by the prison director, we were
left alone in the witness room. A few people whispered.
I concentrated on steady breaths.

One thing about executions: they're punctual. I looked
at my watch, watched the hands move to exactly 9:00 P.M.
Suddenly my watch glowed white, as did the rest of the
room when the curtains whisked open.

Simmons lay strapped in a gurney about eight feet in
front of me. Two intravenous bottles hung over his head.

He looked straight up, into the fluorescent lights of the
chamber, blinking frequently.

Simmons was covered from chin to toe in a white sheet,
with his arms bare and strapped to his side. Catheters were
in each arm.

"I'd say he's pretty well strapped in," one of the witnesses in the front row said.

"He's not a very big man, is he?" another whispered to himself.

The prison director, standing before Simmons, spoke to him, asking if he had any final remarks. Perhaps wanting to confound the living when he left, he said only, "Justice delayed, finally be done, is justifiable homicide."

At 9:02 P.M., the prison director walked behind a door, and Simmons lay there, glancing about him. His head, held tight by a brown leather strap, was unable to move, but he tried to glance about him at the executioner's room.

He then looked once to his right, toward the witnesses. And I could tell Simmons was, perhaps for one of the first times in his life, scared. His eyes were wide, straining to see something, anything, that might let him know what was coming.

So was I. Everything I had learned about this man over the past three months was forgotten: the killings, the pain left in his wake. Of all the deaths that Christmas holiday, the one that bothered me most—that one that most wanted me to see Simmons die—was Sylvia's, the little girl who waited under bed covers to be finished off. The knowledge of dying has to be worse than the act. Now all I could do was wonder what it must be like to be on that gurney, waiting for the fire to pump through your veins.

His eyes returned to the ceiling.

At 9:05 P.M., there were two loud clicks, like from a transformer. Simmons called out "Oh, oh," and began to cough. His eyes shut. He seemed to nod off, as if to sleep.

His body, though, continued to shake, from coughs and convulsions that shook the gurney for four minutes afterward. His fingers and face began to turn purple.

Some witnesses stood to get a better look. Others didn't look at all. I tried to keep an eye on Simmons, another on the witnesses. By 9:10 P.M., Simmons was either dead or at death's door. He didn't move. Neither did we. Four minutes later, he was pronounced dead, and the curtains shut. There would be no appeal.

I wish I hadn't sworn off the tie. Not expecting to be the target of reporter's questions, I had worn jeans and a knit short-sleeve shirt to fend off the June swelter. I looked like a reporter who had just covered an execution for the high school weekly. The first question a television reporter asked me was whether I was legally old enough to witness an execution. Her interview was brief.

The rest of that night was a blur. After a half dozen interviews, I rushed off to write our paper's account of the execution. I drove to the paper, looked over our coverage and went home to stay awake through the night.

A week later I went back to the prison to visit Simmons's grave, an unmarked plot in the prison cemetery. No one had come forward to claim his body, though his gun would later be hot property on the auction block.

From the day of the execution forward, I was a police reporter for years to some. Editors decided I had a knack for crime, and I decided to try to hone a beat.

Maybe it worked. I have covered literally hundreds of bodies, learned the language of cops, taught myself not to flinch at blood, at violence, at what people are capable of. Then again, maybe that means it hasn't worked. I worry sometimes that the naiveté I brought to the Simmons story would improve stories I've done years later. Because I'm not shocked doesn't make a thing less shocking.

Since then, I've also worried less about bringing my own perspective to a story. Perhaps asking personal questions can bring personal answers beyond who died and how. Maybe they get the why.

It can be frustrating. Gene Simmons took that answer to the grave. As we walked out of the witness chamber, I cornered Sheriff Bolin and asked him if he was glad it was over. He said when he stopped dreaming about the bodies, it would be over for him. Then I asked him if he had any theories why Simmons decided that everyone he once loved must die.

Bolin thought about it, dragged on his cigarette and offered this: "I think when you get down to it, Gene was just mean."

I've yet to hear a better explanation.

**Scott Bowles**, 31, is currently a staff writer at the *Washington Post*. He was born in Charleston, S.C., and grew up in Detroit, receiving his degree in history from the University of Michigan. Before joining the *Post* in 1994, he worked as a police reporter for several papers, including the *Atlanta Journal-Constitution* and the *Detroit News*. In 1992, he won the Al Nakkula Award for Police Reporting for, among other stories, coining the term "carjacking" in an investigative project in August 1991.

# TWO

## Dead Prostitutes

### MELVIN CLAXTON

### *The Virgin Islands Daily News*

The newsflash stopped me dead in my tracks.

"There are unconfirmed reports that twenty-eight prostitutes suffocated while being smuggled into the Virgin Islands in a shipping container," the radio announcer said. "According to an unidentified source, the bodies were dumped at sea by the crew of the vessel."

The announcer read the report as if it was an item from Ripley's Believe It or Not. I couldn't blame him, the story had hoax written all over it.

The French newspaper *Le Martin* broke the dead prostitutes story on April 5, 1985. The report created quite a buzz in Paris.

It was a bombshell in the U.S. Virgin Islands.

The prostitutes, Dominican Republic natives living in St. Martin, died while being smuggled into the Virgin Islands in a sealed shipping container, the French newspaper reported.

The newspaper named no sources and never identified the victims. But that didn't stop the story from spreading like a bad case of the flu.

Pretty soon just about everyone, including such

venerable news agencies as the Associated Press and Reuters, were looking into it. Law enforcement agencies on several Caribbean islands also joined the investigation.

The story piqued my curiosity from the start, even though I doubted its authenticity.

It had everything: unscrupulous smugglers dealing in human cargo, dead bodies that couldn't be found and enough unresolved issues for an entire episode of *Unsolved Mysteries*.

With FBI, Customs and Immigration agents helping local police, Virgin Islanders anxiously waited to see if the story was true or an elaborate fabrication.

Jacques Cannezal, the *Le Martin Caribbean* stringer who broke the story, refused to name his source. He insisted, however, that the source was very credible.

But after considerable poking and nosing around, law enforcement agencies and a small army of reporters didn't find a single shred of evidence that any part of the story was true.

Veteran reporters bolstered their position that the story was simply a macabre hoax by pointing out that not one concerned, anguished relative had come forward demanding answers.

Yet I couldn't quite put the story aside.

I may have been the new kid in the newsroom, fresh out of college, but from where I was sitting the hoax story just didn't add up. There was something about it that gnawed at me, something I thought all those highly-trained investigators and reporters had overlooked.

Now all I had to do was figure out what that thing was.

At *The Virgin Islands Daily News* our first piece on the prostitutes was an eight-inch wire story on an inside page. A day later, we ran a more detailed story quoting federal and local law enforcement officials as saying they were investigating, but that the whole thing was probably a hoax.

*The Daily News* is a tiny daily with a staff of six reporters. Back then our circulation was about 11,000 on a good day, and there weren't too many of those. Yet we prided ourselves in tackling just about anything that came our way, and everything and anyone were fair game.

I was working with the newspaper part-time when the story broke. Two months later—two weeks after I left college—I became the newspaper's sixth full-time reporter.

Just days after joining the staff, I was in Managing Editor Penny Feuerzeig's office discussing the dead prostitutes story. Penny is a former investigative reporter who gets visibly excited about a good story.

What doesn't excite her is a story that requires so much digging that it takes time from the reporter's other stories. This one was clearly a "digger."

I told her I didn't think we should write off the story as a hoax just yet, and that I wanted to spend some time looking into it.

Penny pursed her thin lips for a moment, then gave her stock response: a tiny newspaper with just a handful of reporters doesn't have the luxury of investing a lot of time and effort in a story when there is a distinct possibility that it might not pan out.

It was a line I had heard many times before, but this time it had a convincing ring.

We compromised. I agreed to approach the story from a broader angle, making the dead prostitutes part of a comprehensive look at prostitution in the territory. Within minutes of leaving the meeting I was drafting my project outline.

This was my second major project with the newspaper,

and I learned from the first one—a series on public housing done as an intern—that outlines are at best poorly drawn road maps. To follow them blindly is to ignore new leads and information uncovered along the way—the stuff that often gives an investigative piece its zing.

A week later, outline in hand, I met with Penny again. In less than thirty minutes I had the green light, and the prostitution project was on.

I would discover just how degrading and sordid the world of prostitution really was. A world that was far uglier—and a hell of a lot more dangerous—than I first imagined.

From the start, I was forced to juggle my prostitution investigation with daily assignments, no mean feat since reporters were expected to produce at least three stories a day.

When I asked Penny to cut me some slack, she appeared genuinely surprised.

"The brothels are opened at night and you work on your stories at day," she told me. "Why would you need time?"

For some unknown reason, the words "sweat shop" kept coming to mind.

So after work I would rush home to shower and grab a bite to eat, then head for the brothels. A daily routine that did little for my social life.

Although prostitution is illegal in the Virgin Islands, brothels operate openly and freely. Most are in the heart of the territory's main towns and I even found one less than a hundred yards from a police station.

The situation begged the question: Why were the police and other law enforcement agencies not doing more to fight prostitution? Were they just turning a blind eye because they were overwhelmed by other crime?

I sought answers. I believe the ones I found shocked many of our readers. I know they surprised me.

But I am getting ahead of myself.

After getting approval for the project, I spent a week doing background work. This included surveillance of brothels and preliminary checks of police and court records.

Then it was time for hands-on research—in a manner of speaking.

On a muggy Friday night in June, I paid my first visit to a house of prostitution, the popular Clarysol Bar on St. Thomas. The Clarysol, in the center of the capital, was a two-story affair with a bar on the first floor and rooms upstairs where the girls worked.

The landlord, Candida Santiago, was a former hooker with an attitude. She lived on the premises and ran a tight operation.

Just weeks after my visit, she was brutally murdered by her live-in boyfriend who then took his own life. The police later assured me that her murder had nothing to do with my visit or the interview I had with her days later.

On June 19, 1985, Candida Santiago was very much alive and so was the brothel she ran.

That night, as I stepped through the open doorway and into the noisy bar, I was struck by the smell—a pungent mixture of cheap liquor, stale cigarette smoke and human sweat. It is a smell that gets into your hair and clothes and leaves a foul taste in your mouth.

The bar was the kind of place that gives the sermons about Sodom and Gomorrah, which I unwillingly endured as a child, special meaning.

I was both nervous and excited. I had romanticized this moment, seeing myself as a kind of James Bond, sleuthing my way through the corrupt underworld in search of crucial information. I was the detached observer, on a higher moral plane than the Johns and hookers I was covering.

But by the time the project was over, my views had changed substantially. My black and white world of good guys and bad guys had become a world of fine gradations of gray.

I took in the Clarysol with a reporter's eye for the details that would help drag readers into the bar with me. I made mental notes, thinking a reporter's notepad a tad too conspicuous.

The six or seven tables in the bar were dirty and stained. The tablecloths—actually sheets of red and white plastic—were pockmarked with cigarette burns.

Empty beer bottles were scattered on the floor, and even the loud merengue music from two oversized speakers couldn't drown out the shrill laughter and high-pitched giggles of the hookers.

I noted a balding, middle-aged man talking to a fat hooker across from me. The guy took several nervous glances my way.

I would see his type many times, men lured to brothels by lurid pleasures, but consistently wishing for greater privacy. The women liked them because they often paid more and demanded less.

Most of the other men in the bar that night appeared perfectly at home. Regular customers, I gathered, because the women often referred to them by name.

I moved to the bar and ordered a beer. Since I don't drink, I sat nursing the bottle in my hand, trying to hide my distaste whenever I took tiny sips.

I continued making mental notes.

To my immediate right, a skinny, long-legged hooker in a flattering miniskirt sat on the lap of an elderly man who appeared to be getting an inordinate amount of pleasure from the situation. At a table on my left, hookers and Johns haggled and joked, apparently trying to reach some financial arrangement.

I was busy taking all of this in when suddenly I felt a groping hand on my lap. The hand belonged to a full-figured woman whose breasts were firmly planted against my back.

"You want to go upstairs?" she asked in a husky, thick Haitian accent. The boldness of her move—her hands touching parts of me definitely off limits to strangers—caught me off-guard. I mumbled some incoherent mumbo-jumbo. So much for James Bond.

She laughed, keeping her hand on my lap. I reached down and gently removed the offending hand, holding it in mine for safe keeping.

Unfazed, she asked me to buy her a beer and a pack of cigarettes. She lit a cigarette and threw the pack to the guy behind the bar. She didn't even touch the beer.

I made small talk, gently nudging the woman into a conversation about life in the bar. She told me she was nineteen, I would have guessed at least ten years older.

She left impoverished Haiti for St. Martin at sixteen, and within weeks she was working as a prostitute. Two years later, she came to St. Thomas with $120 and the address of the Clarysol Bar.

When I pressed her for more information, she became wary.

"If you not buy sex, I go," she said, turning to walk away. I stopped her, asking if there was a place we could talk privately. She smiled knowingly: "Let's go upstairs."

Pulling on my hand, she led me to the back of the bar. We went up a flight of rickety stairs that creaked with our every step. They led to a narrow corridor with five bedrooms on either side.

The women lived and worked in the rooms. The entire second floor had the musty smell of an old house that had been closed for years.

We went into the third room on the right. A naked woman was sitting on the bed putting on her makeup. She looked up as we entered and reached for her underwear.

She could have been pretty at one time, but now her too-thin face was drawn and tired and even the generous amounts of makeup she applied didn't make her pretty again.

The woman finished dressing, then left. My escort, noting a look of discomfort on my face, assured me she would change the sheets before we got into bed. She then asked me for twenty dollars.

I paid her, and without a word she began undressing. Folds of fat practically tumbled out of her much-too-tight jeans.

Sitting on the edge of the dressing table, I told her to keep her clothes on because I wasn't there for sex.

A look of panic crossed her face, as she pegged me for a cop or immigration agent trying to set her up. It took awhile to assure her that I was only a journalist in search of information. Still, she threw my money back at me, pulled up her pants and fled the room.

I followed quickly, sure that she was breaking the news to some muscle-bound bouncer downstairs. An evening of fisticuffs with an irate bouncer in a whorehouse wasn't my idea of fun and was certainly not in my contract.

As I left the bar, the fresh air felt good on my face. I couldn't remember it feeling or smelling better.

No one had to tell me that my first trip wasn't exactly a success. But at least I knew what to expect the next time out, and I promised myself to be better prepared to handle it.

After the Clarysol Affair, as I came to call it, I carefully planned all future outings. I singled out women who showed a predisposition to talk, preferably in English. And mentally I prepared myself to handle the fondling many of the girls used as a come on.

There were still two things bothering me.

One was making progress reports to Penny. During such reports I often tried to leave out much of the embarrassing details of my trips.

But Penny was insistent that my so-called "lurid details," were in fact the stuff that gave stories the "color" readers craved. Personally, I believed it was color the readers could easily do without.

Don't get me wrong—I care about my readers. But I was convinced that those details brought more color to my face than to the stories.

The other troubling issue was the damage the investigation was doing to my personal reputation—such as it was. In a territory of less than 100,000 people, it wasn't easy to discreetly visit dozens of houses of prostitutions.

Within weeks, several people had begun noticing my newly acquired affinity for the houses. Some of my wife's friends even took it upon themselves to break the news to her. They were genuinely surprised that she took it so well.

Four months into the prostitution investigation my new approach was paying off. I now had the confidence of several prostitutes, although I think most still thought I was a little weird.

As the women spoke more freely, I got rare, intimate insights into the world of prostitution. It wasn't sexy and it certainly wasn't pretty.

It is often said that prostitution is a victimless crime. That simply isn't true.

I have seen the victims.

Women like Helen, a 55-year-old hooker who lost the use of both her kidneys after a series of venereal infections and complications from diabetes landed her in the intensive care unit and near death. When I interviewed her, she was going to dialysis three days a week. Less than a year later, she was dead.

"There is only one thing you learn to do as a prostitute," Helen told me. "That one thing isn't something you can use to get another job."

Then there was the young girl who joined a gang of high school prostitutes and had sex with a sailor for money to buy a class ring. She never wore the ring, too ashamed of what she had done to get it. Like Helen, she too was a victim.

And I can never forget the fourteen-year-old Dominican Republic native, a wisp of a girl with big, sad eyes, who was selling her body to support her parents back home. Her aunt, who ran the house where she worked, had enticed her to come to the Virgin Islands by promising her a job as a maid.

The job never materialized.

"I not so happy with America," she confided in me one night. "But I not do this forever."

I don't know if she ever got out.

Most people have a hard time seeing the women who sell their bodies and perform lurid sex acts for money as victims. But prostitution is a crime that steals not material things, but intangibles. In a way it pulls everyone it touches down several rungs.

On the bottom rung are the real villains. The men and women who lure the girls into the trade and get rich in the process.

Men like Rey Vega, owner of the Hotel El Eco. At one time El Eco was the largest house of prostitution on St. Croix. Vega's business card listed "girls" among his hotel's offerings.

Despite the abundant evidence to the contrary, Vega insisted El Eco was a hotel, not a whorehouse.

The "girls" mentioned on his card were barmaids, he told me, adding, "Men come here because they are friendly."

After several trips to El Eco, I thought the women a little too friendly. So did the relatively inactive police department vice squad, which placed El Eco at the top of its list of known houses of prostitution.

Labor department records showed Vega had only one barmaid, although there were usually more than a dozen women working the bar area.

As a hotel, El Eco was an uninviting place. There was only one entrance, through a rusting wrought-iron gate and filthy corridor, to the second floor brothel. The gate was usually padlocked during the day and opened only at night. Vega insisted this was a special security measure to keep guests safe.

The hotel's phone number was unlisted, appearing only on cards distributed at the bar. When asked about this, Vega expressed shock and said he would have the telephone company correct it right away. Years later, the number remained unlisted.

Not all brothel operators tried to hide their line of work.

Some, like Clara, were open about it. An aging former prostitute, Clara ran a small whorehouse and spent her free time traveling to the Dominican Republic to recruit girls—some as young as 13.

"For many of the girls this life is better than they will ever know in the Dominican Republic," Clara claimed. "In a way I am doing them a favor."

A favor most of the girls said they could easily have done without. Many said they were promised jobs as house girls, maids and cooks. Jobs they never got.

Instead, they found themselves illegal immigrants in a strange country, unable to speak the language, penniless and at the mercy of those who smuggled them in. And the smugglers, they soon discovered, worked hand in hand with the vice lords of prostitution.

A year and four months into the prostitution project I was ready to pack it in.

It wasn't that I didn't have a good story—I had a hell of a story. I just wanted my life back.

Greatly increasing my woes was a heated gubernatorial campaign in the Virgin Islands that had attracted the national media. I was assigned to cover the frontrunner.

Between the campaign, daily stories and the project, my personal life simply ceased to exist. Planning a trip to the movies was as complicated as preparing an extended vacation to Europe.

Election night, I sat at my terminal prepared to write my last campaign story. But halfway through the count it was clear that there was going to be a runoff and that my candidate would be in it.

As luck would have it, I was writing political stories right up to the inauguration.

By the time a publication date was set for the prostitution project, I already had several boxes of notes on brothels and brothel owners and was focusing on the smugglers.

Before my investigation, I thought the main players in the smuggling trade were freelancers who shared information, but little else. I was dead wrong.

Smuggling was not only good business, it was big business. Immigration officials believed a highly organized smuggling ring was responsible for bringing an estimated 3,000 illegal immigrants into the Virgin Islands and Puerto Rico each year.

Most of the illegal immigrants were not prostitutes. Nearly 90 percent of them slipped past border patrols, simply using the islands as gateways to the U.S. mainland.

I had heard numerous stories about the smuggling ring, many from prostitutes themselves. But always the names mentioned in the stories were of boat captains and vessels, not of the men who really ran the operation.

What I had gathered so far made for good reading, but it didn't nail the bad guys. I wanted to nail them.

So with my investigation in a bit of a rut, I decided to go fishing. And the federal courthouse was as good a place to start as any.

I spent hours at the court examining old smuggling cases. I was looking for some fact or detail that authorities may have overlooked or neglected to share with me.

That was how I found his name.

It was in a file of a relatively routine smuggling case. He was a St. Martin businessman whose boat had been confiscated by Customs after it was found with illegal immigrants just off the coast of St. Croix, the largest of the three Virgin Islands.

He had written Customs officials asking them to release his boat. The man claimed he had been gypped by the smugglers into leasing them the boat, believing it would be used to transport legitimate cargo.

Federal officials couldn't disprove his story, and the boat was released. The man sounded like someone I needed to talk to.

Finding him was fairly easy using information in the court files. One day after first seeing his name, we spoke on the phone.

He was a suspicious, cagey guy. He insisted that he call me back at the newspaper to be sure I was who I claimed to be.

When he did call back—hours later—he was still wary. After ten minutes on the phone I had little new information.

This was the story he told me:

Two years before, he leased the boat to a company registered to another St. Martin businessman. He was shocked when he heard about the boat's seizure and cargo.

He immediately wrote U.S. Customs explaining the situation. Eventually his boat was released.

The man who had leased the boat disappeared about the same time the vessel was seized. Nobody had heard from him since.

All this I already knew from the court files. But when I pressed the man for more information he just clammed up, refusing to give names, dates or addresses.

The conversation was going nowhere. He had information I wanted, yet I sensed if I pressed too hard he might shut up for good.

I figured I would give him a couple of days to think the matter over, then call him back. If I had learned anything in this job, it was that most people will eventually talk.

But just when I was getting ready to cut off the conversation, he said something that stopped me cold.

"I don't think I can help you further," he said. "But there is someone I think you should talk to."

That someone, he said, was a friend of his. He would have the friend phone me, he promised.

Two days later, the mystery friend called. The conversation was cryptic.

He said he had information he believed I was after. Would I be willing to come to St. Martin to meet him?

I told him it depended on the information. I waited for him to give the right answer. He did.

"I know the people you are looking for," he said. "I know their names."

Yes, I had struck pay dirt. Now, if only he would deliver.

He refused to give the names on the phone, but said he could meet me the following weekend in St. Martin. I agreed to go.

I made that decision on the spot with little thought. Later, after several hours of quiet reflection, I questioned the wisdom of meeting this stranger in St. Martin.

The newspaper, I was sure, would spring to bring him to St. Thomas. Or perhaps we should meet on neutral ground on a neighboring island.

I had thrown caution to the wind. Now, in retrospect, I was asking, What if?

What if the boat owner was in fact involved in the smuggling ring? I could be walking into a trap.

If, on the other hand, he was legitimate, this could be the break I was hoping for. Even as I wrestled with my thoughts, I knew I was going.

One week later, I was on a plane to St. Martin. I knew my contact by first name and description only, and had arranged to meet him at a popular airport bar.

I was fully aware of the potential danger of the trip and wanted our meeting to be in a very public place. You couldn't get more public than the bar I chose.

St. Martin has often been called the Monte Carlo of the Caribbean, because the tiny island—governed by the Dutch and French—is a place where just about everything goes.

Duty-free goods made the island a shopping mecca. Lax customs and border patrols made it a transshipment haven for drug lords and smugglers.

I planned to keep my eyes open.

My plane landed just after 2:00 P.M., and I went straight to the bar. Less than five minutes later my contact walked in.

The description he had given me was good, and I recognized him right off.

We talked for awhile. The man, I discovered, was once a high-ranking government official.

He was understandably uncomfortable talking in the bar and we decided to finish our conversation in his car, which was parked nearby.

Once in the car, the man handed me a small manila folder. Inside were several pages of hand-written notes and a photograph of two men I had never seen before.

"These are the guys you want," he said, as I studied the picture closely. Both men were white.

One man, in his late fifties, was solidly built and balding. He was casually dressed in Bermuda shorts and a flowered cotton shirt popular with tourists.

The second man was younger and slimmer, his shirt unbuttoned to the waist, exposing a chest matted with thick, black hair. The man's face was partially hidden by dark glasses and a low-brimmed straw hat.

"They are behind everything," my contact said. "The

police know it, the government knows it, but everyone is afraid.''

"Why?" I inquired.

"They are Mafia and nobody wants to screw with them." He was looking right at me when he said that, trying perhaps to gauge my reaction.

"How do you know all this?" I asked, hoping for something solid that I could develop or use in my story.

"I know, the police know," he repeated, adding, "and that's not all these men are into. The smuggling thing is small potatoes. Those guys are moving more drugs through here into the United States than almost anyone else in the Caribbean.''

He was talking and I was taking notes. But the folder contained no secret files or supporting evidence. The hand-written notes turned out to be just some things he had jotted down so he wouldn't forget to tell me.

I had allegations but no proof. My contact never supplied any.

Later, an FBI source confirmed that the men in the photograph were part of a New York crime family. But he said the FBI had no information linking them to the smuggling ring.

I ran the names of the two men by St. Martin Deputy Police Chief Rupert Browne, the man in charge of immigration on that island. He said he had never heard of them.

Browne also said his department never investigated any organized crime figures in connection with smuggling.

My St. Martin contact produced little in the way of hard evidence. He did, however, point me in the right direction.

He gave me an earful and the name of a retired boat captain who had been approached by the smugglers. The captain had turned them down flat, said my contact.

The boat captain lived on Anguilla, just a twenty-minute boat ride from St. Martin. So I decided to look him up before heading home.

Finding the captain wasn't difficult on an island of 7,000 people, where just about everyone knows everyone else.

Getting the man to talk was another story.

I found the graying, middle-aged man at home on the west end of the island. After introducing myself, I gradually guided the conversation to my reason for being there.

I told him I had heard about the offer from the smugglers and asked if it was true.

He looked at me hard, then laughed.

"You shouldn't listen to fairy tales," he said with a frosty chuckle. "You look too old for that shit."

What did I expect? But I pressed on, trying to get him to open up by promising to protect his identity.

"I just want to know who these people are," I told him. "They are criminals and somebody has to expose them."

He stared at me hard, like I was stupid or something, then leaned forward as if about to divulge some great secret.

"I don't know you from Adam and I don't know who gave you my name," he spoke in a slow, easy tone. "But listen to an old man and go home. People have gotten killed for less."

With that he got up and walked inside. I didn't try to stop him. I got the message and didn't see any reason to have it repeated.

I didn't name the two alleged smugglers in my story. There was never enough evidence to do so.

But ten years later, while on the trail of cocaine traffickers in the Eastern Caribbean, the names of the two would again surface. Only this time, just about every federal agency was investigating them.

The last three weeks before publication found me tying up loose ends. I had not forgotten about the dead prostitutes; it was just that the leads were not panning out.

At least that was the case until my final trip to St. Martin.

St. Martin is one of the few islands in the Caribbean where prostitution is legal. It was legalized in the early 1970s after an influx of Japanese fishermen prompted the St. Martin government, frightened that the foreigners might start dating local women, to allow a businessman to open a brothel.

The rules were simple. Brothels couldn't hire local women and hookers had to be examined once a month by government doctors. With local women blocked from the trade, nearly all the prostitutes on the island were from the Dominican Republic and Haiti.

The first brothel, appropriately called the Japanese Club, proved a gold mine. And pretty soon its success bred competition, the biggest being the Sporting Club.

The Sporting Club was a sprawling, open-air complex surrounded by a six-foot wooden fence. The women who worked there, up to fifty at a time, lived in run-down, one-bedroom wooden shacks behind the compound.

I was told the missing prostitutes had worked there shortly before their disappearance. I even had a name of a girl at the club who supposedly knew them.

So on a chilly night in February, nearly two years after the dead prostitutes story broke, I was in St. Martin, heading for the Sporting Club.

It was a Saturday night and business was brisk.

The dimly lit, unpaved courtyard was crowded. I took a seat near the bar and started small talk with a woman who needed to be told she had definitely reached retirement age.

I gave her the name of the girl I was looking for and she left to find her.

Less than two minutes later, the old hooker stepped out of the darkness on my left with one of the most beautiful women I have ever seen.

Her name was Maria and she was twenty-one. Even as we spoke I couldn't help thinking how out of place she looked in a brothel.

She was talkative and spoke reasonably good English— which was important since my Spanish was embarrassingly poor. I didn't tell her why I had singled her out, thinking a bar full of hookers and their patrons wasn't the place to start my inquiries.

I allowed her to lead me back to her room. As we made our way to the shacks, an elderly leather-faced man with a gold tooth stepped from the shadows, blocking our path.

"You pay here," he said, in a gold-toothed grimace I am sure he was trying to pass off for a smile.

I asked how much, and he said $30 would buy me Maria for half an hour. For $50, he said, I could have her a full hour.

I declined the extended period.

Maria's room was dirty, with clothes and personal items strewn about. An empty condom wrapper was on a small plywood nightstand.

She sat on the edge of the unmade bed and slipped her feet out of her shoes. Without a word, she pulled her blouse over her head and began tugging at her body-hugging pants.

I stopped her and her eyes widened.

"I not do nothing kinky," she said with a concerned look. "You want kinky, you can do that with some other girl."

That's when I told her who I was. Well not exactly.

I said I was a friend of one of the missing girls. Did she know what had happened to them?

"What missing girls?" she eyed me suspiciously.

"The ones in the container who are believed dead." I was looking directly at her when I added, "Everyone knows the story."

"What was your friend's name?" she asked. I anticipated this.

"I am willing to pay you for this information," I told her, reaching for my wallet. "It's very important that you tell me everything you know."

For $25 she agreed to talk. I took a seat on the bed beside her.

Maria told me she believed there were only three women involved in the incident, not twenty-eight. She even gave me their names. And then she dropped the bombshell: "I not think they are dead. I know a man who can tell you everything."

She claimed the women left St. Martin for the Virgin Islands in a cargo vessel carrying containers packed with carnival rides. She even gave me the name of a man who worked for the carnival ride company. A man, she said, who knew exactly what had happened to the women.

It was a hot lead on a cold trail, and I spent the next several days tracking the man down. I found him a week later in San Juan, Puerto Rico.

With surprisingly little coaxing, and a promise to protect his identity, the man told me this story:

Four prostitutes were smuggled into St. Thomas on the boat carrying carnival rides from St. Martin. The prostitutes were working at the Sporting Club at the time they arranged to be taken aboard the vessel.

The trouble started when Sporting Club operators tried to stop the women from leaving. Unable to do so, the brothel operators started the dead prostitutes rumor to get U.S. Customs to check out the boat when it docked.

But the story broke first in France—reported by Le Martin's Caribbean stringer—and by the time the media in the Virgin Islands picked it up, the boat had already docked and the women spirited past customs and immigration.

The four prostitutes traveled as passengers and were never put in containers. The women spent seven days on St. Thomas before moving to Puerto Rico and finally to the U.S. mainland.

As proof of his account, the man in Puerto Rico gave me the phone number in the Dominican Republic of the mother of one of the women.

That night, I had a friend fluent in Spanish telephone the woman and ask about her daughter.

"Carmencita is fine," the woman said. "She is in New York and has a new baby."

It appeared that the dead prostitutes had not only survived, they were doing very well.


When I sat down to write the prostitution series I had at least six boxes of note pads and documents. Some of my notes were nearly two years old.

From the beginning, my goals had been ambitious but clear. I wanted to know what made women turn to prostitution, and why so many stayed in the illegal trade even into middle age. I also wanted to know how many of the women, mainly from the Dominican Republic and Haiti, were in the Virgin Islands illegally and who smuggled them in.

I planned to expose the people who ran the houses, to put a dollar amount on the prostitution trade and to identify those pocketing the bulk of the money.

But most important, I wanted to know what dangers these houses posed to the community and why the Virgin Islands government was doing so little to close them down.

I found answers to most of my questions. Some of my findings were reasons for grave concern.

Like the discovery that at least five prostitutes, all still in the business, had tested positive for the deadly AIDS virus and that local law didn't allow authorities to publicly identify the women or stop them from plying their trade. After my series ran, that law was changed.

For the first time we were able to get federal officials to confirm the existence of a highly-organized smuggling ring. And although we couldn't name the masterminds in print, we were pretty sure we knew who they were.

The smugglers, we were able to estimate, netted more than $10 million a year from their human cargo alone.

And I learned that the police were not just ignoring prostitution—they were often active participants in the trade. This became clear after only a few trips to the houses where it was not unusual to find police officers, some high-ranking, among the regulars.

As my investigation continued, I discovered that one of the largest and most lucrative brothels was run by a police officer who kept his girls in line by threatening to have them arrested if they tried to leave. Even after my story ran, he kept his job and his brothel stayed open.

And after spending nearly two years in the filthiest fleshpots in the Caribbean, I was finally able to piece together my own version—based on facts and clues gathered along the way—of the dead prostitutes story.

From the beginning, I knew the story would be a blockbuster if it was true, especially if I located the bodies or nailed the culprits. But a part of me always hoped it was really a hoax.

The tragic deaths of twenty-eight women would simply have made the story bigger, not better. And when I sat down to write that particular story I couldn't help smiling a little, because as long as I could remember I have been a sucker for a happy ending.

**Melvin Claxton**, 38, is a senior investigative reporter at *The Virgin Islands Daily News*. He was born in Antigua, where he worked as a statistician before moving to the Virgin Islands in 1980. In 1995 he won the Pulitzer Prize for Public Service for a series of articles on violent crime. Claxton, who studied journalism and economics at the University of the Virgin Islands, has won more than two dozen national journalism awards for his work, including the Al Nakkula Award for Police Reporting, the Investigative Reporters and Editors Award and the Associated Press Managing Editors Public Service Award—he has been a finalist in the APME awards five times in the past twelve years.

# THREE

—ᴍ—

# The Gatekeeper

## DIANA K. SUGG

### The Sacramento Bee

Through the open car window, from the backseat of the police car, I could see that Officer Pat Higgins had pulled out his gun. Five yards away, a young man stared at Higgins, holding his own gun.

I did what any police reporter would do: I clambered out of the car and started taking notes, thinking I was nice and close, without a crowd around for once.

Higgins, a narcotics officer for the Sacramento Police Department, and the other man eyed each other. Higgins was shouting at him. The man's gun caught my eye—it looked strange, as if the muzzle was broken.

Then I realized it was a sawed-off shotgun. I'd used that description so many times in briefs and stories, and somehow I'd imagined the barrel differently—fatter, maybe. But at that instant I knew I was looking at a sawed-off shotgun. I noticed that I was only about ten feet from the two guns pointing at each other and the men sweating and screaming.

Just moments before in the police car, when the "shots fired" call came over the radio, I had been thinking: this must be a mistake. It was only 3:00 P.M., much too early for a drive-by shooting.

The photographer working the story with me had been complaining that we hadn't encountered enough excitement. No chases or shootings. But after a few months shadowing the narcotics officers for a series for my newspaper, *The Sacramento Bee,* I knew that when dispatchers said "shots fired," it could be anything. I turned to a clean page in my notebook and hung onto the door handle.

Officer Guy Wassather jerked the steering wheel hard, pulling a U-turn and leaning toward the windshield as he sped up Broadway. Less than a minute after the call, the undercover police car was screeching into Oak Park, one of Sacramento's toughest neighborhoods.

Brightly colored clothes flashed by. Kids were walking home from school. I could hear the music from an ice-cream truck.

The police car ran up over a curb, jostling all of us. Before I realized it, Wassather was out of the car, chasing someone. His partner, Higgins, jumped out, shouting. I felt as if I was in a daze, as if all the action was being fast-forwarded on video, and my senses couldn't keep up.

Now, staring at the two men and their guns, I started to step backward. As I walked, trying to get behind the sturdy, black Chevy, the man gave in. He dropped the shotgun, and Higgins shoved him down on the street. "Are you crazy?" yelled the officer.

I could hear the camera clicking as the photographer moved in closer and took shot after shot. I felt numb. Later, in the newspaper, a picture covering almost half the page showed Higgins's gun pointed at the man's head, and the officer's foot on his back. The man turned out to be a Blood gang member.

But that wasn't what I remember. I remember them pointing the guns at each other, I remember not feeling scared—at first. Somehow I thought nothing would ever happen to me as a crime reporter. But that day, standing near the car, my fingers felt fat and thick; the tip of my pen seemed to get caught in tiny bumps on the surface of the paper.

I was scared. I couldn't believe those two men had almost shot each other right in front of me.

Like almost all my days as a police reporter, though, the moment to actually feel, to digest what was going on, to think about it all, was brief and elusive. There was little time to talk over the experience or wonder why the gang member just didn't shoot Higgins. I never considered why I didn't stay in the car.

But I guess I knew the answer to that. I just wanted the story too badly to steer clear. I wanted to see the sweat on their faces, I wanted to hear the words they were screaming, to note the position of their bodies.

As for the larger questions about what I was doing, something always seemed to interrupt those thoughts, to steal away any quiet moment. There were deadlines, editors, other shootings.

This day, in Sacramento's strong March sun, the dropping of the guns didn't end the drama. Wassather was walking back with a second young man in tow. While the officers talked with this man and a few others, the man who had held the shotgun, Carl Webb, sat on the curb, handcuffed. He began looking around and then seemed to have made a decision. A second later, Webb jumped up and started running, his cuffed hands hitting his back with every step.

Cursing, Wassather chased after him through a series of backyards. The photographer and I were left behind with the second man who had been detained. He opened a bag of Cheetos and began to eat.

Suddenly, the street got quiet, and a good, familiar feeling was taking over me—I knew I had great stuff for my series on the lives of narcotics officers. I jotted down every detail: the kids I could hear running and playing, the music from the ice-cream truck. I tried to mentally calculate how long the two men had been holding their guns on each other.

Later, as Officers Wassather and Higgins were doing the paperwork in the booking area of the Sacramento County Jail, I knelt next to Carl Webb and asked him what he was doing that afternoon. It was totally clear to him. He explained, simply, that he and some other Blood gang members were going to shoot up the house of some rival Crip gang members who were infringing on their turf.

When the series was printed in the newspaper, this entire sequence was reduced to one paragraph.

I wanted to describe and explain so much more, but there were practical barriers. The newspaper, like all papers, had only a certain amount of space for stories, and editors, conscious of the public's limited attention span, work to streamline stories as much as possible. Second, my work rarely satisfied me. The words and sentences never seemed to catch the mood or convey the intensity I had witnessed.

Perhaps the most significant obstacle, though—on the series and as a daily police reporter—was the sheer number of anecdotes, details and quotes I recorded. Coming back to the newsroom, I felt the pages of my notebook held gems, individual pieces that I could spread out, select and arrange into a compelling picture for the readers.

It was like pouring the contents of a gallon jug through a funnel into a small chocolate milk carton.

In my darkest moments, I wondered if I was betraying everyone—the readers, the police, the people involved, myself.

During the three months I followed about fifty city and county narcotics detectives, I routinely walked into unforgettable situations. At a rundown motel on a spring night, I watched a mother buy crack from an undercover officer so that she could give drugs to her daughter for her twenty-seventh birthday. I saw roaches crawling on three young girls as they slept, while their mother was next door, buying crack.

Under the red glow of a miniature flashlight, I took reams of notes in the back of police cars. I sat in an old truck with undercover officers, peering onto dark downtown streets that seemed so innocuous by day. These nights, though, the tall trees seemed menacing, houses looked spooky and every stranger appeared to be a drug dealer. I watched as undercover officers became part of that world, trying to buy some cocaine or crank.

One night, after watching an officer go into a house to make a drug buy, I heard a voice hissing into the hidden microphone: "If I find out you're a cop, I'm going to slit your throat." The radio crackled and went dead. The backup officers fought in low voices in the car, agonizing over whether this was another equipment failure or a murder about to happen.

Finally, after five tense minutes, the officer walked out unharmed. He had managed to convince the dealer he wasn't a cop.

Other nights, with permission from a landlord, the county narcs took over an empty duplex. While two or three undercover officers hung out in front, trying to lure in potential drug buyers, at least a dozen of us crammed in upstairs, whispering in the dark and anticipating the coming action. It was like a game.

A stranger on the street approached the undercover officer and then bought some crack. Immediately, there was chaos. A team of officers jumped from the bushes and pounced on the buyer. They hustled the person upstairs into a back room, where with flashlights they set up a booking process.

Detective Jim Cooper shook his head after hauling in the seventh of what would ultimately be more than a dozen arrestees.

"He was in my Boy Scout troop," Cooper said.

Of all the narcotics officers' routines, the most dramatic was serving the search warrant. Officers would meet somewhere near the house they planned to search. One Friday night in March, as cars and families drove by, probably on their way to Pizza Hut or the video store, a team of narcotics officers suited up in raid gear in a windswept parking lot and then piled into several cars.

As the cars turned the corner near the house they were targeting, one by one, headlights went off. The cars swerved to the side of the road, and the officers ran through the night.

Click. Click . . . click, click, click. Guns were cocked. Officers took their positions. Then came the loud banging on the door. "Sheriff's Department. This is a search warrant."

A man inside tried to block the door, a dog was barking, a woman screamed. In two minutes, it was over, with occupants handcuffed and officers busy doing the paperwork, logging how much crack, marijuana and explosives they found.

It was often that way. To get enough information for a

search warrant, officers spent hours watching and waiting in cars, sweaty from the heat and stiff from sitting. But after all the surveillance, serving the search warrant translated into a few minutes of fear and confusion. Officers frantically tried to make sure no one inside had a gun or a pit bull. One detective always ran to the bathroom to catch the dealer before he flushed his stash of drugs down the toilet.

Sometimes, though, the target of the investigation moved faster than expected. In Stockton one afternoon, Sheriff's Detective Dave Pittach had just settled into the backseat of a van to stake out a drug dealer's house. Usually, surveillance was boring and meant long hours of being unable to get food or even go to the bathroom. But this day, Pittach was ready with sandwiches and soda. A breeze floated into the car through an open window.

Suddenly, the dealer got in his car and took off. Pittach scrambled to get back in the driver's seat and started up the van. I listened twice to make sure I was hearing the song on the radio right: "Nowhere to run . . . nowhere to hide." It was Martha and the Vandellas. The van roared out of the parking lot, tires screeching.

"I love this stuff," Pittach said, relishing every word and every moment.

In quieter moments, some narcotics officers confessed that they were almost as bad as the people they were arresting. In their own way, they had become addicted, too. They loved to chase dealers, to speed 100 miles an hour down the Garden Highway, to catch a dealer with his stash.

Their marriages broke up, their health suffered, their circle of trust narrowed. But as Sergeant Gary Gritzmacher said one day in his cramped office, with phone ringing, pager beeping and a line of officers waiting to talk to him: "You can't get people to volunteer to come to narcotics, but once they're here, you can't blow them out with dynamite."

Those two months were the most intense of what became for me a two-year stint on the police beat. But over time, I realized I felt the same way. Many criminals were addicted to crack and crank, the police were addicted to chasing them, and I was addicted to tracking down the stories and getting them in the newspaper.

I loved being a police reporter. I never wanted to cover any other topic. I grimaced when I thought about covering city council or zoning hearings. I was writing about life and death. What could be more important?

It didn't start out that way. When I moved from a small paper in Spartanburg, South Carolina, to northern California to cover general assignment stories at night, I felt sick to my stomach when editors informed me I had been switched to the night police beat. That meant working 5:00 P.M. to 1:00 A.M., Tuesdays through Saturdays, mostly writing small items on car accidents and drownings. I had never covered a beat, and I knew little about police reporting. Worse, *The Bee* didn't have the best of relations with the police department.

The night police reporter typically checked arrest reports, made rounds of phone calls to police and fire jurisdictions—and spent most of his time in the newsroom. The problem was, the paper was often already full of stories by the time I got to work, and I discovered I was mainly a backstop, an insurance policy in case a crisis broke. But I didn't want to write only four-inch briefs, and I wasn't going to hang out in the newsroom, where there were no stories.

So after sleeping late, reading, bicycling and making some calls from home, I headed in to work. Awkward at first in handling the paper's Ford Bronco, which was used exclusively by the day and night police reporters, I soon loved bouncing over speed bumps. My first week, I asked an editor which neighborhoods were the most dangerous, looked them up on the map and took a driving tour.

I started showing up at the police station, eventually working my way inside the old brick building on H Street where the watch commander did paperwork for a few hours before hitting the streets. At first, only Captain Fred Arthur and his lieutenant, Paul Hietala, would talk with me. They were guarded. What they did tell me, in excruciating detail, was how many times *The Bee* got things wrong.

Over many nights, at many crime scenes, they began to see that I worked hard, I got facts right, and I was willing to write the good as well as the bad. I did a feature about the department's new bicycle team, cruising after them on my bike down narrow alleys lit by the moon. I wrote about the pair of cops who cleaned up a part of the city nicknamed "Pebble Beach," because of the abundance of rock cocaine.

Only twenty-four, I started learning the basics from two or three older officers. One sergeant, after determining that a body found in a downtown apartment was the result of natural causes—and not a homicide—called me in to show me what a decomposed body looked like. I was revolted, but I wanted to see. I tiptoed in, afraid I would somehow disturb the room, the air.

Before I could even get a good look, though, a detective arrived at the scene and ordered me out, yelling at me.

Soon I began to see a pattern. Some officers would never talk to me, would in fact go out of their way to avoid giving me any information. Others gave me the basics, nothing more, nothing less. Some would clue me in on stories that would make the department look good. At the other end of the spectrum were a few diehards who would tell me everything, even the unflattering stuff.

It didn't matter if there were only a few, because that was all I needed to tip me off to stories like "Star of the North," a woman in North Sacramento who loved police officers and would allegedly perform sex acts with them while they were on duty.

As months passed by, I began to learn my way around the city. I became more familiar with the language of the beat: 927 for suspicious person, 242 for battery and 187 for murder. There were others, like Code 7, meaning the officers were eating.

One night, months into the job, I met Lieutenant Hietala at The Trails, a cozy spot where waitresses served up plates full of home-cooked mashed potatoes, gravy and chicken. Typically, Hietala and I both had scanners and radios and pagers positioned near us on the table. We talked about work and family. He updated me on what was going on. He was one of the few who believed the police department could best serve itself by being open with citizens and the press.

And he had a heart. He coached me on how to deal with certain officers. He encouraged me when I got down. Paul had become a friend. I knew he still woke in a sweat from nightmares. Sixteen years earlier, on a stakeout for three men who had been robbing bars and their customers, a fourteen-year-old boy was mistakenly shot. It was drizzling that night, and in the dark alley an officer heard someone racking a shotgun. Then he saw someone's shadow carrying what looked like a gun. The officer fired.

Paul was one of the first officers to reach the boy, to realize the stick was a broom handle, not a shotgun. Another officer on a nearby street had racked his shotgun. The boy and two other teenagers had apparently been scoping out targets for the robbers. But holding the boy in his arms, all Paul could think was, "He's just a kid."

For months, for years, he had nightmares of that image, of himself in the alley, shaking the boy and shouting, "Breathe! Breathe!" at the bloodied face. In his dreams, he kept trying to push the foam back in the teenager's mouth and make it oxygen.

The first time he told me this story, he cried. And often when I saw him, I wondered what other nightmares he had. This night, he wasn't saying much, but he seemed to linger over his meal. He ordered a slice of pie and urged me to eat one, too, but after the huge dinner, I didn't have any room left for lemon meringue. A few minutes later, the dispatcher's voice came over the radio in that elevated tone that I knew meant trouble. "187."

Quickly, I shoved my radios and notebooks into my large bag and searched for the Bronco keys. But Lieutenant Hietala kept telling me it was all right to wait a bit. He was the watch commander that night, and I could get whatever information I needed from him.

Paranoid about missing something, I insisted I had to go. I had that feeling in my stomach. It was as if someone had fired a pistol and started a race, and already I was lagging. We were standing at the cash register paying when Paul turned to me: "I just didn't want to eat my birthday dinner alone."

I felt terrible. I wish he'd told me that earlier. Rushing to the shooting, I told myself I was an awful person. Couldn't I have waited just a few minutes? I began to question my motives. Paul was a friend, but also a good contact. He tipped me off to stories. Often, though, he wanted to talk longer than I could. I cut him off on the phone or at the station.

That night, I felt torn. But like the two years on the beat, everything moved so fast that there was little time to consider my relationship with Lieutenant Hietala. For eight, nine, sometimes ten hours a shift, I was tracking down the collective tragedies of the five-county area.

Almost every night, there was blood. The night held the promise of a family feud or a gang shooting. I never knew what was going to happen. I was always anxious for a "good" murder, one with an interesting story to tell. I searched every arrest sheet for some juicy note jotted down near the bottom. I got to know the dispatchers at different police and fire departments, priding myself on creative ways to ask whether there was anything news-worthy going on: "Got any murders-for-hire? Any wild stabbings?"

Often, particularly in the outlying areas, the dispatchers would assure me: "No, thank heavens, everything's quiet." That made them happy, and it made me feel good, too—temporarily, at least—because it meant I wasn't missing some major crime that was going to appear on the eleven o'clock news.

In the newsroom, where the fluorescent light always seemed too bright in the evenings, I sat among rows of empty cubicles, going over my worn list of contacts. But I didn't need to see the numbers anymore. I knew them by heart. Certain dispatchers became almost phone bud-dies. I'd call up Vic in the Truckee bureau of the Cali-fornia Highway Patrol, and we'd discuss our jobs, the weather and the latest shootings.

The joking on the phone, the casual conversations with editors—"We need a good murder tonight," they'd say, helping to make routine something that never should have been. That always became clear when I reached a crime scene.

One November night I rushed to a shooting in Oak Park about 10:30 P.M. Threading my way through the crowd, I reached the perimeter of the yellow police tape. It was almost as if I had stumbled upon a scene from a play.

A quiet crowd surrounded the house. A lone woman, standing on the white porch steps, high above her audience, was completely illuminated in the bright emergency lights. She sank down on the steps, buried her face in her hands and sobbed. She couldn't stand to look upstage, where her daughter's body lay on the driveway.

There is a moment in everyone's life, I believe, when he or she crosses the line, from fairly happy, untouched, to experiencing the horror of death. He doesn't realize how happy he was until the soul of a daughter or a father is ripped away, disappeared in split seconds. Without the tiniest shred of forewarning, all that's left is the body.

That night in Oak Park, it hit me. That's when I always arrived, when these people were on the line or just beginning to cross it, in full view of me, of neighbors. In this moment, they were beginning to realize that nothing would ever be the same again.

I wanted to know why the person died, whether they tried to fight back, what they were screaming, and in the end, what they whispered to the neighbor who found them. I wanted to describe everything. That was my job.

This night, after trying only two people in the crowd, I got a hit. I found a neighbor who knew the woman on the porch and the man who supposedly had shot two of this woman's daughters. The neighbor told me the story casually, and as I was writing, struggling to see my own scribble in the dark, I thought to myself, "Bingo." It was unbelievable how much neighbors knew, and I wondered why writers ever had to invent stories, when there were so many good ones cropping up every day.

The daughter in the driveway, Donna Suggs, 26 (no relation), had a bullet in her heart. Another daughter, Sandra, 25, was shot in the neck and was bleeding in the backyard. The man who did it, the neighbor told me, was a popular handyman on the street who helped the sisters' mother with taxes, pulled weeds from her garden and mowed the lawn.

I learned that night, and police later confirmed, that Marcellious Dewayne Tucker shot the sisters because they owed him $5. He was later convicted of two counts of second degree murder.

Sometimes I was so desperate to get the information, to find the killer detail that could make the whole story, that I went too far.

The day after Christmas, just a few minutes before my shift was supposed to end at 1:00 A.M., a dispatcher announced a shooting at Caselli Circle, one of the most crime-ridden streets in Sacramento. Grabbing my bag and shoving a portable radio and a new notebook inside it, I rushed across the street to the parking lot. By the time I was climbing inside the Bronco, a second shooting victim had been located. As I was speeding down Highway 99, the dispatcher had changed "double-shooting" to "triple-shooting."

At Caselli Circle, I saw a cap in the middle of the road. I stopped and got out. Next to the cap was a puddle that looked like oil. Getting closer, I realized it was blood. A house door slammed behind me. I could hear the distant sound of screeching tires and saw a police car speed by a few streets over. It was a clear night, and I looked up to see a slew of bright stars overhead. I thought about Christmas.

Walking closer to the puddle, shiny in the street light, I wrote down the descriptions: "thick, wet blood; red spots—stained baseball cap.'' The street seemed deserted. I felt exposed, as if someone was watching me. I realized I had gotten there before police had located the three bodies, set up a perimeter and started searching for suspects. I got back in the Bronco and began looking for the cops, for the place roped off by yellow tape and attended to by people with guns.

There, I could get most of the facts I needed: age of the victim, number of times shot and where, names of suspects and possible motive for the crime. I could see my favorite crime scene investigator, who took pictures of the body.

Huddling in my coat, dictating the story over the portable radio to an editor, things were clear-cut.

But I didn't end up with a story in every case. Sometimes, no one was hurt in the incidents—like when a drunken man had barricaded himself in his house or a mentally ill person had wandered from home. Often there wasn't a crime, just a long, painful situation that had boiled to the surface and caused someone to call 911.

One dark evening, I stood in the chilly Sacramento wind, in the shadow of red and blue blinking lights, in earshot of police radios and curious neighbors. It was a familiar place for me. But this was one of those stories that wouldn't make it into the paper, a story too long, too complicated, of a mentally ill man and the family who had to live with his sickness. This chapter was being played out on the roof.

It was a slow night, and I found myself transfixed by what was happening. I watched for an hour as the man, wielding a steak knife, held off several officers who tried to get him down. Police flashlights exposed him in eerie shafts of white light. Private tragedy had turned public. A crowd had gathered.

I thought of my own family, and my autistic sister, who had rammed her hand through a window and punched my parents and siblings. Police had been called. Ambulances pulled into our driveway. Our neighbors got used to it. Now, I was 3,000 miles from home, and I felt as though I was watching a scene from my sister's future. I wondered what sense a reporter would make out of her story.

After several attempts to get down the mentally ill man, the officers finally used a taser to temporarily shock him. The crackle of electricity on that man, and the way he screamed, still rattle around in my mind.

I scribbled lots of notes that night, for I knew this was a story. But no one had been attacked; there would be no charges and the man was being sent to the psychiatric ward. It wasn't the kind of story we put in the newspaper.

On disturbing nights like those, I found comfort at the small bar on the first floor of my high-rise. Walking down the steps from the parking garage, I could just barely hear the music and the chatter from Gilhooley's. All I had to do was angle myself a little more to the left, and instead of walking toward the elevator, to get to my fifth floor studio, I was walking into the bar.

There, I could gossip with the bartender. Or after particularly crazy, violent shifts, I could act out recent crimes for the entertainment of the regulars, showing them where people were positioned when the shooting happened.

Some police officers had drinks there after work, since it was just down the road from the downtown patrol station. Sometimes we didn't even acknowledge each other; other nights, we talked about work. Every once in a while, one of them would walk by me and suggest I check out something.

One such tip, from a sergeant who had never told me anything, was to stop by a family's house downtown. A

Vietnam veteran who lived there had just committed suicide. It didn't sound like the sort of thing we could write
about, until the sergeant said to me: "There's just something about that family. You've got to go over there."

I stopped by the next day after making the rounds at
the jail. Knocking on the door, I was prepared to have the
door slammed in my face. Soon, though, the family welcomed me inside, put me in their most comfortable chair
and brought me a cold glass of lemonade. They reverently
showed me the case that held a twin set of identical medals, won by father and son in their respective wars.

The son, Ray Fernandez, grew up hearing the glory
stories of his father fighting in World War II, and when
the Vietnam War arrived, he dropped out of school at age
seventeen and signed up. He earned the Bronze Star, the
Purple Heart and the Combat Infantryman's Badge, just
as his father had.

But Ray Fernandez was forever changed.

On the previous Friday night, twenty-one years after
returning from Vietnam, he shot himself in the head. His
mother found him in his bedroom, in the same room
where his army uniform and treasured hat still hung in
the closet. Too shaken to walk, Delia Fernandez crawled
to the front door and called to her husband, who was
working in the yard.

I wrote the story. Above it ran a large photo of Ray
Fernandez's parents, holding all they had left of him: his
picture and the medals.

Some of my fellow reporters thought detectives were
the best sources for stories. But patrol officers—like the
sergeant who tipped me off—are on the streets every day.
They respond to all sorts of calls. Writing the story about
Ray Fernandez taught me that even painfully private
deaths like suicides could make the front of the metro

section if the family felt comfortable and wanted to tell their story.

After I had nearly a year on the night shift and three months with the narcotics officers, the editors moved me to the day police shift. I didn't want to change my hours. I loved working nights, hanging out at the police station, getting to the crime scenes. I worried there wouldn't be much action during the day.

In fact, there was more to keep up with during the day, between follow-ups from crimes the night before to anything that happened after the night reporter got off at 1:00 A.M. I had to adjust to a newsroom full of people, to new editors and waking up early. At night, as one of only three reporters, I had felt protected and secure.

During the day, some of the night's excitement seemed to fade, as if the flashy police lights were part of a dream. The allure of the dark began to seem fake. I met more families, and I began sorting out the daily tally of deaths, which were homicides, and which were accidents. The problem was, sometimes the accidents got to me more than the murders.

Like so much in life, there wasn't a clear-cut villain, just a stupid mistake or a broken machine, like the box compactor that cut off the head of Miguel Quintero, a twenty-year-old who was supporting his mother and seven siblings by working as a dishwasher. There was always someone left behind, someone sobbing inside the yellow police tape, standing near the blood, or holding the T-shirt left behind by paramedics—who'd ripped the clothes off in their efforts to stop death.

Sometimes, family members would catch wind that there had been an accident, or a shooting, and they would come running, only to confront head-on the one thing they had never wanted to see.

One beautiful, spring Friday afternoon the dispatcher's voice came over the police scanner, repeating "accident on golf course" with that edge, that emphasis that told me I should be there. A huge tree on the Bing Maloney Golf Course had cracked and split, landing on top of a cart carrying three people.

Hitting the gas pedal hard, I sped over the fairways in the newspaper's Ford Bronco, following the procession of fire trucks and police cars and television vans. At the fourth hole, firemen were calling into the fallen tree. Its trunk was too large for two men to wrap their arms around.

"We need a chain saw! A chain saw!"

The police officer was yelling in a high-pitched voice. I resisted the temptation to stare at the frenzy of rescue workers around the tree. Whipping out my long, skinny notebook, I shoved my bag over my shoulder and began approaching the golfers and the gawkers, trying to find someone who had been there.

"The wheels were just spinning. He was in reverse. He couldn't get out of the way." The words tumbled out of Bob Morris's mouth.

"We got there right after it fell," added Dan Martin. "But there was just no way to lift the tree. It was too heavy."

As I took down these awful accounts, word soon spread that one man had struggled out. Officers were talking to a second man under the tree. His eleven-year-old daughter was with him. The saw started buzzing furiously. Then I heard a woman behind me asking in a shrill, trembling voice about her daughter and her husband.

One paramedic, taking her by the arm, calmly explained that they were getting her husband out. But what about her daughter, she asked. The paramedic couldn't tell her anything else.

"Please, tell me my baby is alive. Tell me my baby is alive. Tell me!" screamed the woman. She was dressed in a matching skirt and blouse, as if she had come from work. Oblivious to the crowd and the afternoon heat, she was pacing back and forth, saying over and over, "Baby, don't die, don't die on me."

I couldn't take my eyes off her. I struggled to stop staring at her. I tried to focus myself, searching for more witnesses. Wiping away the sweat on my face, I scrawled out another bystander's quote: "He just kept saying, 'Get my daughter out of here.' "

Soon firemen were loading the woman's husband into an ambulance, and the frantic activity around the tree stopped. The workers appeared to be figuring out how to free his daughter.

But they weren't rushing. In one awful moment, silence spread through the crowd. People tried to look at the woman out of the corners of their eyes. I saw the paramedic walking up to her.

"No!" She cried and collapsed on the ground, beating it with her fists, crying, screaming, praying, Lord, bring back my daughter. I stood there watching as the woman's friends tried to lift her up and take her away. But she didn't want to leave her little girl, and she broke free from her friends, running toward the tree, falling near it and clawing at the manicured green lawn. I couldn't hear anything but her sobs. Staring down at my notebook, I tried to write exactly what was happening before me.

But even as my pen was moving up and down, I was torn, wondering if I belonged on that golf course, watching this woman at the moment she was told her daughter was dead. The moment she crossed the line. Maybe a stranger shouldn't be recording this woman's pain in a flimsy note pad.

All I ever saw of her daughter was the yellow plastic, the standard cover for corpses. The police and deputy coroner usually leave the body in place for at least an hour, so that they can gather information for reports. So the girl's body stayed there, as they walked around it, photographing and measuring.

With white-gloved hands, the crime scene investigators from the police department jotted down notes on clipboards. They chatted in low voices with the deputy coroner about their kids and their lives.

I knew these officers. They weren't cold people—but they saw too many bodies to let it eat at them. After several months on this beat, I, too, was learning not to let all the victims in my heart. I was beginning to feel worse for those left behind.

That Friday, one by one, the people drifted away, the television vans drove off, and there were only a few officers left. The corpse was still there. And I was going back to write the story for the cover of the metro section, complete with color photo.

As the victims began to pile up, I became more and more convinced that my own family had escaped fate. None of us had been raped or shot or even robbed. I wrote about a steady parade of victims, many who were ordinary people, on their way to work or just watching television, when they were killed.

Often it seemed there would be a string of them who were all model citizens and adorable, lovable children whose school pictures looked great in the newspaper, next to the stories of their deaths.

Connie Cornelius, a 44-year-old mother of four, PTA leader and Girl Scout troop leader, a woman whose daughter called her "my best friend," a woman who had finally earned the teaching degree she always wanted—was killed by a drunken driver on her way home from chaperoning a sober graduation party for high school seniors.

Heather Brown, a toddler who ran around the house singing parts of songs, who had been rocked to sleep by her father one Friday night on the living room sofa, was killed by a high-caliber bullet in a drive-by shooting. The family had just come back from a trip to McDonald's for ice cream. Later, detectives found the killers hit the wrong house.

Ten, twelve and fourteen hours a day, the dispatchers' voices came over the scanner, efficiently announcing assaults and domestic "disturbances." And every day it was a juggling act. Most people have to prioritize tasks at work, but for me, it wasn't accounting and marketing reports, it was rapes, assaults and murders.

By late morning, I usually had compiled a list to go through with my editor, Loretta Kalb. We were very efficient, and we made sure to take into account specifics of each case. If we had a few rapes, for instance, the one where the victim barricaded herself in the bathroom and called police on her cellular phone would get into the paper. An assault with an interesting twist or particularly horrific element could also land in the metro section.

But there were so many victims and so many stories that never made it into the paper. I had to be cruel and make the cuts. There wasn't room for all of them, and along with my editor, I was the gatekeeper.

In my own life, I started to become paranoid. The lonely gas-station attendant who asked me one too many questions began to seem dangerous. Callers who hung up when I answered the phone made me think twice. I learned to take nothing for granted. Considering my parents, brother and four sisters, I wondered which of us would be the first to die. I pictured myself being the victim of a crime and tried to figure out if I would fight back or if my fear would paralyze me.

If my mother was upset about one of my siblings back East, I thought I was consoling her by saying, "Well, at least none of us has been raped or killed."

The job wore on me in other ways. I hit the soda machine by 9:30 A.M., and by 4:30 in the afternoon, I was on my fourth or fifth Diet Coke. A Snickers or KitKat helped me hang in there if I didn't have a chance to grab lunch. The *Bee*'s cafeteria—open all hours and stuffed with a salad bar, grill and plenty of good food—was only one floor up from the newsroom, but it seemed miles away. I just didn't think I could spare the time.

Loretta once told me that she'd look at me and think I wasn't going to make it through the day. It wasn't just the constant high-pitched beeping of my pager that unnerved me, or the scanner's constant babble. The problem was, I didn't think I was doing enough. I considered becoming a social worker or a foster mother; I was guilty about my middle-class life.

The next year, on a journalism fellowship in a friendly midwestern town, I woke up night after night from dreams filled with sirens, deadlines and victims. I suffered from terrible migraines. Gradually, over weeks and months, I came to see that there was another world, of walking slower, of calm, of people untouched by horrible crimes and death.

Still, in the thick of things in Sacramento, I was so wrapped up in the police world that I could not see that. I was tired until I got a new tip or another body was discovered. Chasing down a story, getting the clincher interview, was like a small triumph.

I learned to keep tissues with me, to expect to feel awkward and out of place in the middle of tragedies. Yet no matter how concerned I was or how much I tried to immerse myself in it, I knew I could never fully understand. No one close to me had ever been murdered or raped or grown up in a housing project where gunfire could be heard almost every night. I was pure and removed. I slept in a safe apartment, sealed in the air-conditioning.

I didn't know why I had that privilege or why my family hadn't yet crossed the line, was still naive about the horror of crime, or death. And I didn't know what the families thought when I showed up—all neat and efficient—and questioned them about the worst moment of their lives. Amazingly, they were almost always willing to talk. They wanted to talk. It seemed to make them feel better. It gave them a chance to publicly share the good things about their family member, to erase the dirtiness of crime now forever linked to their relative's death.

More and more, I wanted to make sense of each death. I started looking for clues, for details that would somehow pull the tale together. I found myself staring at corpses pulled out of rivers, or in caskets. The youngest corpse I saw was that of Randy Harlan.

I was several blocks from the newsroom and two hours to deadline when I found myself alone, in a funeral home, looking at a coffin small enough for me to pick up and carry away. Viewing hours had just started, and I knew others would be coming soon. I walked closer to the casket, and there was the subject of my story: Randy Ray Harlan, five years old.

I quickly scribbled down my observations: powder blue

suit, navy shirt and matching bow tie, child's arms wrapped around a teddy bear, long, brown lashes, hair combed neatly to the side.

As an infant, he had received a beating that almost killed him. That afternoon, his father—strung out on Jack Daniels and methamphetamine and angered that the baby was crying because of a wet diaper—threw Randy's body against the walls. He grabbed him by the ankles and shook him upside down.

"He left fingerprints on that child's body," Randy's grandmother, Velda Wills, whispered to me that afternoon. "It happened all over the house . . . Randy was still a tiny, tiny thing."

The baby survived the beating, but ended up blind, almost completely deaf, with broken ribs and spinal damage. His brain, severely damaged, deteriorated piece by piece, until his whole system shut down and he died, five years later.

Looking at Randy, I was suddenly angry at myself for intruding into this peaceful place, for thinking that this dead boy was somehow going to tell me what I should feel, how I should write his story. For one moment, I thought I could almost see his chest move. I wanted to believe that he was only sleeping in that miniature coffin, and I stayed by his side for several minutes, watching him. I fought back an urge to reach out and pick him up, to hold him and rock him.

Then it clicked: this little boy is finally resting, I thought.

Earlier that day, Randy's grandmother Velda, had wondered proudly what her grandson might have become had he stayed healthy.

"We was beautiful before all this happened, perfect in every way," she said.

\*     \*     \*

From the top of the television set, a color portrait of Randy distracted me. His big, dark blue eyes seemed to pull me in. I turned my head and tried to concentrate. I focused on seven-year-old Lisa, playing with a Barbie doll on the living room floor. She had watched her daddy hold Randy upside down and shake him. For weeks afterward, Mrs. Wills told me in a shaky voice, Lisa ran around the house repeating what she'd seen and pulling out her hair.

That's when the vision of Randy's beatings became too much for me. I could hear my scanner babbling about stolen cars, suspects and warrant checks. It was stuffed inside my oversized, black and tan purse, along with my notebooks, my pager and the portable radio I used to talk with my editor. A brush, barrettes and makeup were also jammed inside, ready to pull me together on long days, which were most days.

I wasn't thinking about any of that. I was imagining the sound of Randy's body hitting the wall. It was like watching a movie I didn't want to see. For a few moments, I allowed myself to forget my job. I leaned back in the chair, staring at Lisa and Mrs. Wills.

But I knew I had a deadline. I knew there were at least a dozen calls to make when I got back to the newsroom, checking in with all the fire and law enforcement agencies. As the police reporter for a 350,000 circulation morning daily paper, I didn't have the luxury of following one case for a month or even a week. There were briefs to write about a body found in the river and a fatal accident on Interstate 80.

And on top of this, I realized that Randy Harlan made a great story, a story sure to hit the front page. I was excited and revolted at once. I knew I'd be bringing a prize back to the editors, that they'd compliment me and think I was good. I wanted that. And I also wanted to tell people about Randy Harlan. I wanted people to know what had happened to him. So did his family.

It seemed all of our motives collided.

Mrs. Wills's voice and my notebook pulled me back. She told me about the boy who endured several major operations and outlived every doctor's expectations. The only sound he ever made was the mewing of a kitten. Every once in a long while, one side of his mouth managed to turn up just far enough that his family could say, "He smiled."

Borrowing the 8-x-10 inch portrait of Randy, I gathered all my things and shook Mrs. Wills's hand. I wasn't hungry for my missed lunch. I'd forgotten I had to go to the bathroom. That Wednesday afternoon in Sacramento, I was too caught up in the rush of a story that had to be told.

In the newsroom, I walked to the desk where all the portable radios were stored and quickly snapped mine back in its battery charger. Like a soldier returning from the field, I marched straight for my editor's desk, before going to the bathroom, before hitting the snack machine. Ricardo Pimentel turned his attention to me.

"How'd it go?"

I was standing in the narrow aisle between his desk and the news editor. Reporters and editors kept trying to squeeze through. This was the busiest place in the newsroom, where about forty-five reporters got their assignments and hashed out stories with several assistant city editors. The phones were always ringing. Reporters waited their turn to speak to editors.

Behind me, two editors debated what stories should go on the front page. Other reporters were scattered about in short, neat cubicles that made the newsroom look much more efficient and clean than any from the movies. The phones were ringing, the police scanner was beeping and talking. But that wasn't why I couldn't manage to speak.

My throat felt swollen to twice its normal size. I swallowed hard, squeezing my hands into fists and telling myself not to cry. Then I told Ricardo about Randy's little smile, about his grandmother's guilt over failing to stop the beating, and about his sister, who kept interrupting the interview to ask, "Where's Randy?"

But my voice wasn't working right. My face felt hot. I knew it was red.

"It was bad," I said. Right then, I didn't care about the front page. I just wanted to cry.

Ricardo opened his eyes a little wider; he looked at me a little closer. "Can you write this story?"

I wasn't sure if he was worried about me or about getting his story, or both. It didn't matter, though, because something like a switch turned on in me, and I knew what I needed to do. I felt like a robot.

"Yes, of course. I want to write this story," I said, glancing at the clock, which read 3:30. "I'll be done by 5:30."

I charged over to my desk, taking out my notebook, signing onto the computer and calling the coroner's office all at once. Randy's death was officially classified a homicide because he died from the injuries he suffered in the beating. But since his father had been killed while drunk driving three years after the incident, he would never face charges.

I looked again at Randy's picture. I opened a clear screen on my computer, and the first line almost typed itself: "A little boy rests at last."

They were the words that I heard, over and over in my

head, in the funeral home. Nothing else came automatically. Sitting at my terminal, perched on the edge of my seat, I took deep breaths and felt some comfort in the cold metal of the chair against my stockinged feet. I struggled with words and phrases and paragraphs, putting them together and ripping them apart, shoving my hair into a messy ponytail and twirling it as I stared into the dark green screen.

I couldn't hear the rapid keyboard tapping, the chatter of editors and the incessant ringing of phones that reaches its crescendo in the late afternoon of a newsroom. At one point, I realized an editor, Maury Macht, was standing next to me. He patted my shoulder. Later, I could hear someone calling, "Diana, Diana," from far away. I struggled to pull myself out of the story and saw the night photo editor a few feet away from me. I glanced at the clock. It was almost 5:00 P.M. I realized he wanted Randy's picture.

Within two hours of arriving in the newsroom, I was writing the last words to Randy's story: "Long, brown lashes hung over his eyes, and just for a second his chest seemed to move—as if he were only sleeping."

I hit the computer's "send" button, cleaned up my desk and headed to the bathroom. Inside the stall, I covered my face and cried. I learned to do that when the crimes got too brutal, when the victims touched me too deeply, when I felt I couldn't control my emotions anymore. Mentally, I'd yank all that sadness and upset back inside me and walk calmly to the bathroom, nodding and smiling to whoever was at the copy machine. Then I'd slam the door of the bathroom. Inside my tiny, private space, I could question why this happened to a little boy. I could wonder what he might have become. I could cry.

Eventually, I developed a pattern at work and at home.

I made the routine cop checks. Certain murders didn't seem to bother me as much. They arrived on my list of things to do and then disappeared so quickly. I couldn't find the detail or the interview that I needed to turn the death into a full-fledged story. Many victims were drug dealers or gang members. Family members wouldn't talk. I felt those stories turning into formulas. That bothered me.

I wanted to feel; I wanted to hurt. If I didn't feel anything, I thought, the readers of my story wouldn't either.

Still, I was supposed to be detached, and other reporters criticized me for being "too sensitive." I rarely socialized or ate with them. I was too caught up in the daily crime tally and the latest victim. On my time off, I met cops, eating dinner on their shifts or drinking beers at their hangouts. I got more tips, I began to understand this other world.

Any worry about becoming callous never lasted long. Some incident always sucked me back in. The misery was neatly summarized and listed by police district: a grandmother who jumped from her ninth-floor balcony on Christmas Eve, or the one-year-old girl who was fatally stabbed when her mother used her as a shield during a fight with her husband.

There were so many words I wanted to say to the victims' families. I wanted to tell them that they were right, that life was cruel and bizarre and strange, that they had reason to be outraged. There were so many people I wanted to hug, to hold, to make better and heal somehow. But my notebook was there, and I'd record and watch and listen to the narcotics officers knocking on the door of a middle-aged couple's home, telling them their teenage son had been arrested for dealing crack.

The home was in a good neighborhood. The father

didn't understand. His son had a nice stereo, an allowance, loving parents. They had moved to Sacramento to get away from the gangs in Los Angeles.

Then the father put his hand over his eyes. His wife whispered, "Our older son was killed by the Crips a year ago in L.A. Now it seems we're losing the other one."

Walking away from the house that day, I felt like I had hit bottom. I didn't know if I could see another heartbroken family.

A few months later, after many beers at Gilhooley's, it was close to 2:00 A.M. I sat on one of the outside benches, talking with a veteran detective.

He described a domestic disturbance call he responded to as a young patrol officer. It was in the middle of one of Sacramento's scorching summers. When he pulled up to the house, he saw several young children under a big fig tree. They each had a pot or pan, and with the help of spoons, they were making music.

"It was beautiful," said Detective Gary Kereazis.

Inside, he discovered that the family was living in a burned-out house. The children's toys had been destroyed.

"I opened my big mouth and said, if the parents didn't mind, I'd like to take the kids and get them a set of drums," Kereazis said.

So on his day off, he picked up six or seven children under the age of twelve in his old station wagon and ferried them to toy stores. But they couldn't find any drums. Eventually they wound up at a pawn shop, staring at the only set of drums they could find, a $500 set.

"I kept trying to find them cheaper, but those kids just wore me down," Kereazis said. "I made a promise."

So even though he was going through a divorce and had little money, he whipped out his credit card. After a stop for hamburgers, he brought the children home and unloaded the set of professional drums. The children set them up right then and there. And the music sounded wonderful.

"They were worse off then I was," he said.

The winds had picked up. It was after 2:00 A.M. Then he confided to me: "You know, that's the best thing I ever did."

This story never appeared in the paper. It had happened years before. But I realized later it was probably the most important one I ever came across, for it helped me finally understand why the police beat held such power over me.

It was the charge of chasing a story and getting it on the front page. But even more, it was that while I was seeing the worst in people, the police beat also showed me the best in people: the children who brought so much joy in only two years of life, the parents who had the strength to serve me lemonade just a few days after their son had committed suicide, the ninety-two-year-old woman who managed to grip my hand so strongly even after a savage beating.

Somehow, along the way, along with the pain, I'd been gathering the joy, just like Kereazis, who ignored the poverty and the fighting parents, and instead chose to see the children and hear their music.

**Diana K. Sugg**, 30, is a reporter at the *Baltimore Sun*. Before coming to the *Sun* in 1995, Diana covered crime at the *Sacramento Bee* in Sacramento, California, for two years. She won the first Al Nakkula Award for Police Reporting, a national prize. Previously she worked as reporter at the *Spartanburg* (S.C.) *Herald-Journal* and the Associated Press in

Philadelphia. She earned her master's degree at Ohio State University on a Kiplinger Public Affairs Reporting Fellowship in 1992. She graduated Phi Beta Kappa with a double major in English and Honors from Villanova University in 1987.

# FOUR

—〰—

# The Practice Homicides

## WILLIAM HERMANN

### The Arizona Republic

Sooner or later every police reporter must confront the fact that there are real homicides and there are practice homicides. With the beheading of Angela Brosso I finally began to understand the difference between the two.

I was the night police reporter for the *Arizona Republic* and wandering around in the dark in the North Phoenix desert looking for Angela's head. Perhaps 200 yards from me, huge, portable lights illuminated a small crowd of homicide detectives crawling over every sandy centimeter of the murder scene.

The cops said this was no "practice homicide," but was a very real homicide. Not only was it a real homicide, it was a *real big* homicide. I couldn't know then that though I wouldn't solve the real big one, I would stumble upon the answer to a bigger question.

The scent of mesquite and palo verde trees, creosote bush and saguaro cactus laced a light breeze. It was late fall, but the temperature was a little above 60 degrees— the kind of weather that in just fifty years has turned a cowtown into a desert metropolis of more than two million people.

Cowtown crimes have given way to big city crimes, so many we have stopped paying attention to most of them. But if the victim of a crime is the right sort of person, or if the crime is particularly hideous or bizarre, then we pay very close attention.

If the victim is the right sort of person *and* the crime is hideous and bizarre, then the victim becomes a guest of page A-1 for days.

The date was November 9, 1992. Angela Brosso's naked, headless torso had been found beside a bicycle trail in a desert park about 100 yards east of her North Phoenix apartment complex. The 22-year-old victim wasn't just naked and headless. She had been disemboweled.

Earlier in the afternoon, a TV cameraman's long lens had taken me up close to see that her torso had been ripped open from her throat to her pubic hair. Her breasts lay to her sides, near her armpits.

Angela had gone out about seven the evening before for her regular bike ride, which usually lasted about ninety minutes. When she hadn't returned home by 11:00 P.M., roommate and boyfriend Joseph Krakowiecki called police. The cops told the twenty-four-year-old that if Angela didn't turn up by morning, they'd conduct a search.

The next morning came, but Angela didn't. The search began. About 9:30 A.M. police found the headless body, clad only in socks and tennis shoes. Her blood-soaked clothing was heaped nearby.

Angela would have been twenty-two years old on the day her body was found.

Angela's purple, 21-speed Diamondback mountain bike was missing. As was her head. It had been severed cleanly just below the chin, as if with a surgical saw.

The cops at the crime scene gave reporters little information. As usual, they kept all media away from investigators; our information came through a public information officer.

Detective Leo Speliopoulos, the P.I.O., was a veteran of countless ghastly crime scenes, but even he was shaken after viewing Angela's body.

"I don't remember anything—nothing in recent memory—that was anything like this," he said.

Speliopoulos admitted that homicide detectives had little evidence. They had concluded that Angela had not been beheaded and cut open where her body was found—not enough blood. But investigators had not found the site where she had been slain.

Police turned up no witnesses and had received no phone tips of any use.

At 8:00 P.M. homicide detectives were still working the scene. Patrol officers and reporters alike scoured the surrounding desert for Angela's head. The cops and the media all regarded this as one of the biggest cases, one of the biggest crime stories, to come along in years. It was the realest sort of real homicide.

The previous year, during my first week on the police beat, I'd learned the distinction that most cops and journalists make between real homicides and practice homicides.

Then it took me almost two years to learn that we all were wrong.

One chilly January night I'd heard my police scanner squawk that a body had been found near the railroad tracks at Jackson Street and 19th Avenue. I was at the scene in ten minutes.

The young woman lay sprawled on the cinders, a gash in her throat, her eyes glassy-dead. She wore dirty denim shorts and a sweatshirt. She had a high-top tennis shoe on her left foot; its mate lay among oily cinders between the tracks.

It was my first up-close homicide, and I tried frantically to get information from the lone investigator at the scene so that I could phone in the big story.

The detective was a kindly sort, and he set me straight gently. It went about like this:

"Look, Bill, this isn't a real homicide," he said as he stood casually smoking a cigarette and gesturing toward the body. "This is what we sometimes call a 'practice homicide.' Our experience has been that your paper usually only wants to know about real homicides."

So what the hell is the difference, I'd demanded, between a real homicide and a practice homicide?

The detective said, "This lady here—let's call her Lupita Lopez—is a prostitute and a crack addict. A crack whore. She screws guys for $10 a throw, she sleeps wherever she can flop, she pees in the street. Women like her get killed. It's what they do, finally.

"Now, it's not that we don't care that this poor woman is dead. Oh no, we care. We will try to find out which of the thousands of lowlife bastards who live around here offed her, and we will try to send him to the lethal injection table, or at least get him a few years in the joint.

"But this poor whore's death isn't a real homicide, and we're not going to call out the cavalry to solve it."

Then the detective held up a hand with a finger pointing in the air, emphasizing that something of importance was coming.

"On the other hand," he said, eyes widening, eyebrows raising, "If Mrs. Harold Radcliffe III, of the Biltmore Estates, is clipping roses in her garden tomorrow and someone drives by and shoots her, we by God won't rest until we have that clown by the short hairs. Because, you see, the death of a *Mrs. Radcliffe* would be a *real* homicide.

"You see?"

I remember laughing a little nervously, then consulting by telephone with my editor about this real and practice homicide business. He concurred, in general, with the detective. I'd learned my first lesson on the police beat.

Thereafter, when a Lupita Lopez or a Rogelio Martinez or a Lawanda Jefferson or a Clarence Washington died while walking the streets, fighting another gang member, mugging another homeless person or battling another drunk over a wine bottle, I would usually write something like the following: *The body of a Phoenix woman was found about 10 p.m. Friday near the Southern Pacific railroad tracks at Jackson Street and 19th Avenue. Lupita Lopez, 32, had apparently been stabbed to death, officials said. Police still were investigating the case late Friday.*

But if a middle-income couple were driving down the freeway, and a gang member shot one of them because he thought he'd been cut off in traffic, or if a woman who lived in a good neighborhood was raped and murdered in her home, or if a businessman walking to his car outside a nice restaurant was waylaid, robbed and shot to death, why, then we'd be looking at sixteen to twenty column inches, and let's definitely try for some art: a photograph while the scene is hot is best, a map or some other graphic will do.

I didn't like the fact that we blew off so many murders, but I understood why. In any big American city there are hundreds of homicides every year. Reporters (and editors) are looking for *news*, and in most cities it no longer is news when a gang member, prostitute, transient or drug dealer gets zapped. It's seldom even news when some kid wanders into the line of fire.

Happens all the time.

In any event, the horribly brutal murder of the young, honest, hard-working, white, Angela Brosso seemed as real as a homicide can get, and the cops were acting accordingly.

So were the reporters. We talked to neighbors for blocks around ("And this always seemed like such a nice neighborhood."), talked to every cop who strayed outside the crime scene and talked to each other to try to swipe information.

I finally got sick of talking to people who didn't know any more than I did, so I busied myself peering into mesquite bushes, looking under palo verde trees and rustling the underbrush, wondering if I'd fall over in a faint if I found the head.

I'd only seen a severed human head once before.

About a month before I'd gone to a car/pedestrian accident in northwest Phoenix.

After being hit, the victim flew onto the hood and his head went through the windshield, where it was severed from his body, but somehow came flying back out of the car along with his torso.

The head bounced along the road until it came to rest beneath a rear tire of the car, which had eventually stopped about one-hundred-and-fifty yards from the point of impact.

The torso had fallen beneath the car after it came off the hood, and under there it was shredded, sliced and diced, leaving a leg here, another there, arms on opposite sides of the street, and intestines and other viscera down the center of the road for more than one hundred yards.

I called the desk with the story of the mutilated pedestrian. Unfortunately, my information so disgusted the editor that it was decided the accident would be left out of the next morning's news altogether.

I guess it was a practice pedestrian death.

Of course, if I had found Angela's head that night—or if I stumbled across her entrails—that was guaranteed front page. Or if I could point toward a suspect, that would be terrific. I wondered if this murder was as much a "whodunit" as it appeared. Maybe it was just the old story: the man closest to the dead woman did it.

For I'd also learned early on that every day in every way boyfriends kill girlfriends, husbands kill wives. And when a man is found dead, the woman closest to him is the first suspect—though the fact is, men kill women about four times as often as women kill men.

Which left me, most of the other reporters, and certainly the cops wondering if the boyfriend, Krakowiecki, had snuffed Angela.

Earlier in the day I'd worked the Woodstone apartment complex on Cactus Road where Angela and Krakowiecki had lived together. Krakowiecki was not home. Neighbors said little more than that the two seemed like pleasant young people and appeared to get along well.

But the daytime cop reporter had found friends of Angela's who said that she and Krakowiecki were "having problems." One friend said Angela had confided that she intended soon to move out of the apartment.

That was enough to make us craft the first story on the murder in a manner so as to hedge our bets.

We couldn't say explicitly that the boyfriend was a suspect, because the cops hadn't said that. But we could put in the quotes about the two having problems so that if the boyfriend were later arrested we could say, "Well, we knew it all along, but couldn't just come right out and say it.''

It was a common journalistic sleight of hand. But not a writing technique I would have taught my English students. (As it turned out, Krakowiecki was never charged with any crime in connection with Angela Brosso's murder.)

I had, improbably enough, been a high school English teacher and then principal before coming to the newspaper. Most of my career was spent at an inner-city Catholic school attended by about 50 percent Hispanic, 10 percent African-American and 40 percent Anglo students.

Some of them were from middle-income homes. Most, however, were from homes where the cost of tuition was a profound sacrifice. The parents wanted their children to get a good high school education, go to college and never again have to live in a neighborhood where violence was commonplace. A neighborhood where "practice" homicides claimed so many young lives.

During my education career, I had sold freelance stories to several newspapers, and when, in a fit of midlife crisis, pondered whether at forty-three years old I was destined to die a high school principal, I asked the *Republic* for a reporting job.

Improbably enough, I got one.

It hadn't gone well at first. I was assigned to write a light, gossipy "around the town" column that would include lots of names of society and business types. I never could quite get that chatty, friendly, in-the-know slant those columns must have and after about a year begged to be switched to the news section.

Like many newcomers to the city desk, I was assigned to the night police beat. I soon understood why that beat is among the least popular at any newspaper.

Nobody wanted to spend their nights hanging around practice homicides. Nobody wanted to cover death after death that would go largely unreported. Few wanted to wander around in the desert looking for a human head.

Including me.

I gave up on Angela's head about 9:00 P.M. and began driving south on Interstate 17, into the heart of the city.

I was on fire with plans to make a special project of the Brosso murder. This was, I knew, the biggest case I'd worked on yet. If I could follow every step of the investigation, get the inside scoop, be the first to know of an impending arrest, I would have one of the year's top stories on my hands.

As I drove along, I had my police scanner on low, having long since learned to screen out reports of assaults, burglaries and auto thefts and come to attention when the word "shooting" was broadcast. As one part of my mind plotted how I would take hold of the Brosso story and not let go until someone was in jail, the other listened to the radio traffic.

I would get to the bottom of this, I would go back to the apartment where the murdered girl and her boyfriend lived, I would learn everything there is to know about killers who . . .

Suddenly on the scanner a voice shouted something like, "I think we've got a shooting here, 27th Avenue and Indian School."

Then a few moments later "Hey! We. . . . Hey! 999, 999!"

999. Officer needs assistance urgently.

It's the call that makes cops slam the accelerator to the floor and race to the rescue—in this case, at Indian School Road and . . .

Christ, I thought, I'm *right at the Indian School exit!* Now I'm going off, I'll get through this parking lot, there's 27th Avenue, Jesus! What the hell?

Getting out of my car . . . Chaos, screaming, people running, ducking, cops circling someone . . . Then BLAM, BLAM, BLAM, BLAM, the cracking smack of gunshots . . . then more gunshots, screaming . . .

Someone going down.

On the few occasions when I have stumbled right into the middle of a violent situation I have had only a dim idea of what was going on. This was one.

When guns fire, when knives flash, when fists connect with flesh, when injury or death is at hand, few of us are able to keep our wits about us enough to be careful observers. It took me about a half hour to figure out what I had "witnessed" in those few seconds.

What I learned was that a few minutes before the first 999 call went out, a man named Ricky Gillin had been picked up near 27th Avenue and Indian School Road by his estranged wife and her fourteen-year-old son in the wife's van.

Gillin had claimed the driver's seat and driven west on Indian School Road. He and his wife had begun to quarrel. Gillin had shouted, cursed, waved his arms, threatened them both. Then the boy told Gillin to calm down.

Gillin whipped a pistol out of his waistband and shot the boy in the face from a range of about six inches.

The van was pulling into the intersection of 27th Avenue and Indian School as the boy slumped down, dead almost instantly. But there, in the intersection, a motorcycle patrolman was sorting out a traffic accident. He'd heard the gunshot, quickly realized something terrible had happened in the van and made his first call.

Patrol cars already on their way to the accident now came screaming in from three directions, officers unholstering pistols, a sergeant grabbing his shotgun, other calls for assistance going out.

Gillin had stayed in the van for less than a minute before climbing out the driver's-side door, dragging his screaming, hysterical wife. He stood by the driver's door and held her by the neck in front of himself as a shield.

Three cops—two officers with pistols and a sergeant with a shotgun—sidestepped around in front of Gillin, trying to get into a safe position from which to shoot.

Suddenly the wife broke away, Gillin lowered his pistol and everyone opened up.

That's about when I pulled up and heard gunshots, saw figures ducking, running, shouting, screaming.

Within seconds Gillin was on the pavement with several bullets and a good helping of buckshot in him. Nobody else was hit.

The mother ran to the van and began clutching at her son, hideously disfigured and dead on the seat. I walked up to the van as she began screaming high and madly.

Those dreadful shrieks filled the intersection, filled the night air and silenced the police and gathering crowd.

I will carry to the grave the sound of that poor woman's screams.

Gillin was trundled into an ambulance, paramedics assuring me he would soon die. He did not. He lived to be convicted of murder and followed one part of the police adage that says, "Shoot a bad guy fifteen times in the head, neck and torso, and somehow he will live. Shoot a cop in the elbow and he will surely die."

After the forty-five minutes or so it took me to put together in writing just what in the hell I had blundered into, I phoned my story to the paper.

They cut the story down to forty-seven lines.

This tragedy was, after all, something of a practice homicide. For one thing, it happened in a lousy part of town. For another, the folks involved weren't exactly the country club set. Finally, it happened late. The presses had begun to roll with the first edition, and the death of a poor boy shot in a poor part of town just wasn't important enough to start remaking the newspaper.

But mostly it was just another shooting. Of course, years ago in Phoenix, when the homicide count for one year was only thirty or forty, this story would have been a sensation. But with the murder count moving into the one hundreds then two hundreds through the 1980s and 1990s, more and more killings have moved from the real homicide to the practice homicide category.

It was almost midnight by the time I began driving back to the paper, and all I could think of was the terrible scene at the intersection. I doubt that I thought of Angela Brosso at all.

That's how it would go for me in my efforts to follow the Brosso investigation. It's that way for most police reporters.

You cover a murder, maybe follow that story the next day, and then you move on to the next homicide. Between January 1992 and January 1995, I covered about three hundred homicides. Most were practice homicides, of course, but some rated twelve or even twenty column inches. There simply is not time for a police reporter to devote himself to following one murder investigation to the exclusion of all else.

But Angela was good for at least three or four days. The next day I came into work early, hoping to get in on whatever was breaking on the Brosso killing.

I went to the fourth floor of the police department to talk to Detective Speliopoulos.

Got any suspects? Do you think we have a serial killer

on our hands? Have the Phoenix cops asked the FBI's help in compiling a psychological profile on the murderer?

"No," to the first question, "Who knows?" to the second question, and a rather unpleasant smile for the third question.

"We've asked for the FBI's help in the past, and may do so in this case," Leo said. "Typically, what happens is, we give them the facts of a killing in which the perpetrator seems to be, shall we say, a little unusual, and we hope they can give us some solid information about this person.

"Usually, the FBI geniuses will send a terrific profile on the killer. It will say something like, 'this person likely had a very disrupted childhood. When he angers, he becomes highly agitated. He may have considerable animosity for women . . . ' like that.

"Very, very helpful, always leads us right to the killer."

Thank you, Leo.

In the next few weeks I covered five or six homicides, and every one of them involved a gang member or drug dealer. Each got a few lines of agate on B-2. But I wasn't particularly concerned about these practice homicides because I was trying to ferret out what the cops were doing on the Brosso investigation.

I learned that policewomen dressed in sportswear were riding bicycles in the evenings throughout the area where Angela had been found, hoping to bait the murderer. Every officer on a bicycle had a squad of officers watching her, and hundreds of hours were expended peddling and watching.

Other police scoured the area for miles around the Brosso murder scene, searching for the woman's head and her bicycle. Scores of phone tips were pursued.

Zero.

A large irrigation canal ran near where Angela's body was found, and police divers spent many hours searching the dirty waters. Divers went into the canal three times, the last time, early in the day on November 17.

Later that same day Angela's head was discovered.

It was found in the canal about a mile and a half from where her body had been discovered. It was spotted by a rather interesting character.

Mark Qualls was a free spirit, an eccentric, and spent many of his days wandering along the canal bank, looking for useful items and fishing. Now, the fish in Arizona's irrigation canals are not trout, nor are they any sort of fish most of us would like to put on the table. They are bottom-feeding carp, big, ugly brutes, and it would take a very hungry or very indiscriminate eater to consider them a delicacy. Qualls, known throughout the neighborhood as the "Fisher King," practically lived on those creatures.

The thirty-nine-year-old told police he saw the head washed against a grate in the canal where it crosses under Interstate 17.

Of course I wanted to know what condition the head was in, but cops weren't talking. It took me a couple days to learn that the head was in very good condition indeed.

"The sick bastard who killed her probably has been keeping that head in a refrigerator," a police source confided to me. "We don't know why he finally got rid of the head. Maybe he thought it was talking to him. But he's keeping the bike. We're sure he considers it a trophy. These guys who do shit like this like to take trophies and gloat over them."

Qualls was flattered to be the subject of intense television and newspaper publicity. What he didn't know was that we smiling, affable journalists were setting him up as the murderer of Brosso. The poor man smiled, talked a bit in his slow and shy way and was quite polite.

The cops looked hard at Qualls but would only tell me that several key factors eliminated the man as a suspect.

A sensational story like the Brosso killing is guaranteed page A-1 the day it breaks. There will certainly be an A-1 follow-up story the next day even if there is really nothing new. By the third day of nothing new the story usually moves to page B-1, and then, if nothing turns up, the story goes to sleep.

Angela hit A-1 twice, then B-1 twice for the four days after her body was found. There was similar treatment when her head was found. Then the stories petered out, with now and then a "nothing much new" brief.

During the next several months we received lots of telephone tips about the Brosso case. The cops, of course, received hundreds.

Most of the tips were about seeing Angela's missing bicycle. Some of the calls were from psychics indignant that the police were not using their services and offering us a bargain basement price for a consultation.

The day cop reporter spent much more time on the Brosso case than I did. Then I got switched to days, poked around the aging case a bit, but found nothing. I still spent most of my time on no-account practice homicides, trying to sex up the death of some bum so I could at least get B-1, but usually with little success.

On Wednesday, September 22, 1993, I'd started the day as usual in my office at the city's main police station, which is located in the heart of one of the worst sections of downtown Phoenix.

The station itself is a four-story, squat, concrete cube with slits for windows. The office I share with another newspaper reporter and a radio journalist is just off the main lobby and is about the size of a large bathroom. Police scanner radios constantly blare in the little workplace and robbery or assault victims, prostitutes or transients often wander in.

About 10:30 A.M. I was pounding out a brief about some poor wretch who'd been run down by a truck when I heard some scanner traffic about more cops needed at the 451 scene at the Arizona Canal, just off Interstate 17.

What 451 scene?

I drove north on the freeway, parked at a technical college nearby, and saw Leo Speliopoulos standing on the south bank of the canal. On the north bank I saw Lt. Sharon Kiyler, head of homicide, staring down into the water. Three other detectives crawled around in the weeds and bushes on the north bank, and about six patrol officers walked the canal banks searching for something.

"This wouldn't be a homicide, would it Leo?" I smiled.

"That's a distinct possibility," he sighed. "In fact, it's a distinct possibility that the body of a seventeen-year-old girl was found in the canal about ten this morning by a jogger."

I looked up and realized we were barely a mile from where Angela Brosso's body had been found about nine months before.

"Tell me quickly, Leo, was this girl beheaded."

"Now don't even start that nonsense," Leo snapped. "But you might as well know, she was riding a bicycle along here last night . . ."

"And the damned bicycle is missing!?"

"You win the prize."

During the morning I learned that Melanie Bernas, an honors student at Arcadia High School, often went for evening bicycle rides, usually alone.

The popular, attractive girl was last seen early Tuesday evening, September 21, by her mother at their home, about six miles from the crime scene. When Mrs. Bernas returned home from dinner with friends, about 10:00 P.M., Melanie was gone. When her daughter still had not returned at 2:00 A.M., Mrs. Bernas called police. A missing person's report was taken, and Mrs. Bernas was left to fret.

About 10:00 A.M. Wednesday, a bicyclist noticed blood on the bike trail beside the canal and called police. Cops then found Melanie's body floating in the canal near the point where it crosses under Interstate 17. Which was right where Angela Brosso's head had been found about ten months before.

"OK, Leo," I wheedled. "She has a head, but what was done to her chest?"

"Can't comment on that right now," Leo said quietly.

Soon we would learn that Melanie had massive wounds to her chest, that her green, 1992, 21-speed Hardrock Sport mountain bike was missing, and that police wanted to talk to a thinly built Anglo male who was seen near the canal during the past several days.

"You think this Anglo male is the guy?" I asked Leo.

"Christ knows," he said. "The guy was seen around here a lot, and maybe he saw something himself, or maybe . . . anyway, we want to talk to him. Say as much in your story, if you please."

"So here it is, Leo. Will you guys say that this case certainly seems strangely similar to another case—which you might remember—that took place in this neighborhood?"

"No."

I wandered about the crime scene. I walked on the footpath on the east side of I-17, and looked back at the area on the canal bank where the blood trail was found.

It seemed likely that the murderer had either used some pretext to stop Melanie as she rode along the canal bank or had jumped from bushes and pulled her off her bicycle.

Interstate 17 is a divided, six-lane freeway linking the Valley with the northern part of the state and is heavily traveled day and night. Some part of the assault upon Melanie took place less than seventy-five yards off the highway, and if anyone driving by had just turned and looked at the right time, they would have witnessed the attack. If the killer had dragged Melanie out of view of freeway traffic and into the bushes, any of the people who walk, jog and ride along the canal bank could have meandered into the midst of the murder.

Just as, ten months ago, someone who used the trail where Angela rode her mountain bike could easily have chanced upon the murderer as he either dragged the young woman away or killed her in the area.

This killer had incredible nerve or was too nuts to worry.

Lacking anything solid to write about at the crime scene, I went to find out what I could about Melanie.

As I drove toward Arcadia High School, I used my cellular phone to check my phone messages. There was a long, emotional message from Bill Barber, a friend and fellow teacher from my education days.

Bill taught at Arcadia, and Melanie had been one of his prize students.

Bill told me that he, the other teachers and the students were stupefied over the news of the popular girl's death. He advised me not to come to Arcadia—journalists already were trying to get on campus to talk to students and were being turned away—but to call him in the English Department office and he would meet me nearby.

We rendezvoused at a small sandwich shop near the campus. Bill sat across a formica table from me and repeatedly shook his head from side to side and said, "I can't believe it, just can't believe it!" He ordered a meal but ignored it.

I am ashamed to say that not only did I eat the roast beef sandwich I ordered, but I ate Bill's sandwich as well. I am also not proud to note that almost no homicide— neither shooting nor stabbing nor strangling—has ever completely extinguished my appetite. I deserve to be obese but have stayed about 160 pounds since I was twenty.

In any event, Bill told me what everyone who knew Melanie would repeat. Excellent student, charming, pleasant young woman. Full of promise . . .

And best of all for my purposes, Melanie was white and from a nice family. Add to that the bizarre nature of her murder and it was as real as a homicide can get.

I threw myself into the Melanie Bernas story. I had, during the last few months, spent less and less time on practice homicides, and now I whisked through them like lightning. In fact, one day when I learned about a body having been found in a poor neighborhood in South Phoenix, I simply ignored the killing altogether because I was on my way to talk with Melanie's mother.

Our conversation was brief.

"I don't think I can talk about this," she said in a low voice as she stood in the doorway of the middle-income, pleasant, ranch-style home she had lived in since Melanie was a little girl. Mrs. Bernas was divorced, her older children were grown, and Melanie had been the center of the woman's life.

"I know this is hard," I said, "but maybe if you give

us some information, it can help find the person who did this."

Mrs. Bernas—late forties, trim, attractive—was trying to be polite to yet another journalist wanting to talk about the most painful thing in her world.

She took a deep breath. "You cannot imagine how much I would like to have the person who did this found. You can't imagine how much I would like to have my daughter back. . . . You just can't . . ."

The woman stopped and stared at me with a look that went beyond sorrow or despair. It was a look I have come to know too well—the look worn by a parent who has lost a child.

I will eagerly walk into the midst of gun battles, knife fights, train wrecks, car accidents, riots and fires for the sake of a good story. But I go dead in the heart when I have to face a parent whose child has been killed. When parents learn the terrible news, they howl and shriek and scream, and they double over as if they have been struck in the stomach. And they are never, never the same again.

When you lose a child to violence, something inside you is simply extinguished. And you wear the look of your loss the rest of your life.

Mrs. Bernas wore that look.

"Listen," she said, "the detectives begged me not to tell any details that haven't already gone out. If we talk I'll probably mess up and say something I shouldn't. Would you please come back later, when the detectives say I can talk?"

I left and drove the seven or eight miles back to the crime scene and walked around the area for the entire afternoon. The next day I reread the Angela Brosso police report, then went back to the north Valley and walked up and down the bike path Angela had ridden. As I trudged about, I tried to imagine what had gone on in the mind of the monster who had slain two innocent young women.

What the cops wouldn't say publicly, they conceded privately: the lunatic who had butchered Angela Brosso was almost certainly the same person who had killed Melanie Bernas.

"And he likely has several from the past—probably in other cities, other states we don't know about," a detective told me. "And worst, he'll have others in the future. He seems to like his work, and he's fearless."

Two days after Melanie's body was found, I was deep into a book on serial killers when the city editor called me. She wanted me to go out to a crime scene from the night before. A girl who lived in a miserable neighborhood had been killed in yet another drive-by shooting—about the 100th for the year. The night police reporter had done a brief story, which, typically, would have sufficed.

"I don't know," the city editor said. "Sometimes I think we need to pay a little more attention to these things. See what you can dig up."

I grudgingly went. I could easily guess what I would find: poor people, few of whom would speak English, mourning a lost soul and cursing young thugs with guns.

What I knew as I drove to the seedy, Central Phoenix neighborhood was that Vianette Mungarro, 14, had died of a bullet wound Monday night. It had been, police said, some sort of gang altercation. Great, I thought, yet another gang shooting, yet another poor Hispanic kid dead.

Yet another practice homicide.

As I got out of my car a tall, slim transvestite walked up, tears flowing down his heavily made-up face. His long, auburn hair looked as if it had recently been permed; his nails were perfectly manicured and polished.

He asked if I was a reporter and I confessed I was.

"Then someone needs to write something *real* about this death," he said. "That was a little teenage girl that was shot down and your newspaper story made it sound like, like . . . just nothing had happened."

The transvestite introduced himself as Candy and led me to the small, shabby apartment complex where Vianette had lived in three rooms with her mother, three sisters and two brothers. Two young women stood out in the small yard of the horseshoe-shaped complex. They spoke quietly, as did a group of young Hispanic men standing nearby.

One of the young women was Vianette's sister, Carolina. She was thirteen. She said she and Vianette had been standing in that same spot the evening before.

"We was just standing there, Vianette holding my sister Griselda's baby, when these guys came up," Carolina recounted in a soft voice. She took deep breaths and wrung her hands as she relived the previous night's horror.

"They said they were gonna get us for our friends doing a drive-by. We tried to say we didn't know anything about . . . but then one of them shot in the air twice, BANG! BANG!

"Vianette and I fell to the ground, and she was trying to protect the baby."

Carolina said she and her sister lay on the ground a few moments, then got to their feet, with Carolina taking the baby.

"Then they shot again and hit Vianette," she said.

"She screamed out, and turned toward our front door . . ."

Just as Vianette's mother came running to the door.

Carolina told me that Vianette cried, "They've killed

me, Mama! They've killed me!'' as she fell into her mother's arms.

As Carolina told her story, Candy was standing nearby weeping.

"Vianette was laying on her back, and her mother had her head in her lap,'' Candy interrupted, using a small, flowered hanky to wipe away his tears.

"The poor mother was just hysterical, and I took Vianette's pulse, and nothing, just nothing,'' Candy sobbed. "The worst thing was that Vianette's poor mother just couldn't be consoled.

"She stayed out in the yard all night and wouldn't go in. And all of us in the neighborhood lay in bed and heard her crying all night for her little daughter, who was dead.''

I looked at Candy, I looked at Carolina, I looked at the young men who were, I knew, plotting revenge. And I looked at a small woman standing in the shadows inside the doorway of the sad little apartment. I didn't have to see her face to know that her eyes would tell me that something had gone dead inside her. Just as it had for Melanie Bernas's mother.

And I finally figured it out.

I realized that this was, after all, a real homicide and a real story, one that belonged on A-1. Which is where it would end up in the next edition of the *Republic*.

And I realized that too often I had turned my back on stories because they involved illegal aliens or gang members or poor people in a nasty neighborhood. Because they involved people our society seldom wishes to read about.

And I finally realized what was real and what was practice.

I knew that in the future I would better understand the significance of deaths like those of Angela Brosso and Melanie Bernas. They were tragic, they were heartbreaking, but *they* were, after all, the "practice" homicides.

For the fact is, Angela and Melanie had died at the hands of a freak, a madman of a type that has existed for centuries, is blessedly rare, and signifies little or nothing about the society in which he pops up.

He is crazy, he murders until he is caught, and that's all.

A madman striking down innocent people may hold a horrid fascination for many of us but is no more typical than a lightning bolt.

But the death of a Vianette Mungarro, or Lupita Lopez or any of the scores of people whose deaths we so often consigned to a few lines of agate type on B-2 are the homicides that tell the tale of our cities.

They are the real stories of our nation. Stories of teen-age boys with guns slaughtering thousands yearly. Stories of drug dealers, gang members, society's bottom ranks, shooting their wretched neighborhoods and the people in them to tatters. Thousands and thousands of these killings every year, many times more in the United States than any other nation.

Our newspapers too often give life to the deaths that, ultimately, mean little while we bury the murders that are killing us.

Now, every time I go to a poor neighborhood and cover the death of a gang member or a prostitute or a homeless person, I try to think of a way to craft a story that will claim A-1. Usually, I fail. But I succeed now and again, and my work is better for the effort.

Still, I carry two pictures in my reporter's notebook.

Each is of a bicycle. One, Angela's, the other Melanie's. Both bikes still missing, the killer still at large.

Every month or two Phoenix police get a lead that they hope will point them toward the killer.

So far every lead has led nowhere.

I sometimes imagine the killer gloating over his bicycle trophies and plotting how he will kill again.

Providing some reporters with a story about a real homicide and some reporters a story about a practice homicide.

**William Hermann** was born in Indianapolis, Indiana, in 1946, and his family moved to Arizona in 1951. Hermann graduated from Arizona State University with a B.A. in English literature in 1969, and he spent fourteen years as an English teacher and six years as a high school principal. Hermann's freelance writing, as well as a quiet midlife crisis, drove him into journalism in 1989, and he has been a police reporter for the *Arizona Republic* since late 1991.

# FIVE

—៳៳—

# Witness

## PAULA BARR

### The Kansas City Star

Every so often, a story I'm covering grabs me by the heart and refuses to let go.

Usually the story is intriguing because it's bizarre, mysterious or challenging. The unsolved murders and dismemberment of several young women found in the Missouri River is one such case.

Another involves a conspiracy murder investigation foiled by the disappearance of a key witness. The witness told federal authorities that a woman hired him to kill her business partner, who was murdered in July 1991. Days after his statement, the witness met with that woman. The next morning, he dropped out of sight. Without him the case has stalled.

But hardest to forget are the cases that involve children.

One of the most compelling stories was the case of an eight-year-old girl who saw her stepfather shot to death by an armed robber on April 14, 1994, in Independence, Missouri.

As Robert Newton lay dying, young Sarah Yates said a short prayer, and then she phoned for help. Later she would provide the detailed information to investigators that would help them apprehend the gunman and his accomplices. Her straightforward, heart-wrenching court testimony would help convict the cold-blooded killer and send him to Death Row.

From the murder to the sentencing, Sarah's courage never wavered, even after she learned that the gunman who had let her live, hadn't meant to spare her life.

Sarah was one of five children to have witnessed a fatal shooting in Independence from January to May of 1994. Two others—a four-year-old and an infant—had seen their mother murdered late in the evening of January 31. A masked intruder had slipped inside the small, brick ranch, then lurked in the dark kitchen until Diana Ault and her children returned home.

Two weeks after Sarah saw her stepfather killed, a twelve-year-old boy stood outside the home of his mother's boyfriend, where the man had briefly held the boy's mother hostage. Minutes after police went inside, the boy heard them shoot and kill the boyfriend.

A month later, a nine-year-old boy returned home from school to find his dying parents on their bed, minutes after the father had shot the mother, then himself.

Even though children witness more violence than ever before, cases where they see their parents murdered still are rare in the Kansas City metropolitan area.

In fact, homicide is relatively rare in Independence, where a "bad year" might include three murders. During that four-month period in 1994, however, six fatal shootings occurred in the city of 112,000.

Sarah's story worried me even before I found out that the robber had tried to kill her. If we let people know that children can help police find suspects, will murderers leave no witnesses, regardless of age, I wondered.

My editor, Connie Bye, and I weighed our responsibility as journalists. Running details of the story could prompt potential killers to consider murdering future child witnesses.

But when someone murders a parent in front of a child, the news is compelling and cries to be told. The public deserves to know when such monstrous killers are in their midst.

And sometimes, learning of a murderer's cold-blooded actions is what finally motivates a crucial witness to come forward.

So we run the stories. And we pray the children will be safe.

I first learned of Robert Newton's murder on the late-night television news. Cynthia Lozano, then our night police reporter, heard the call about 10:00 P.M. on the scanner: A young girl had seen her father shot at a small eastern Independence gas station. The girl was still on the scene.

Patrol officers, detectives and police administrators were at Campbell Oil Company when Cynthia arrived. But they would tell her only that a 53-year-old Blue Springs man had been shot and killed during an apparent robbery attempt.

Nearby, a young girl sat in a patrol car, clutching a stuffed animal. Certain she was the child police had referred to on the scanner, Cynthia approached the maroon Ford cruiser for more information. A friendly, beautiful, no-nonsense young woman, Cynthia easily elicits information from even the most crusty police officers.

That night, officers refused to let her near.

The next morning was Friday, and it was my job to follow up. I headed to the three-story concrete Independence police headquarters to talk to detectives. The tan building with narrow tinted windows sits on the fringes of Independence Square, where covered wagons once started their westward journeys and Harry Truman took his daily strolls.

The windowless, first-floor detective unit had worn, burnt-orange carpeting that ran partway up the waist-high cubicles. The walls, file cabinets and Formica tabletop desks were painted an ugly greenish-yellow. Tiny windows near the ceilings of a few smaller offices were shaded by an overhang and let in no light.

Despite the dismal decor, Independence detectives were a jovial bunch, often ribbing reporters or playing pranks. But with journalists they trusted, they usually were willing to share details of a case.

Unless it was a homicide.

Unlike Kansas City detectives, who deal with murders nearly every day, Independence investigators have been reluctant to discuss homicide cases until they are solved.

In the hours after the Newton murder, detectives were somber, rushing in and out of the bureau without speaking. Many were strangers to me—investigators from area agencies who had formed a Metro Squad to search for clues.

Sgt. Al Hainen, a tall, unflappable man in his mid-fifties was in his small inner office. I plopped down into a chair in front of his desk as he rifled through reports.

He knew what I wanted. The press release on the police wire had provided some details. But I needed more.

Press releases typically offer only a few basic facts. This had more than usual for Independence.

On April 14, 1994 at about 9:56 P.M., Independence, Missouri Police officers were dispatched to 316 North M-291 Highway to the Campbell Oil Company to investigate an armed robbery. Upon arrival, the officers located the body of Robert L. Newton, a

53 year old Blue Springs, Missouri resident and attendant of the service station. Mr. Newton was dead at the scene from an apparent gunshot wound. The victim's nine year old daughter was present during this armed robbery and did witness the death of her father. The nine year old girl was also threatened by the suspects in which the suspect had pointed the weapon at her but she was not harmed.

The release went on to describe the three suspects. Two were tall black males, each with a medium build and short black hair. One was twenty-five to thirty-five years old and the other was between fifteen and twenty-five. The older one wore a white tank top and long pants. The other wore a white or green T-shirt, baggy, blue, knee-length shorts and a baseball cap with white numbers or letters on it.

The third suspect was a black female with a heavy build. She wore a white T-shirt and baggy blue jeans. Their car was a light blue Chevrolet Camaro or Corvette that had some rust on it and white dots or circles on the sides.

So far, Hainen said, the police had no idea who the suspects were.

He corrected the girl's age in the press release, fielded my questions and offered some information on his own.

According to the police reports, the two men entered the station Thursday night while a woman waited outside in the car. The men robbed the gas station, then took Newton to a back room. The girl stood by his side.

The gunman fired, pointed the 9 mm. pistol at the child but did not shoot, Hainen said.

Hainen was appalled and disgusted.

"People don't respect anything or anyone," he said,

shaking his head as he leaned back in his chair. "They're willing to kill for a few dollars or a perceived slight."

Back in the sunshine, I knew I needed to find Bob Newton's friends. I headed east from the station along a sparsely populated section of Truman Road, then turned north on Missouri 291. The stretch of four-lane highway was under construction. The pavement had been ripped up, leaving a rutted, dirt pathway.

There were few businesses and no houses along that stretch of highway. Off to the east, underground caves housed several warehouses. On the west, about seventy-five yards south of Campbell Oil, another gas station appeared deserted. One car was gassing up outside the scene of the murder.

I pulled into the crushed stone lot and parked near a grassy area that bordered woods. On the south end of the building was a single-bay garage. The north corner was glassed in, revealing most of the inside.

As I grabbed my notebook and pen, a thin man wearing a worn baseball-style cap finished pumping gas and walked into the station. I took a deep breath, got ready for the possibility that I would be tossed out of the building and strode to the front door.

Jim Foster, a wiry man who looked to be in his late fifties or early sixties, turned to greet me. Behind him were shelves lined with motor oil and other auto supplies. To the left was a small room with a few wire rack displays of chips, crackers and other snacks and a cooler full of soft drinks.

Behind him, inside a short hallway, I could see the door to the storeroom where the murder had occurred. No one opened it the whole time I was there.

Foster smiled, looking at me curiously. I introduced myself.

"I'm doing a story on the murder," I told him. "I need to find friends of Bob Newton who'll tell me a little bit about him."

"Oh sure," Foster said, settling onto a wooden stool at the small wooden counter.

Just then, Foster's afternoon replacement, Richard Stone, walked in. Stone, taller and heavier than Foster, walked back and forth in the small room as he prepared to start his shift. Both men wore work clothes and boots. They spoke quietly and their faces were solemn.

"She's here about the murder." Foster told him. "She wants to know about Bob."

Bob was a nice guy who would drop everything in order to help you if you needed him, the men agreed.

The small group of retirement-age men who worked at the station all were close, and everyone was badly shaken by the murder, Foster said.

There had never been trouble before at the station, each insisted.

"This is the first time in five years I haven't wanted to come into work," Stone said, looking away from the back room. "I'm pretty uneasy."

Foster had not heard about the murder when he arrived that morning. But he knew something was wrong when he saw Newton's pickup truck still in the parking lot.

Newton had replaced Foster at 3:00 P.M. the previous day. Sarah had not been with him.

Foster had spoken with his boss, who told Foster what police had said about the murder.

Sarah had arrived sometime in the evening, Foster related. While she was there, two men and a woman had purchased $1 worth of gas. They returned about a half hour later, at closing. The men entered the store, stole

Newton's pocket change and less than $450 from the change drawer.

Foster believed that Newton would have obeyed a company policy that prohibits employees from challenging robbers. He said Newton had told him he would not resist.

Apparently, it had not mattered.

Quietly, in disbelief, Foster explained what he heard had happened next.

One of the men forced Newton and Sarah into a back room at gun point, Foster said, indicating the closed door with his right hand.

Inside the room, the gunman aimed the gun at Newton and fired. The killer then turned to little Sarah. He pointed the gun right at her.

But thankfully, he didn't shoot, Foster said.

"The last thing Bob said was 'don't kill my daughter,'" Foster said sadly. "Then the guy shot him in the head."

The room was silent for a long moment. Then, to ease their fears and grief, the two men chatted about Newton's retirement from General Motors after twenty-five years. Bob was planning to open a bait shop near the Ozark Mountains, Foster said.

I needed to head back to the bureau to verify their account with police. So I thanked them, left my card in case they heard anything new and then headed back to the bureau in southern Independence.

I was horrified by what I'd heard. During the drive to the office, I mulled over their statements and worked on some tentative leads for the story.

It took about ten minutes to get back to the office, located in a heavily commercial section of the working-class suburb. The county seat, Independence consists of single-family homes, several historic buildings and a few high-rises for its large elderly population. East of Missouri 291, Independence is mostly rural.

Our office is near the busiest intersection in the city, where Interstate 70 crosses Noland Road. The most heavily traveled roadway in the city, Noland Road is crowded with fast-food restaurants, retail and department stores, motels and gas stations.

My desk is about eye-level with traffic on Interstate 70. When I returned that day, I grabbed a cup of coffee, picked up the phone and began verifying with police most of what the men had said.

Their insight answered some of the questions left by the police reports. But a story like this one would touch people's hearts and cried for reaction from the family. People would want to know how little Sarah was doing and how her mother was coping.

This is the worst part of my job—calling relatives of murder victims to see if they'll talk. I'm always amazed when someone agrees to share memories and details about the victim. Some see it as a chance to memorialize their loved one in print. Others are angry and find a release in sharing their feelings.

A few refuse to talk at all. I don't blame them. I wouldn't be half as polite as most are when I call.

There are a number of ways to locate families of victims. If I'm lucky, someone slips me the names and numbers. More often, I find them in the phone book or the city directory. Once the obituary is phoned in to the newspaper, I can use it to find additional sources and the names of other family members.

All too often, those sources come up empty, and the obituary is nonexistent or arrives too late to help me. That's when I have to dig. It might mean calling people who live near the family or checking with my sources to see if they've heard something that could help me. Sometimes, it means knocking on the family's door.

This time, it was easy to find Astrid Newton's phone number in Blue Springs. But when I called, I got an answering machine. I left a message, asking someone to return my call.

No one did.

A police officer who knew the Newtons gave me the name of their pastor. But when I finally reached him, he confirmed what I had been hearing.

Astrid Newton and her family did not want to speak to any reporters

For Saturday's *Kansas City Star,* I focused on the new information from police and the statements from Newton's coworkers at the gas station. By the end of the day, police had nothing new to report.

Over the weekend, I pondered new angles and ways to get information. Who among my sources might have known Newton and could help me reach his family? Should I get experts to speculate on the type of person who would murder a child's parent in front of her, then threaten her life for a few hundred dollars? Which investigators would be more likely to share information about the case?

Meanwhile, spurred by Sarah's courage, detectives worked round the clock to track down the gunman and his helpers.

On Monday investigators were tired and frustrated. They had no leads on the three suspects. And the car with the white spots still had not been located.

Despite my attempts, no friends of the family would talk to me. But my luck changed when I walked into the detective unit that morning. Detective Mike Johann told me that Astrid Newton had decided to speak with the media, hoping that more publicity would help police to nab her husband's killers.

Detective Johann, a dark-haired, intense and somewhat reserved detective, recommended she talk to me. The *Kansas City Star* is the biggest paper in the area, and I could give the case the most publicity. Johann knew from the Diana Ault case that I could be trusted and that I kept my word when going off the record. And he was certain I would be compassionate when I interviewed Astrid Newton.

We met in a large conference room and sat at a long wooden table. Astrid Newton sat stiffly as she talked with me about her late husband.

A plainspoken man with simple needs, Bob Newton accepted Astrid's seven children and treated them as he did his own daughter. He was especially close to Sarah, the only child who still lived at home. The little girl adored him and called him Daddy.

Bob had already built a swing set on the property he and Astrid had purchased down south in Clinton, Missouri. They had planned to move there later in the year, and Bob was going to buy a pony for Sarah.

He had taken the job at the gas station eight months earlier to pick up some extra cash, his widow said, sighing.

After a while, Astrid relaxed a bit and settled more comfortably in the chair. She shared with me the premonitions she had felt before the murder, and she told me what had happened that evening.

A month earlier, a "creepy feeling" about Bob's working at the gas station came over her. Anxious, she begged her husband to quit. It happened again one week before Bob Newton's death. But he assured her nothing was going to happen to him and told her she was frightened over nothing.

Around 8:30 P.M. on April 14, Astrid was suddenly overcome by the urge to see her husband. She and Sarah left the house, got into the car and drove to the gas station. Astrid wanted Bob to come home on time, so she offered to help count the cigarettes before he closed. But Newton had already finished that chore.

Sarah asked if she could stay with Bob until the station closed, about an hour or so later. It was a quiet evening, so Astrid agreed to the special treat. She kissed her husband good-bye and headed home to Blue Springs, a growing, white-collar suburb east of Independence.

But during the twenty-minute drive, she had the feeling that she should have stayed with him. As soon as she arrived home, she dialed the station.

"I said 'Is everything fine?' " she recalled asking her husband.

Her voice began to quiver as she continued her story.

"He said 'Yes.' Fifteen minutes later Sarah called me."

Astrid recalled that her daughter had been calm on the phone. "She said, 'Mommy, daddy is dead and I'm scared. A black man came in and shot him in the head.' "

When she heard her daughter's words, Astrid said she became hysterical.

"I was so scared. I wasn't sure if she was OK."

Astrid told Sarah to call 911 to reach Independence police. She wanted to get to her husband but knew she was too distraught to drive. Astrid called her son-in-law, told him what had happened and asked him to drive her to the station.

The rest of that night was a blur, Astrid said.

She told me that Sarah had kissed her stepfather at the funeral and wiped off a tiny bit of blood from his nose that the undertaker had missed. But even then, Sarah had not once cried.

At that point in our conversation, Sarah walked into the room, greeted the detectives and sat next to her mother. She had waist-length brown hair, large hazel eyes and a heart-shaped face. She wore a loose T-shirt and shorts. She looked innocent and vulnerable. How could anyone have wanted to hurt this little girl, I asked myself.

Anita Townsend, Astrid Newton's older daughter, hovered protectively over Sarah, then sat close behind her when Sarah slid into a chair next to their mother. Townsend spoke little during the interview.

I looked into Sarah's eyes as we talked. Her face remained impassive and her voice was matter-of-fact, but her eyes were guarded. The sparkle usually seen in the eyes of a child was missing. Even if I hadn't known about the murder, I would have guessed she was hiding pain.

Sarah munched pizza and drank root beer while her mother and sister discussed Bob Newton. She and her stepfather often watched television together, Sarah said.

"I liked to go shopping with my daddy," she added.

The youngster's expression didn't change as she talked about the shooting. She described how the robber had made them walk into the back room. Sarah was standing next to her stepfather and had looked away for only a moment when she heard a gunshot.

The noise hurt her ears, she said.

She looked at the gunman, and he pointed the handgun at her. Sarah said she pleaded with him not to hurt her.

"He looked at me kind of funny," she said matter-of-factly, watching Detective Johann as she spoke. "Then he just walked out."

Astrid began to cry as she explained why they agreed to speak with me. The detectives listened silently across the table from her.

"I want the killers to see how happy we were," Astrid said, and tears rolled down her face. "I want them to see what they've done to us. They took a piece of me and a piece of my daughter.

"I don't know how I'm going to live without my husband."

Sarah inched closer to her mother and put her small hand on Astrid's arm. Her own pain remained locked inside.

By the end of the interview, my own cheeks were wet. I ran fingers quickly over my face to brush away the tears, thanked the three of them for talking with me and gave Astrid a number where she could reach me. Then I headed back to the office. The interview had gone well, and the story was easy to write.

Astrid Newton's plan worked. The front-page story ran the next day, April 20. Soon after the investigation picked up. Tips began pouring in. Television reporters clamored for their own interviews, which they ran on the evening news.

That night, police received a phone call from an anonymous tipster who gave them the information they needed to identify the killers. On Thursday, Major Dave Emmons filled me in as detectives updated him.

By midmorning, police had arrested Leon Taylor of Kansas City, the man believed to be the gunman. Independence detective and Kansas City narcotics and robbery units surrounded his home and arrested 36-year-old Taylor. He was charged with first-degree murder.

It wasn't the first time he'd been in trouble with the law, Major Emmons added.

Meanwhile, uniformed officers were on their way to a Kansas City residence to arrest his accomplices, Major Emmons told me. But he wouldn't tell me their names until they were caught, only that the three were related.

Later that afternoon, police arrested the other two suspects. Investigators found them in a Kansas City house, about to watch a television news story on the murder.

Their mistake was a common one made by many criminals—they had bragged about the shooting to someone. He then tipped off police.

Major Emmons told me something else, something police hoped to keep from Sarah. In a low voice, he explained that the "funny face" the killer made when he pointed the gun at the frightened young girl was not a sign that this cold-blooded killer had had a change of heart and had decided to let her live. Instead, he said, the killer wore the strange expression after realizing that his semi-automatic had jammed as he attempted to pull the trigger and kill the young eyewitness.

In a rage, Taylor had then returned to the getaway car parked out front in order to get another gun. But when he tried to go back to kill Sarah, his accomplices wouldn't allow him to leave the car.

Aghast, and angry that anyone could have wanted to kill that sweet little girl, I rushed back to the bureau to get to work. I had a lot to do. Contact my "ears" in the community. Check the clips for the name *Leon Taylor*. Call the state to check his driver's license for an address. Find people who knew him.

I stocked up on chocolate candy, refilled my coffee mug and sat at my desk, jiggling my knees up and down nervously as excitement ran through my body.

Leon Taylor, I learned, had been involved in murder once before.

I pieced together the alleged killer's history with the help of our library staff and the Missouri Department of Corrections. What I learned was shocking.

In 1975, when Taylor was seventeen, he was arrested for the stabbing death of a sign painter in Warrensburg,

Missouri. He pleaded guilty to the murder in 1979 and was sentenced to eleven years. But he was paroled just two years later.

In November 1981, three months after his parole, Taylor attempted a robbery in Lafayette County. He pleaded guilty in 1982 in exchange for a five-year sentence. Again he was released early. Then, in July 1985, he pleaded guilty to an armed robbery, also committed in Lafayette County. That sentence was for ten years.

Taylor was released from the Missouri prison system in June 1992, after serving seven years of his sentence. Until his arrest for Newton's murder, Taylor had worked as a dishwasher at a cafeteria, located one-half mile north of the Campbell Oil gas station.

On April 21, Taylor was charged in Jackson County Circuit Court with first-degree murder, robbery, assault and three counts of armed criminal action for his part in the Campbell Oil incident. His arraignment was scheduled for the following day.

That night, one news station disregarded the police's request and ran the information they had been asked to keep confidential. In her home, Sarah Yates watched as the newscaster detailed how Taylor had intended to return to the back room and finish her off.

Astrid Newton and Anita Townsend showed up at the courthouse the following morning for the arraignment, but they made Sarah stay at home. The two women waited nervously for the alleged killers to be brought to the third floor of the brick, three-story Independence courthouse in the historic center of town.

"I didn't know that was going to be on the television," Astrid Newton told me as we waited for the alleged killers to arrive. "We're not sure what effect that will have on her."

As reporters crowded the hallway, the elevator door opened and the three suspects shuffled out. Taylor, a balding man with wire-rim glasses and a black mustache, wore leg shackles as well as handcuffs. He looked straight ahead, without making eye contact with anyone.

His handcuffed half-brother, Willie Owens, grinned and waved at cameras as sheriff's deputies escorted him to the holding cell. Following behind was his sister, Loutinia, whose hands also were handcuffed in front of her.

During the arraignment, prosecutors described how Loutinia Owens had waited in the car while her two brothers entered the gas station. Willie Owens brought the cash back to the car while Leon Taylor pushed Bob Newton and Sarah into the back room.

After the proceedings, an emotional Astrid Newton told reporters she hoped Taylor would get the death penalty. Half a dozen television cameramen and journalists followed the three as they were taken back into the tiny holding area and put in separate cells.

Taylor, the alleged gunman, refused to speak to the media. But the Owenses remarked about how they had intended only to rob the place that night.

Taylor went to trial in March 1995. Joe Lambe, our Kansas City court reporter, covered the trial. His accounts of the trial were chilling, and I followed the trial through his stories.

Willie Owens, a cocky, thin young man with short black hair, testified that Taylor had talked about Sarah when he returned to the car.

"She was watching her daddy bleed, and she put her hands up in the air and said, 'I'll do anything you want me to,' " Owens said Taylor told him. "He said he had to go get her. He asked if there was another gun in the car."

Loutinia Owens, a heavy-set woman with a deep voice, testified that Taylor came out yanking at the gun and cursing it.

"He said he had to go back in and shoot her," she said. "We drove off and he was still trying to get the gun unjammed."

According to Loutinia, Taylor announced that he should have just choked Sarah to death.

His only explanation for the shooting was that "a little man on his left shoulder made him do it," Taylor's brother, Willie Owens, testified.

Sarah, as calm and courageous as she had been throughout the ordeal, recounted the events of the murder for the jurors. Her demeanor impressed prosecutors and apparently convinced the jury of Taylor's guilt.

Astrid Newton took the stand and tearfully told jurors that her young daughter was still suffering from the trauma of witnessing her stepfather's death.

"She's told me she wants to be dead and she wants me dead, so we can all be together," Astrid testified.

Defense attorneys and witnesses portrayed Taylor as a victim of his childhood. He never knew his biological father, they said, and his mother was an abusive alcoholic who died in 1983.

Taylor shot Newton by accident, Assistant Public Defender Janice S. Zembles insisted.

In an ironic twist, one of Taylor's uncles testified that his nephew had seen his own stepfather shot to death in 1968.

Jurors soon found Taylor guilty of first-degree murder but couldn't decide on a sentence. When they deadlocked 11–1 in favor of the death penalty, the decision fell to Jackson County Circuit Court Judge William F. Mauer.

Taylor's next court appearance was held on May 4. It

was at that sentencing that Astrid Newton stood up to read a letter from Sarah to the judge.

"The best thing in my life was destroyed," Sarah wrote. "It's lonely out there with no dad. It's dumb for the sweetest, kindest dad to be killed for a lousy $450.

"I've never had so many nightmares. I'm so unhappy."

At the end of the hearing, Mauer sentenced Taylor to death, plus life in prison and 315 years. Taylor listened, stone-faced as the judge read his sentence.

Willie Owens was to get an eight-year sentence after his testimony at the trial. Prosecutors dropped charges against Loutinia Owens, apparently because their case against her for murder was not very strong.

The story of Sarah Yates will be forever etched in my heart.

I believe her life was spared so that she could lead police to her stepfather's killer.

I hope with all my heart that the lives of other children will be, too.

A transplanted New Englander from Sterling, Massachusetts, **Paula Barr** has worked for the *Kansas City Star* for nine years. Currently, she covers crime and animal issues from the *Star*'s Eastern Jackson County bureau in Independence, Missouri. Her work also has appeared in *Woman's World, Massachusetts Audubon* and newspapers in Massachusetts.

# SIX

—〰—

# Who Killed Carol?

## J. D. MULLANE

### The Bucks County Courier Times

The cop asked: Are you sure you want to see these pictures?

Yes, I said.

They're brutal, he warned.

He looked at a half-dozen 8½ by 11–inch black and white photos, winced, then slid them across the table to me.

The little girl lay on her back. Her eyes were open in a death stare, her head wrenched violently to the right. Her black corduroy pants were yanked to her knees, and her left arm lay straight out, fist clenched, indicating that she had been in great pain as she died.

The photographs of Carol Ann Dougherty, 9, had been taken by the police nearly thirty years before. And still their power to sicken hadn't diminished.

I've seen plenty of gruesome stuff: bloody car crashes, gunshot victims, bloated corpses pulled from the Delaware River, even a headless body.

But these pictures left me heartsick. Through the years,

a couple dozen small-town cops had tried to solve her mysterious rape and murder in the choir loft of St. Mark Roman Catholic Church in Bristol, Pennsylvania. All were unsuccessful.

I excused myself from the room. I needed air. I went to the fire department garage and leaned my forehead against a soda machine.

Harry Crohe, a Bristol town councilman, saw me and said: "Hey, what's wrong with you? You look like you've seen a ghost."

I'm a reporter for the *Bucks County Courier Times* in Levittown, Pennsylvania, a daily newspaper in the Philadelphia suburbs with a circulation of 72,000.

My interest in resurrecting Carol's unsolved murder in the summer of 1992 began with a simple question: How could someone walk into a church, lock the doors, attack and rape and strangle a little girl, then walk out onto a busy street and vanish?

When I moved to Bristol in 1991, I registered as a parishioner at St. Mark's. Fellow parishioners would mention the murder from time to time. Some talked of a nervous, middle-aged priest who had been suddenly transferred from the parish after the killing. Others spoke of a man who had confessed to the crime but was let go by police.

Each had a different idea of who killed Carol. But no one could prove it.

"I think the person who did it was questioned, but for whatever reason, he slipped through the cracks," said Gaspar Favoroso, one of the cops who had helped investigate the case in 1962.

As the thirtieth anniversary of the murder approached, I decided to find out why.

Bristol Borough is a small town on the Delaware River.

It's old, founded a year before Philadelphia, in 1681. Italian, Irish and African-Americans built it and ran its mills and factories throughout the town's lusty industrial past.

Bristol is Aunt Bea and Opie and Floyd the barber. It's waking to Sunday church bells or an early morning coffee at Katy's Kozy Korner. It's catching up on the latest neighborhood gossip, porchside.

It has what all towns have: sex, scandal, political chicanery.

And it has murder.

October 22, 1962. A warm, clear Monday.

Carol Ann Dougherty was a fifth grader at St. Mark Roman Catholic Elementary School in Bristol. She boarded the school bus at 7:40 A.M., began classes with a prayer at 8:10, played and sang at noon recess and returned to her home in nearby Landreth Manor by 3:00 P.M.

She changed into her play clothes and told her mother she was going to return a couple of books to the Bristol Library on Dorrance Street, about a mile from her home. She was told to be home by 4:30 P.M. Carol got onto her blue and white Londoner bicycle and was off.

On the way, she stopped at Tommy's Luncheonette on Farragut Avenue. She had a Coke with a squirt of cherry in it, her favorite. She laughed and giggled as she raced a couple of factory workers to where Lincoln Avenue meets Radcliffe Street. St. Mark's was on the corner.

The children at St. Mark's school were taught to stop and say a prayer if they passed a church and had the time, and so after she rounded the corner onto Radcliffe Street, she parked her bike out front by the stone steps and went inside. It was 4:00 P.M.

About fifteen minutes later, a women who stopped at

the church each day after work tried the front doors. They were locked. That was odd. She gave the doors a good shake. She paused for a moment and considered going to the rectory next door to find out why the church was locked. But she changed her mind and left.

About 4:45 P.M., Carol's father, Frank, returned home from work. He and his wife, Dorothy, and their youngest daughter, Kay Ellen, 2, ate dinner. By five o'clock it was getting dark, and Dorothy Dougherty began to worry about Carol. She called a few neighbors and some of Carol's friends.

No, Carol isn't here, they said.

Dorothy got into the family car and drove toward the library. As she passed St. Mark's, she saw Carol's bike with the library books still in the carrying rack. She opened the big church doors and peered inside. It was quiet and empty.

Without checking the choir loft, she left and drove to the library. Carol wasn't there, either. She swung the car around and drove back to St. Mark's. The bike was still there. She checked the church again. Still no Carol.

She drove home and told her husband about the bike, the books in the carrying rack, the empty church, the library. The Doughertys took Kay, got into the car and drove to St. Mark's.

Msgr. E. Paul Baird, St. Mark's pastor, was speaking with a parishioner when he heard pounding on the rectory door. Frank Dougherty burst into his office and was screaming something about his daughter having been raped and murdered in the church.

Msgr. Baird hurried to the church, climbed to the choir loft and saw Carol's body.

"Dear God in heaven . . ."

5:40 P.M.

Sgt. Hubert Downs was working the switchboard at the Bristol police station when the monsignor called.

"Sergeant, send a car to St. Mark's immediately. It's an emergency."

Downs asked what was wrong.

"It's terrible. I'd rather not tell you on the phone, but I think she's dead."

Downs pulled up a few minutes later. Msgr. Baird was on the sidewalk trying to calm the distraught parents. Downs went toward the monsignor.

"She's inside," Monsignor Baird said.

"Should I call the rescue squad?"

"No. They won't be needed."

Across town, Police Chief Vincent Faragalli was sitting down to a spaghetti dinner when he got the call from his secretary.

Chief, she said, we've got a murder—a little girl in St. Mark's Church.

Faragalli was forty-three and had been on the force eighteen years. He was a short, stocky man with a large, bald head and a wide mouth slit across a doomsday face.

He ruled his department like a tyrant, and his gravelly voice could boom through the halls like a foghorn on the Delaware River.

He could handle the violence, the gore and the corpses that came with his job, but a victimized child tore him to pieces.

The night Carol died, Faragalli sped to the church. Police and fire cars were everywhere, their driver-side doors wide open, lights flashing, radios crackling into the damp night. Reporters with pop-flash Speed-Graphic cameras were arriving.

Faragalli went to the choir loft.

After regaining his composure, he began giving orders:

the church and churchyard were to be searched, and the neighborhood was to canvassed for witnesses.

Outside, about a hundred police, fire police and fire-fighters swarmed through the neighborhood, their high-powered flashlights throwing long cylinders of light through darkened backyards and into black alleys. Patrol-men went door-to-door asking:

Did you see anything?

Did you hear any screams?

The day after the murder, Bristol awoke to a blur of screaming headlines and a cold drizzle.

1:30 P.M. Tuesday, October 23. It had been twenty hours since Carol had been found dead in the choir loft.

The phone rang at the town hall. A man's voice said: "Tell the police that the next one isn't going to be a little girl."

An hour later, the same voice: "There are lots of little boys in town. There's lots in the playground at the ele-mentary school."

An unmarked envelope was mysteriously left at the po-lice station. The envelope contained a photograph clipped from a newspaper and showed a group of people seated in an auditorium, as if assembled in prayer. The sender had blotted out a woman's head with an asterisk and had scrawled an inky blue taunt: "Carol, come to the loft."

On Mulberry Street, Faragalli and a team of county and state police investigators had set up a command post at the old town high school. They sifted the evidence and had some leads, but from the start of the investigation they were hamstrung by a lack of witnesses who could give them anything solid.

The investigators began working eighteen-hour days to

find the murderer, but they weren't making much headway.

Tuesday, October 23: Suspects were questioned, alibis checked, leads chased.

Faragalli to reporters: "I won't rest until I get this guy."

Wednesday, October 24: More suspects were questioned, more leads were chased.

Faragalli: "I still feel we're on the right track."

Thursday, October 25: It had been seventy-two hours since Carol's body was found and still no arrest.

Faragalli, frustrated: "So far, we have very little to go on."

Investigators chased leads through the winter, spring and fall of 1963. In a last, desperate hope, exactly one year after the murder, a Pennsylvania state trooper sat concealed in the darkened church waiting for the killer to return. No one came.

The trail of evidence had run cold.

In July 1992, I pulled the yellowed news clips of the Dougherty murder from our library and began reading.

There was nothing about the nervous parish priest and only a sketchy report about the man who had supposedly confessed and was let go. The newspaper had covered the story extensively in the first months but after the winter of 1963 had written nothing substantial.

In one news clip, on the twenty-fifth anniversary of the murder, there was a piece of information that struck me. Chief Faragalli, who had long since retired, was quoted in the story as still having a picture of Carol, a picture he had kept on his desk at the police station for seventeen years, until he left the force.

\*     \*     \*

If there was an answer to the mystery, I figured the clues lay in the police file. I had to see it; otherwise I'd have to write a story based on breathless but insubstantial news clippings and the foggy recollections of aging investigators.

Within a few days, I began pestering the Bristol police to let me look at the Dougherty murder file. Because there's no statute of limitations on murder, the case was still technically active, and each time I asked to see the file the police gave me the same answer: No. Now get lost.

I continued pestering, but the answer remained the same. By mid-September, I had gotten nowhere. So I approached a couple of political sources in town to lean on the chief to let me see the file.

A few days later, the Chief called: Okay, you can see the file, he said. Come down on Monday morning.

Within a week, I'd find the clues I had been looking for.


Daily newspaper reporting isn't glamorous, despite the images that Hollywood has promoted through the years.

What college professors didn't tell you as you slogged through their journalism courses is that you'll spend most of your time writing routine stories, not streaking into the newsroom shouting over the din of Teletype machines and ringing phones: "Stop the presses! Replate the front page! I got a story that's gonna crack this town wide open!"

You spend much of your time informing the public about how some guy in Tullytown grew a 300-pound tomato in his backyard. Or taking police briefs from a snarling desk sergeant who hates the paper because it didn't cover the department's annual charity golf tournament. Or explaining for the third time to some reader on the phone that no, this isn't classified, this is the newsroom.

There's nothing sexy about working crazy hours and sustaining yourself for days on Cheez-its and Coca-Cola from the cafeteria vending machines. There's nothing rewarding in running into dead ends, getting burned by sources or having to write a correction. And after the lonely torture of writing is over, there's nothing more frazzling than arguing with some tin-eared editor who's convinced that your clever turn of phrase is really editorializing.

And yet sometimes a story will come that makes all the mutant-vegetable reports and the legion of cranky cops fade. When you have a story like that, you put in fifteen-hour days and work on the weekends. Your social life is placed on hold, and your family is relegated to second-class status.

Maybe it's the pursuit of some injustice. Maybe it will crack the town wide open. Maybe it's just a great story. Whatever the case, it burns inside you, and you're possessed.

That's what Carol Dougherty's story became for me.

The Bristol police set me up in a small interrogation room. Before I could see the files, they had some ground rules.

First, I couldn't make copies of any of the police reports, and the only way I could review the file was if an officer sat with me the entire time.

Second, if I wrote a story, I was not to give any indication that I had seen the police file.

Third, I wasn't allowed to take written notes. I had asked to *see* the file, and that's the request police would honor. I didn't object to these criteria. I was afraid that if I complained, the file would be taken away and placed back in the dusty attic storage room where it had sat for years.

One of the news articles in our library had mentioned that within a month of the murder, the police had compiled enough reports to fill a file cabinet. But all I was given were two folders. A cop told me that Chief Faragalli had kept the Dougherty file in his office. After he retired, a new chief tossed most of it to make room for himself. Great.

By the second day, the cop assigned to sit with me became bored and left me alone the rest of the week. I wasn't permitted to take written notes, so after he left I began dictating the reports into a microcassette recorder. For some reason, the police weren't bothered by this.

I spent five days sorting through a jumbled mess of photos, reports, scribbled notes (some in unreadable shorthand) and faded state police telexes.

Each night, I'd return to the newsroom, transcribing and arranging the information in my computer. Often, I didn't leave work until 2:00 A.M.

As I read the musty reports, the portrait that emerged was of an intense investigation with more twists and turns than the staircase to St. Mark's choir loft. Notes in the file showed that detectives were desperately searching for the killer in the days immediately following the murder, but this was all they knew:

The county coroner estimated that Carol had been dead about two hours when her father found her. Witnesses said they saw Carol park her bike and enter the church about 4:00 P.M., so the investigators pegged the attack between 4:00 P.M. and 4:30 P.M.

Carol's left sock had been found beneath her body. It was neatly rolled and damp with saliva, indicating that it had been stuffed in her mouth to gag her screams.

In her left hand were two brown public hairs, probably from the killer.

Death had been from strangulation. Doctors performing her autopsy noted that there was an impression on her neck, perhaps made by a metal buckle when the killer tightened a belt around her throat.

A semen analysis showed a low sperm count. Forensics experts with the state police in Harrisburg said it indicated the killer was either a young boy or an older man.

As the investigators searched, puzzling bits of information surfaced.

For example, Carol had a single, large, roundish bruise on her left hip. The police couldn't figure how it got there.

It was unlikely that the injury had occurred during the attack, since the absence of other bruises indicated that there hadn't been much of a struggle; Carol had been easily overpowered. Mrs. Dougherty told detectives that her daughter had no bruises the night before she was killed. Carol wasn't a rough-and-tumble child, so it was unlikely she had acquired the injury while playing.

There were items found on the choir loft floor: Three Wrigley's chewing gum wrappers, half an Acme supermarket matchbook cover, three burnt matches, one unlit match, and a half-smoked Winston cigarette.

Had the killer been waiting for a victim?

Then there was this: Witnesses saw Carol park her bicycle near the steps, pause, then enter the church. But about fifteen minutes later, a parishioner who had tried to enter the church found the doors locked.

Could the killer have lured Carol into the church, then locked the doors? If so, it must have been someone she knew and trusted. Or was he a stranger who had followed her into the church and then locked the doors?

Based on the autopsy, the semen analysis, the hair

found in Carol's hand and the items found on the floor, the investigators put together this profile: The murderer probably was Caucasian, either an adolescent boy or an older man, possibly a smoker.

The profile was vaporous, but it was all they had.

Within two weeks of the murder, the police had questioned dozens of men, taking pubic hair from each and comparing them with those found in Carol's hand. Neighbors were calling the police anonymously and ratting out neighbors. Dozens of anonymous letters were sent to the police, each with a name or a suggestion as to who the killer was.

Police gathered absentee lists for the day of the murder from nearby schools. Each student listed was questioned.

The three priests at St. Mark's, all respected men in Bristol, were not above suspicion. Each was interviewed at the rectory, which was a short walk from the church. Msgr. Baird, Father Michael Carroll and Father Joseph Sabadish said they had been away from the church on the annual parish visitation. A patrolman was assigned to check their stories.

Francis Patterson, the church sexton, was questioned, too. He said he had been in the church on Monday to fix an electric wire. He left about 1:30 P.M. and spent the rest of the day a block away at the parish convent, painting window frames.

No, said Patterson, he hadn't seen anyone in the church, but the police should know this: It's not unusual on Mondays to find drifters searching the pews for loose change dropped during the Sunday collection.

The same day that Faragalli was quoted in the newspaper saying there was little evidence to go on, the police picked up a suspect. He was sixty, illiterate, never married and had a history of exposing himself to little girls—once to Chief Faragalli's daughter.

The police department erupted in shouts and whoops when an officer burst out of an interrogation room shouting: "He did it, Chief! He says he killed her!"

Frank Zuchero was taken into custody after witnesses told police they saw him drunk and staggering near St. Mark's about the time of the murder.

His account of the murder was chilling, but after questioning he was released and never questioned again.

Zuchero told the investigators that he had been drunk on Monday, October 22. As he walked home from a bar, he passed St. Mark's and saw Carol's bicycle parked by the stone steps. He went inside.

As Carol knelt at the altar, he slid the bolts and locked the church doors. He said he approached and grabbed her arm. Carol broke free and ran for the locked doors. When she couldn't get out, she turned and saw him coming down the aisle for her. With her back pressed against the doors, she began crying and then screaming: "Someone, please help me!"

Carol panicked and blindly ran into a pew, which explained the bruise on her hip. As she bounced off the pew, Zuchero said he grabbed her and dragged her to the choir loft. He took off one of her shoes and socks and stuffed the sock into her mouth. He raped her; then he strangled her with his hands. Then he unlocked the doors and went home.

The police took Zuchero to the church and had him lead them through the murder sequence. Much of what he said fit the pattern of evidence the police had. But almost immediately there were doubts about his story.

When Zuchero was brought to the police station, he was questioned by a lone officer, and no notes of the interview and his "confession" were kept. Afterward, Zuchero told his nephew that the only reason he confessed was because the cop had threatened him.

At the reenactment in the church, Zuchero kept contradicting himself, first saying he did it, then denying he was ever in St. Mark's on the day of the murder.

Later that night, Zuchero was taken to a conference room in the town hall and was questioned by Paul Beckert, the Bucks County district attorney. A tape recorder was clicked on, and Zuchero again contradicted himself, saying he did it, then saying he didn't do it, and then saying this:

Q: Why did you lock the church doors, Frank?
A: I didn't want to make nobody come in. Somebody come in, they get you right away.
Q: Is that because you had in mind that you were going to do this?
A: That's what the brain said to me.
Q: What?
A: That's what the brain says you do. If you don't, they will straighten you out, the brain says.

To Chief Faragalli, Zuchero's version of the killing seemed so delusional that he released him and never questioned him again.

The next day, Faragalli received a phone call from a woman in nearby Morrisville who said she knew who murdered Carol. Meet me at the Bristol train station, she said.

Come alone.

Faragalli waited in the train station parking lot.

A man and woman drove in and pulled up next to him.

They identified themselves as Alfred and Pauline Kalman. Mrs. Kalman told Faragalli that she suspected her son, Wayne Roach, of raping and strangling Carol.

Wayne had been known to lasso his younger brother and sister around their necks with a belt—and wasn't it in the newspaper that Carol had been strangled with a belt?

Wayne often visited churches and would ask clergy for money.

Then Mrs. Kalman told Faragalli this: She found a notebook in one of Wayne's jackets with the name *Carol Ann Dougherty* written in it.

Faragalli took the Kalmans to the police station for questioning.

Roach was nineteen, a short man who occasionally played guitar in a local rock and roll band. Mrs. Kalman said he had been a "problem child." While on probation for auto theft in August 1962, he had left home. The Kalmans didn't know where he was, but a strange incident made them believe he was still in the Bristol area.

Within hours of the murder at St. Mark's, someone had entered their house on Delmorr Avenue and took two of Wayne's jackets and some coins. They believed it was Wayne. Mrs. Kalman told Faragalli: "Find Wayne, and you've found your murderer."

Faragalli asked Mrs. Kalman where the notebook was that had Carol's name on it.

Mrs. Kalman said, "I burned it."

Police found a witness who identified Roach as being near St. Mark's at the time of the murder. They also found that he might have tried to enlist in the navy the same day.

The police took Roach's picture to the Navy recruiting

station at the Bristol Post Office, across town from the church.

Yes, said recruiting officer John Gordon, a guy who looked like that had been in here about 4:30 P.M. on October 22. Gordon and another recruiting officer remembered because the guy had scratches on his face, like he had been in a fight. They began a massive hunt.

On Tuesday evening, October 30, 1962, Chief Faragalli received a phone call from Rocco DeRosa, a detective in the nearby Falls Township police department.

A Falls housewife had told them that a few weeks before the murder a Bristol man had made threatening and obscene sexual advances toward her. The man was a priest at St. Mark's Church. She had a tape-recorded telephone conversation to prove it.

A few days later, Faragalli and a police officer waited in an unmarked car on Swain Street in Bristol. They were closely watching Father Joseph Sabadish, a priest at St. Mark's, as he made his rounds visiting parishioners.

Father Sabadish emerged from a house. Faragalli stepped from the car and called to him.

Father, could you come here?

Sabadish came over.

Faragalli asked him to get in the car.

Without telling the priest their destination, Faragalli and the police officer drove to the Bucks County Courthouse in Doylestown.

The county district attorney, several detectives and a lie-detector machine were waiting.

Sabadish was taken to a conference room.

The priest was nervous. Faragalli knew that nervousness could skew the results of a lie-detector test, perhaps rendering the results inconclusive. In his best heart-to-heart manner, Faragalli gently spoke to the priest to relax him.

Sabadish was forty-four and had been a priest for seventeen years. He had grown up in Branch Dale, a small town in the coal regions of Schuylkill County. He was stationed at parishes throughout the region, and sometimes heard confessions and said Mass at the House of the Good Shepherd in Reading, a Catholic girls' home.

He had come to Bucks County in the 1950s and in 1962 was transferred to St. Mark's in Bristol. After the murder, he helped rededicate the desecrated church and was one of seven priests who assisted Msgr. Baird at Carol Dougherty's funeral.

The day after Carol's murder, Faragalli and State Police Sergeant Andrew Kutney went to St. Mark's rectory and interviewed the priests. Father Sabadish, Msgr. Baird and Father Michael Carroll said they had been away from the church visiting parishioners at the time of the murder.

Patrolman Gasper Favoroso was assigned to check the priests' stories. Msgr. Baird and Father Carroll's stories checked out, but Sabadish's didn't. The investigators found that he had not been at the homes at the times he said he was, and when they eliminated the places he hadn't been, there were at least thirty minutes unaccounted for, the same time frame in which Carol had been murdered.

In the course of checking Sabadish's background, the police also found that he had been purchasing ladies' clothing for a girlfriend at Dorothy Binder's Fashion Shop in nearby Hulmeville, and they obtained receipts of his purchases.

Then came the housewife's phone call to the Falls police department.

The woman said she had known Sabadish when she was at the House of the Good Shepherd, the girls' home in Reading. She had lost contact with him after he was transferred.

The woman had since married and moved to Lower Bucks County and had heard that he was stationed in the area. About a year before the murder, she called him to say hello. Sabadish had dropped by her home three times: once in the afternoon and twice late at night, while she was in her nightgown and her husband was working late.

She told the police that three to four weeks before Carol's rape and murder the priest had made lewd sexual advances toward her and said he wanted to fondle her. He said he wanted to visit her at her home. She refused. He said that if he came to her house, he'd force himself on her.

The woman told her husband about the priest's phone calls. He attached a tape recorder to the phone and called Sabadish. He asked the priest if he had made the phone calls to his wife. Sabadish apologized and said it wouldn't happen again.

The unaccounted time on the day of the murder, the purchase of ladies' clothing and the taped phone conversations made Sabadish a suspect.

At the courthouse in Doylestown, the investigators confronted him with the information.

Then they asked him: Do you suspect anyone in particular of causing the death of Carol Ann Dougherty?

No.

Do you know for sure who caused the death of Carol Dougherty?

No.

Rev. Sabadish passed the lie-detector test and was cleared as a suspect.

That's where the police file ended and my reporting began.

Charles "Scoop" Lewis was a reporter for the *Courier-Times* and had covered the Dougherty murder for the newspaper in 1962 and 1963. I called him at his retirement home in Florida to talk to him about the case.

Botched from the beginning, he said. Small-town police force, small-town investigators. The Bristol cops never asked hard questions of the suspects, because many of them were their own neighbors.

"It was a case of trying to question people you were born and raised with," Lewis explained. "The police just couldn't question them the same way an outsider would."

Lewis remembered telling Chief Faragalli: "Vince, you've got to get outsiders to do the questioning. An outsider can ask deep questions."

I asked him who he thought did it. He couldn't say for sure. But there was an odd incident with a priest that he never forgot. Scoop had known Father Sabadish when the priest had been stationed at St. Michael the Archangel Church in Levittown in the late 1950s.

A few days after the murder, Lewis was in the newsroom when Father Sabadish called. He told Scoop he was broke and wanted to borrow $25 train fare to get to New York City. Lewis told the priest that he was on deadline and hung up.

"Think you'll find out who did it?" Scoop asked me.

"I don't know," I said.

"Good luck, kid. It's a hell of a story."

\* \* \*

I went to the Doughertys' old neighborhood. The wounds of that awful time were still raw. Many neighbors were resentful. One slammed a door in my face, saying she hoped Frank Dougherty would punch me out if I tried writing about the murder.

I kept pressing for information and found that the Doughertys had moved some twenty years before to Berwick, a small town in upstate Pennsylvania. Mrs. Dougherty had since died.

I called directory assistance for Berwick. Frank Dougherty wasn't listed. I called the Berwick town hall and asked them to check land records: if Frank Dougherty owned a house, it would be listed. It was. I took the address and wrote him a letter, asking if I could talk to him about his daughter's murder.

Chief Faragalli had retired from the Bristol police in 1979 and was living in New Jersey. I called him and asked if I could talk about the investigation. He was reluctant at first ("Why do you want to bring that up?"), but then he agreed. I set up an interview for 7:00 P.M. the following Wednesday.

I arrived at his house and rang the bell. He opened the door. He was baggy, droopy and wrinkled. He looked pissed.

"You're late," he grumped.

But it's only a minute after seven, I said.

"In New Jersey we consider that late."

He invited me into the living room. His recollections of the events were vivid, and much was confirmed by the police reports he had written thirty years before. We spoke for almost five hours.

When he arrived at the church that night, he stepped

from his car and into chaos. A crowd of several hundred had gathered outside St. Mark's. The Doughertys were at the curb. Mrs. Dougherty was hysterical.

He went to the choir loft and saw the body. It still bothered him. "When you're a police officer in a small town, you see everything. You get used to it. And during my career I don't think there was anything in law enforcement over the course of thirty-five years that I didn't see. But when I went upstairs and saw that kid laying there, boy, let me tell you, to the day I die I will never forget it."

He called for assistance from the county DA's office and the state police. As he waited in the choir loft, he had a recurring thought about the killer. "You son of a bitch, I'm gonna get you if it takes the rest of my life."

The investigators came, shot photos, collected evidence. Then, to press the urgency of finding the killer, Faragalli ordered each of his officers to the choir loft to see Carol's small, broken body.

The first weeks of the investigation were exhausting. He'd grab two or three hours of sleep at the police station, get up, dictate reports and chase leads. That October, and for months afterward, Bristol's streets were deserted after dark.

Then came a break: Frank Zuchero's confession.

I asked: Why did you let Zuchero go?

Zuchero didn't do it, the chief said. Couldn't have. He was a drunk and a town nuisance, not a killer. Sure, he had exposed himself to kids, but he never tried attacking them, he said.

The day of the murder a couple of parents waiting outside St. Mark's school for their kids had seen Zuchero staggering drunk toward the church. He was so drunk that he had to hold onto the school's black iron fence railing to stay up. It's unlikely that a sixty-year-old in that condition could have the presence of mind to go into a church, lock all the doors, capture Carol, drag her up the stairs to the choir loft, rape her, kill her, then unlock the doors and walk out onto a busy street, unnoticed.

Besides, Faragalli had some compelling evidence to let Zuchero go: his pubic hairs didn't match those found in Carol's hand. The hairs were the best evidence and were used to clear each suspect.

What about Wayne Roach? I asked.

Roach didn't do it either, he answered.

After Roach's mother and stepfather fingered him as the killer, the investigators searched the country for him, finally tracking him to a trailer park in Midway, Virginia. Three Bucks County police officers were sent to get him. Roach was taken forty miles west to a state police barracks in Culpeper and given several lie-detector tests. He passed all of them. Witnesses said Roach had been working as a laborer installing driveways the day of the murder.

Still, the cops brought him back to Bristol for questioning. He was given a few more lie-detector tests. Again, he passed them. When he was released, he pleaded with police to let him spend the night at the station. With all the publicity, he feared he'd be lynched. Faragalli could never figure out why the kid's parents believed he was the murderer.

"They told me their son was capable of doing this, and you figure you're dealing with an animal. But when he came back, he was such a gentleman, it was pathetic. He had nothing to hide, he was real cooperative."

And Father Sabadish?

The least likely suspect of all, he responded.

Sabadish confessed to the investigators that he had been at the ladies' boutique in Hulmeville at the time of the murder, which is why his alibi of visiting parishioners didn't hold up.

"He was up front with us as to where he was at the time of the murder," Faragalli explained.

The police file doesn't mention whether pubic hairs were taken from Father Sabadish. Why? I asked.

"We didn't feel it was necessary," Faragalli said. "He passed the polygraph, he confessed he had a girlfriend."

Then Faragalli told me something that wasn't in the police file, something that still frustrated him: the strange reluctance of the church pastor, Msgr. Baird, to cooperate with police. Baird might have been the key to solving the case, but from the beginning he fought Faragalli. It was the reason Sabadish had been snatched from the street corner; Baird would never have allowed police to interview the priests a second time.

"I hate to talk about him cause he's dead," Faragalli said. "But I'll tell you the truth. The only thing that kept me from getting in a real tangle with the monsignor was the fact that he was a member of the cloth. Had that guy been a civilian, he'd have been in a lot of trouble. I might have locked his ass up."

Within a few hours of the murder, Baird had ordered Faragalli to get the body out of the church and to clear the crowds from the sidewalk. The chief refused, saying nothing would be removed until the crime scene had been thoroughly investigated.

Next, police interviewed the parish housekeeper. She told them she had been removing flowers from the altar at about 4:00 P.M.—roughly the same time police believed Carol and her killer were there. The woman recalled seeing a man kneeling in prayer in a pew at the rear of the church.

He was in shadows, and she couldn't give a clear description.

Faragalli figured the man might have seen something—or maybe *he* was the killer. When he suggested that the woman be put under hypnosis, she agreed. But only if Msgr. Baird said it was okay.

The monsignor said he would think about it.

Meanwhile, newspaper reporters covering the case learned of the shadowy man, whom they called the mystery witness. The chief asked that they not go public with the information, but when the *Philadelphia Evening Bulletin* published an account, Msgr. Baird became enraged. He accused Faragalli of leaking the tidbit to the media as a pressure tactic; then he forbade police from putting the housekeeper under hypnosis.

I asked: Couldn't you have leaned hard on Baird to cooperate?

"He would have told me to go to hell, in plain English," he snapped. "Until the day he died, I don't think he ever forgave me. He probably still thinks I gave that story to the newspapers. You don't know how frustrating it is when you're only trying to do your job, and you know you got a guy who can help you, and he doesn't want to."

As the investigation progressed and police began questioning children at the St. Mark's school, Msgr. Baird became more belligerent, once stopping the chief on the street and lambasting him: "Faragalli, you're a Catholic, and you're persecuting Catholics with this investigation."

Faragalli shot back: "No, Father, I'm a cop and I'm trying to find out who killed that little girl in your church."

"What about fingerprints?" I asked. "There's no mention in the reports of any fingerprints."

"What were you going to fingerprint?" Faragalli asked.
"How about the mystery witness? He probably put his hands on the pew."

"Well, we did some dusting, but I don't remember after all these years."

No, Faragalli said, the killer was a drifter, someone who had met Carol by chance and had gotten away with murder.

As I left the house, the last thing he said to me was: "I still have her picture."

The weaknesses in the investigation were becoming clear: no fingerprints taken, a drunk who recounted chilling details about the murder but was let go, a church pastor permitted to run roughshod over the investigators, and a suspect priest who wasn't subjected to the same police scrutiny as others.

I tracked down other investigators and as many cops as I could find who had been on the force at the time when Carol Dougherty had been murdered. Each had different theory.

"You may not have had the killer, but you had his pubic hairs," I told them. "And they didn't match those of the suspects, with the exception of the priest."

Pay no attention to those pubic hairs; they meant nothing, one retired county detective advised me. The detective still had the notes he had taken at the crime scene. He told me that the choir loft had been dusty, and many hairs had been collected from the floor that night. It was quite possible, he theorized, that the hairs found in Carol's hand were strays, picked up by the little girl during the attack.

The best evidence was probably no evidence at all.

A few days later, I interviewed another investigator. My tape recorder was rolling when I asked him who killed Carol. He motioned to me to turn off the machine.

"Are we off the record?" he asked.

OK, I said.

It was Zuchero.

How do you know?

The guy confessed, he said.

But he could have been coerced.

No, he wasn't. And besides, there was a piece of evidence that police never made public.When they searched Zuchero's house, he told me, they checked the man's dresser drawers. They found socks.

So?

The socks were rolled exactly the way the sock stuffed into Carol's mouth had been rolled.

On October 3, a Saturday, Frank Dougherty called me at the newsroom. Yes, he said, he had received my letter, but I had the wrong address. He had moved from Berwick years ago to Huntington Mills, a tiny town in Luzerne County. The Berwick postmaster, a friend of his, saw the envelope and forwarded it along.

Frank had pondered my request for several days before deciding to talk with me. Other than his late wife, he hadn't spoken to anyone about the murder for thirty years.

Huntington Mills is three and a half hours from Bucks County. The brilliant autumn day I drove there with photographer Art Gentile, WOGL, the Philadelphia rock and roll oldies station, was featuring songs from 1962.

Frank was waiting for us at the door, a big man with white hair and a soft voice. He lived alone in a cabin on a lake with his dog Stripe. This wasn't going to be easy for him. Each time we began to talk about 1962, he gently dodged the subject, switching instead to a discussion about his TV satellite dish or his dog or to offer us more coffee. Finally, after about thirty minutes, we settled at a table in his living room, a huge portrait of Carol smiling behind him.

I told him what I had already learned. Then I asked him to draw from his recollections of that day.

Carol had gone to the library, he said. When she did not return home for dinner, he and his wife went searching. They went to St. Mark's, where Carol's bike was parked outside.

"That bike was her pride and joy," Frank said. "I knew that where that bike was, she wouldn't be far away."

Frank Dougherty remembered going inside and, in the semidarkness, checking the pews, behind the altar, the confessional boxes. Nothing. There was only one other place Carol could be. He headed for the steps of the choir loft. He reached the landing and, in the twilight, he saw what looked like a large doll lying twisted in a heap, its clothing torn away.

It was Carol.

He knelt and felt for a pulse.

Her arm was cold.

He screamed, then ran from the church, bursting into the rectory. Msgr. Baird was there, speaking with someone in his office.

"Father, you've got to come quick," he said. "My daughter's in the church, and I think she needs the Last Rites."

Frank returned to the car. He told his wife: "You stay right here; there's been some sort of bad accident. I think Carol's gone."

The rest of that night was a blur of police, the crowds outside the church and pushy newsmen—one of whom tried to force his way into the family's living room.

Frank wept at the memories and the pain they brought. "It's been thirty years," he said. "You'd think you'd forget about it. It never stops."

I told him about Frank Zuchero and Wayne Roach. I told him about the shadowy mystery witness the housekeeper spotted in the church and Msgr. Baird's reluctance to cooperate with police. I told him about the hairs found in Carol's hand and how Father Sabadish had been a suspect.

He had never heard of Zuchero. He vaguely recalled Roach. But Sabadish, yes, he remembered Sabadish very well. Sabadish and the two other priests at St. Mark's had never called on the Doughertys after the murder, a routine gesture of spiritual support one might expect from parish priests. That was something that bothered Frank.

"I always wondered about Sabadish," he said. "There was just something there that didn't strike me as right. I asked him one night in the confessional, I said, 'Father, am I wrong in assuming that a priest could have killed my daughter?' He knew who I was, and I just figured I'd get it right out in the open. He said, 'You're entitled to your opinion.' "

For a year after the murder, their youngest daughter, Kay, would cry each night. The Doughertys took turns holding her until she fell asleep, then would creep on hands and knees from her bedroom.

They moved from Bucks County in 1968, when Frank got an offer to buy into a publishing business in Berwick. They discussed the murder frequently, but never with Kay. The figured the less she knew, the better.

Dorothy had a heart attack and died in February 1975. Frank retired in 1981. Kay married and had a daughter, whom she named Carol Ann.

Frank was still angry, still wanted vengeance.

"If I had gotten my hands on him, he wouldn't have lived until the next day. Even when my son-in-law found out that you were coming up here today, he said if they have any good leads, Frank, we'll go down and find him."

I told him that I could make no promises about the story. It was possible that I could bring new light to the case, but after that, it would be up to the police to decide if they wanted to do anything with it.

"Still," I said, "it's something."

The list of suspects in the police file was long. Seventy-five men had their pubic hair yanked from them by the Bristol police, most in the first two weeks after the murder. I decided to focus on the three prime suspects: Frank Zuchero, Wayne Roach and Father Sabadish.

Zuchero had died in 1984, and his relatives wouldn't talk. Wayne Roach couldn't be located. Neither could his mother and stepfather, who had fingered him as the killer.

That left Father Sabadish.

Using a Philadelphia archdiocesan directory, I traced him to Norristown in neighboring Montgomery County, where he was the head chaplain at Sacred Heart Hospital.

I called and asked if I could interview him about the murder. I didn't tell him I knew he had been a suspect, fearing it might scare him off.

Sure, he said.

For me, this would be difficult. I'm a Catholic and attended twelve years of parochial school. I, like many Roman Catholics, have an inherent respect for priests.

But as a reporter you set those feelings aside, or try to, so you can ask the tough questions. I've never had a problem doing that. I once wrote a series of stories about a group of renegade cops working the midnight shift in Bucks County who were known as the Black Glove Squad because of the menacing leather gloves they wore when they pulled over motorists and roughed them up.

As the stories were published, I found myself being tailed by police cruisers late at night and, in a cheap attempt at intimidation, the renegade cops scared the hell out of my dad when they sent a patrol car to my parents' house to say they wanted to talk to me.

Over the years, asking tough questions and writing revealing stories has taken its toll, mostly on my car, which has been vandalized a half dozen times. Oven cleaner has been dumped on the paint, and nails have been driven into the tires. This mischief always happens at night, and while I have my suspicions, I've never been able to prove who did it. I've been threatened and shoved and surveilled and sued, and still I don't shrink from asking the tough questions, not because I'm a tough guy, but because it's my job.

But this was a first: I had to talk to an aging priest about sex. And rape. And the murder of a little girl in his church. And ask him if he did it.

We sat in his office on a sunny Saturday afternoon. I had my list of questions written in my notebook, the last one being: Did you do it?

Father Sabadish was seventy-three, short, cherubic, with a touch of upstate Pennsylvania brogue. He looked like the kind of guy central casting might send over when a Hollywood movie director needs someone to play a lovable Catholic priest who can teach a bunch of street thugs how to sing "Amazing Grace" in angelic harmony.

He doted: Did I want coffee? A soda? I made small talk, told him I was a Catholic and that my grandmother had come from Mahanoy City, near Branch Dale, his hometown. Twenty minutes later, I was still staring at his Roman collar, still nervously making inane small talk.

Boy, what a nice day, isn't it, Father? Say, did you know a nun named Sister Grace? She was my fifth grade teacher . . .

I ran out of dopey things to say and, after an uncomfortable silence, I looked at my notebook and began asking questions. I tossed him the softballs first:

How long have you been a priest?

Forty-seven years.

When were you transferred to St. Mark's?

Can't recall.

When were you transferred out?

Can't recall.

When did you find out about the murder?

That night. He said he had returned from the rectory. It was October, and all three priests were away from the church on the parish visitation, where priests call on each parishioner's home to chat, bless the family and ask for a donation. He saw crowds outside. He went into the rectory. Msgr. Baird told him what had happened. Everyone was terribly upset.

I notched up the heat: "Do you recall Mr. Dougherty very well?"

"I don't. I never knew him."

"He told me he went into a confessional one night and he asked you, 'Am I wrong to assume that a priest could have killed my daughter?' "

"I don't recall that at all."

"You told him he was entitled to his opinion."

"That I couldn't recall. See, the good Lord gives us, I guess, a sense that we forget what was told to us in confession."

"But when a man comes into confession and asks a pointed question like that, would that be something you would forget easily?"

"No, I don't think it would."

"Did you ever stop by the Doughertys' house afterward and offer them any kind of condolences?"

"Not that I recall. See, I didn't know the Doughertys. I didn't know them at all."

"In such a crime, though, wouldn't you feel obligated to tend to one of your parishioners? You were at the funeral Mass."

"Well, ordinarily we do go when they're our people . . ."

"She was a student at St. Mark's."

"Well, I didn't know her."

"Didn't you read any of the newspapers?"

"No. All I know is what was told to me the day it happened."

"Mr. Dougherty said none of the priests ever called or stopped by."

"That I couldn't tell you."

"He said they could have used some spiritual comfort."

"Well, I imagine."

I told him I knew he had been a suspect. I told him I had read the police file and that Faragalli and the other investigators had told me how his alibi had fallen apart. I told him the name of the Fairless Hills housewife who said he had made sexual advances to her over the phone.

"She said you had made some graphic remarks to her and that she hung up. She told her husband and he called you . . ."

"I don't remember that name at all."

". . . and he got you on the phone and said that you didn't deny the conversations, but you apologized."

His voice turned angry.

"That is absolutely, positively a lie. I don't even know the woman."

"Why would the detectives tell me that you had made these advances on this woman? Didn't they ask you these questions when they polygraphed you?"

"Not that I recall," he said.

"Did they say you had some other lady friends in the area?"

"Oh, well," he chuckled, "you must remember this. When you're in a parish, you do make friends. You're just not a hermit. You make friends with people in the parish."

"Well, how friendly were you with these women?"

"With whom?"

"With the women the police say you were intimate with?"

"I don't even know them. I don't even know those women. This is the first time I'm hearing this."

"So you didn't have any close physical relationship with any women at the time?"

No, he said. In fact, he always played it safe. If he knew he would be out with a woman parishioner, he always made sure that at least one other person was with them. "There is, as they say, safety in numbers," he said.

I knew what he meant. A priest once told me a story about how he had returned to the rectory late one night after having dinner at a restaurant. There was a message that the pastor wanted to see him. The pastor had received a complaint from a parishioner. The parishioner had spotted the priest at the restaurant in the company of an attractive woman and told the pastor that she thought it was "disgraceful."

As it turned out, the attractive woman was the priest's

sister, and they were out celebrating her birthday. It only takes one parishioner with a suspicious mind to indict a priest.

Father Sabadish denied all of it: the lewd advances, buying clothing for a girlfriend, being suddenly transferred from the parish after the murder.

My questions came quicker. What about being whisked to Doylestown by Faragalli?

"If Faragalli is saying that, he's lying."

What about the receipt with your name on it from the lingerie store?

"I would like to see that receipt."

Why would police say these things about you if they're not true?

"They're crazy."

I stopped, hovering on the edge of the next question: Did you do it? When a reporter asks a question like that, he or she knows what the answer is going to be: No. But getting a direct answer isn't the point. You hope that the suddenness or the gall of the question will throw the interviewee off balance, and the truth will come out in other, albeit more subtle, ways—awkward body language, a stammer, eyes that shift too quickly.

I looked at the question in my notebook.

Sabadish sat impassively across from me.

I tried to say the words, but I couldn't. I just couldn't ask a priest if he had raped and killed a little girl in his church. Quickly, I shifted gears and clumsily backed into it: "As a priest, as somebody who deals with spiritual well-being, how do you suppose somebody who commits a crime like this could keep it on their conscience for thirty years?"

"Well, that's a good, hard question to answer. If the person were guilty, I suppose it would gnaw at them. He would think of it quite a bit."

No stammering, no shifting eyes, nothing. He was ice.

In four weeks of reading the police file and interviewing, I had accumulated a thick file of notes. The story was originally going to be a one-shot Sunday feature, looking back thirty years at an unsolved murder. But with the cast of characters and plot twists, I knew I could write something with more weight.

My problem: How do I report thirty-year-old news and make it riveting?

Newspapers are at a strange place in their history. Readership keeps sinking; papers keep folding. Some say we're doomed to extinction. In a world of CD-ROMs, online bulletin boards, talk radio, CNN and tabloid television, newspapers are the eight-track tape of the mass media.

I didn't want to write one of those lumbering multi-part news stories that begins with a trite anecdote and then blathers over into two inside pages that leave readers awash in an inky pit of gray type, dull graphics, predictable photos and a couple of giant-sized quotations pulled from the copy. Big city metros and respected suburban papers excel at churning out those kinds of monsters. An editor sends an anointed reporter or two into semiretirement researching a single story. Then six months or a year later, after the piece is written, they christen it with some awful colonnaded title like, "Stiffed: How the Hairspray Cartel Controls Your Coif." Someone pass me the No-Doz.

These are "I-get-the-point" stories. Read the headline, read the first three paragraphs, look at the picture, okay, I get the point. Has anyone seen the comics section?

I've never been a fan of those kinds of stories. I know they're important. I know there's an incredible amount of work that goes into them. They often win all kinds of impressive journalism awards, so somebody must be reading them. But I rarely do, usually because they're as exciting as a bowl of room-temperature tapioca.

I didn't want the Dougherty story to be that. I didn't want stock lines like "A two-month investigation by the *Bucks County Courier Times* reveals . . ." I didn't want any paragraph to begin with that flatulent little word *Indeed,* as in "Indeed, it was one of the most intensive murder investigations in Bucks County's history."

I wanted a story that flickered inside a reader's head like a movie. But this wouldn't be make-believe. This was real life. The murder was real. The people were real. The dialogue, taken from police records, was genuine. It would be written like a book, a real-life whodunit told in three quick chapters.

I told my editor, Guy Petroziello, what I wanted to do. He liked the idea but had to get the okay from Len Brown, the then *Courier Times*'s executive editor. Brown wanted an outline, so I wrote one. He liked it but said he wanted six chapters, not three.

It was October 12. The series was to begin on Sunday, October 18. That left about a week to transform several hundred pages of notes into the equivalent of a seventy-five page book. That's not a lot of time. In fact, the week the series was published, I still hadn't completed the last two chapters. They were written literally on deadline, the day before they were published.

Worried that readers would become bored, I ended each chapter on a "cliff-hanger," so that anyone caught up in the story would have to buy the following day's paper to find out what happened next.

I mentioned the story to a feature writer, Steve Hedgepeth. He asked to see the first installment. He was hooked. He spent hours editing the series and, as we say in newspaperland, made it sing.

As I was writing, Petroziello came over to my desk.

We needed to give the story a title. I wanted "A Death in Bristol" or "A Prayer for Carol."

"What are you writing, a murder story or a sympathy card?" asked a smart-assed copyeditor.

Brown came up with an ear-catcher—"Murder in a Choir Loft." Our graphic artist designed a small logo for the series in which the word "murder" was scrawled as if in blood. Beneath it was a church bathed in the light of a spooky full moon.

"It looks like a horror movie," I whined.

"Look," Petroziello said, annoyed, "you don't tell the graphic artist how to do his job, and he won't tell you how to write your story."

I arrived at the newsroom each day by 8:00 A.M., incredibly early for me.

The story began this way: "*A year after the murder, this is all the police knew for sure: The little girl had been raped and strangled in the choir loft of St. Mark's Church. But how do you catch a killer when the church pastor who may hold the key to the case won't cooperate? When witness after witness can only attest to seeing shadows and fleeting glimpses? When the best evidence may not be evidence at all?*"

The night before the first installment was published, I went to the newspaper. At 12:45 A.M. the presses began to roll, and I watched as the first editions came off. Some people need shrinks or Prozac or booze to soothe their hurting souls. Give me a few minutes watching the newspaper fly off the presses with my byline on the front page, and it's Christmas Eve and I'm 5 years old again. Corny, but true.

"Murder in a Choir Loft" was a hit. As the week progressed, our circulation rose by six hundred. Copies of the paper sold out in Bristol. Readers began calling me at work, pleading to know who did it.

You'll just have to read the paper, I told them.

Thirty years after Carol had died, readers sent sympathy cards and asked that I forward them to Frank Dougherty.

On October 23, the day the series finished, I called the Bristol police. Randy Morris, who had been appointed the department's sole detective just a few weeks before, had become interested in the story after he saw me going through the police file. He told me he wanted to reinvestigate the case.

The police still had the forensic evidence, including the hairs found in Carol's hand and the hairs collected from the suspects. Using DNA testing, there was a pretty good chance the killer could be found, he said.

Chief Frank Peranteau cautioned: ''There are a lot of loose ends in this case. We may go nowhere.''

That Sunday, we bannered a Page One story: ''Search is on for Carol Ann's Killer.''

I continued pursuing the story.

A police officer who had worked on the original case called me with information about Father Sabadish. Within a few minutes of the murder on October 22, the cop said, Sabadish was seen at Popkin's Shoe Store on Mill Street, a short drive from the church. He was acting nervous and kept asking the clerk for the time, even though he was wearing a wristwatch. The clerk, after hearing about the murder, thought it was odd and called the Bristol police to tell them about it.

Another cop called me. He had been at the church the night of the murder and saw Sabadish smoking in the church, which he thought was highly disrespectful, especially for a priest. Later, when the cop was told that a half-smoked cigarette had been found in the choir loft, he

went to Sabadish and asked him: Father, do you smoke?
Sabadish said no.

On October 27, a week after the series was published,
Father Sabadish called me at work. He was angry. He
didn't mention the story, but said he was going to send
me a Mike Royko column about how the press bashes
people unfairly.

I asked him about being seen at Popkin's Shoe Store.

"That's a lie. There was no clerk in that store," he
said.

Steve Shuman, Carol's cousin, called me. He was nine
when Carol was murdered. He remembered being at Murphy's funeral home, across the street from St. Mark's, just
before the funeral mass began. As he watched the crowd
outside the church, he was overcome by a "sudden, terrible feeling."

"He's here," he remembered telling his mother. "The
guy who killed Carol is here. He's watching."

Again, during the mass: "Mom, he's here. I know he's
here."

Karen Fox, a local news producer for the CBS affiliate
in Philadelphia, called too. She wanted to do a story about
the murder for the Channel 10 news and wanted me to
"star" in it. We've had experiences with TV people at
the Courier Times, usually bad ones. It's a typical come-
on. They stroke your ego, use you to give them a guided
tour through the story, and then, when it's time to broadcast, cut you out, crediting only "published reports" or
worse, making it appear as though they dug up the story
themselves.

I turned her down. Another man called. He identified
himself as a film producer who had done work for PBS.
He wanted to turn the story into a screenplay.

"What a wonderful indictment of the Catholic church," he gurgled.

I hung up on him.

By December 1, 1992, Detective Morris said fifteen people had called him after reading the story to give him information about the case. But it was slow going. "I'm one man back here and we have a hell of a caseload," he told me. "A lot of this is being done on my own time."

A few days later, I ran into a lawyer, Tom Hecker. Hecker had been an assistant district attorney in Bucks County in the 1970s and now handled municipal work for a large law firm.

He was also a member of the Vidocq Society, a Philadelphia-based social club of some of the East Coast's best police investigators. The eighty-two-member group was named for Francois-Eugene Vidocq, who founded the French de Sureté in 1809. The group formed in 1991, when several law-enforcement officers met for lunch and began discussing unsolved cases, particularly homicides. Its members lent their expertise to police departments stumped by tough, unsolved murders.

Hecker tipped me that some Vidocq members had read the series and were considering joining Morris in his investigation.

Chief Peranteau confirmed that, yes, he had spoken with them, and he and Morris were going to make a presentation of the case at the society's quarterly luncheon.

On a rainy December afternoon, the members met in an upstairs dining room at City Tavern in Philadelphia. Peranteau and Morris were there to ask for help. Peranteau passed around the crime scene photos. Eyes narrowed, faces grimaced.

He said: "These harsh photographs still touch some of

us who've been in law enforcement for years. I brought them hoping that they would touch something in you, hoping that you would give us a hand in this case.''

Morris took over. He led them through the events of October 1962. When he told them about Frank Zuchero, who had confessed to the crime but was let go, someone in the back of the room let out a low whistle.

I and a TV reporter, Dave Murphy from the ABC affiliate in Philadelphia, were asked to leave. We did, and the doors to the dining room were closed.

An hour later, when the doors opened, the Vidocq Society had unanimously decided to take on the case.

During the closed session, Morris had told the members about new evidence that had been uncovered since October. He wouldn't say what it was.

Chief Peranteau said: "There are several suspects. I don't want to say anything about who either of them are.''

After reviewing the evidence, the members unanimously decided to take on the case. I called Frank Dougherty in Huntington Mills. He wept and said it was the best news he'd heard in thirty years.

On January 5, 1993, Morris and Peranteau met with eighteen of the society's members. Committees were formed to keep track of interviews, forensic evidence, and files. As the team was about to begin their investigation, Bucks County District Attorney Alan Rubenstein spoke with Chief Peranteau. Rubenstein had read the series. He was convening a grand jury and felt the Dougherty case might be a good one to put before it. But this meant the Vidocq Society—which had no legal standing in the case—was out of the picture.

Some in the Vidocq Society grumbled that this was headline grabbing by Rubenstein. For sure, it grabbed headlines. But then again, Rubenstein wasn't just talking.

Since 1987, his office had brought convictions in eight unsolved murders, all using the grand jury's powerful tools to subpoena and compel testimony from reluctant witnesses. One of the murders had been fourteen years old.

March, 22, 1993, our front page: "Bucks grand jury will probe 1962 church, rape, murder."

Frank Dougherty was incensed. "It doesn't seem right to me that an organization like the Vidocq Society that came and volunteered to help is down the drain. I'd love to see this thing solved before I die—and I don't have much time left. Hell, I'm sixty-nine years old."

The grand jury went to work, and I continued working on the story. Several people told me that Dorothy Binder, the woman who owned the ladies' boutique where Father Sabadish had been purchasing ladies' clothing, was dead. But I was able to track her to Florida. I interviewed her by phone.

Yes, Mrs. Binder said, she remembered the priest quite clearly. He had come into her shop three or four times. Once, he had visited with a young, attractive woman. She picked out some clothing, and Sabadish paid for it. He also came in on the day of the murder, sometime around 4:30 P.M. She remembered because he asked if she sold shoes. She didn't. But she told him if he hurried, he might be able to make it to Savage's Department Store in Newtown by closing time, 5:00 P.M.

"He seemed to hang around," she told me. "He acted strangely. I was perturbed about the whole thing, and then a policeman came and asked me about it. For him to say he was never at my place, well, that's wrong."

The police file mentioned that Carol had stopped at Tommy's Luncheonette on Farragut Avenue just before heading off to the church. It said she had spoken to a waitress at the counter. I set out to find that waitress. It was a long shot, but maybe Carol had told her whom she was going to meet. Problem was, I didn't know the woman's name.

Tommy's had long since closed. I peeked inside the dirty windows: the place was a museum piece from an early 1960s malt shop, dark and filthy with dust and grime. Tommy Rosackis, the owner, was in his 90s and an invalid. I tried interviewing him, but he was in such poor health that it was impossible.

After attempting to interview Mr. Rosackis, I stood outside the shuttered luncheonette. It was a Tuesday, and it was pouring rain. I was soaked. But I needed to find that waitress. I quizzed anyone who passed by, "Do you know who the waitress was who worked here in 1962?"

One old-timer looked at me and said: "Are you all right, son?" Then he crossed the street, turned and shouted over passing traffic, "That's a long time ago."

I never did find her.

One year after the series was published—eight months after the case went to the grand jury—there was nothing new to report. Rubenstein, the DA, wouldn't talk. Neither would Detective Morris or Chief Peranteau. Both had been sworn to secrecy by the grand jury. Even most of my sources had clammed up. A curtain of silence had been drawn around the case.

Under a thick black headline, "Unsolved mystery," I wrote, "A year after Bristol Borough police began reinvestigating Carol Dougherty's 1962 rape and murder, detectives are no closer to finding the little girl's killer than they were thirty-one years ago."

There were few new clues, no new suspects, and no one had been subpoenaed, I reported. I was wrong, but I wouldn't find that out until much later. A few days after that story appeared, I received a letter at the newsroom. It was postmarked Philadelphia, October 22, 1993.

The anonymous sender strongly suggested that he knew who killed Carol. The letter said if I wanted to talk, I should place an ad in the newspaper's classifieds, with a time and phone number where I could be contacted. It was signed "12."

In any highly publicized story the cranks and crazies come crawling from under the rocks. On this story, I checked out every tip, no matter how nutty. I met tipsters in bars and diners and at the Bristol wharf. Once, late at night in a vast shopping mall parking lot, I met with a short, chubby, middle-aged woman with badly dyed hair who was convinced her ex-husband was the killer.

"12" wasn't the only anonymous tipster, just the eeriest.

I put the ad in the paper. It said: "12 Got your letter. Call me 12PM" followed by my newsroom phone number. The ad ran for three days. Each afternoon, I waited at my desk, but 12 never called.

The Sunday after my cryptic ad appeared, I went to the 10:15 Mass at St. Mark's, as usual. When I returned to my car, there was an envelope tucked under the left windshield wiper. I opened it. Inside was a piece of paper. On the paper was typed "12," nothing else.

I looked around the parking lot, which was nearly empty. Across the street, the pastor, Father Kostelnick, was in front of the church chatting with a few parishioners. I checked the envelope. Nothing.

12—what did it mean? A house address? A floor in some building? Maybe it was the same person who had mysteriously left an envelope at the police station the day after the murder with the message: "Carol, come to the loft."

At the time, the investigators wondered if it was from the murderer, but that was never determined. Now, more than thirty years later, I stood in the parking lot of St. Mark's wondering: Did 12 know the answer? Was 12 the killer? Or was this just another crackpot? Whatever the case, this was certain: 12 knew my car and my habits.

I was being watched.

A few months after the series was published, I received a phone call from Mary Chiverella of Mountain Top, Pennsylvania.

In March 1964, her nine-year-old daughter, Marise, had been abducted as she walked from St. Joseph's Memorial School in Hazleton, a coal town about two and a half hours north of Bristol. Marise was found tossed in a strip mine, raped and strangled. The murderer had never been found.

The upstate papers had picked up on the Dougherty reinvestigation. For years, there had been suspicions as to whether the same man who killed Carol had also killed Marise.

At the time, investigators were struck by the similarities: both were tender-aged children, both were Catholic school students, both were raped and strangled, both had pieces of their clothing stuffed in their mouth to gag their screams.

And in both cases police found brown pubic hairs at the crime scene. One of the most intriguing aspects of the Chiverella case was this: The night before Marise was murdered, about 1,000 people from Bristol were in Hazelton to watch the Bristol High School basketball team compete in the state semifinals. Had the killer been among them? Had he stayed the night and then attacked and murdered Marise the way he had attacked and murdered Carol?

In 1966, the FBI had compared the hairs found on both

girls. The results were inconclusive. No connection had ever been made.

Mrs. Chiverella asked me to send her a copy of my series. Then an upstate reporter who was working on the Chiverella story tipped me: the state police were investigating the case, trying to connect it to Carol's murder. What if there is a connection? What if I was looking at an early 1960s serial killer? One who preyed on kids. As with the Dougherty case, I figured the clues lay in the murder file.

I called the state police in Harrisburg. Yes, a special homicide unit was looking into both cases, but that's all we can tell you, a sergeant said. I worked for months to develop sources within the state police. I sent my murder series to investigating officers. It panned out. One called me. He said it would be possible, if I kept quiet, to see the Chiverella file.

That winter, the East Coast was socked with eighteen ice and snow storms. Each time I made arrangements to see the Chiverella file, it snowed or iced so badly that my appointment had to be postponed. Finally, in April my source set up a fourth meeting at the diner in Chester County, just outside Philadelphia.

April 28 was beautiful, bright and warm. I decided to ride my motorcycle to work. But with the record number of winter storms came record amounts of salt and cinder dumped on the roads of Bucks County. I hit a patch at 35 m.p.h. and lost control, sliding across a highway with the bike on top of me, the pavement tearing my clothing and skin. If I hadn't been wearing a helmet, I would have left half my face on that roadway. I tried to get to my feet but collapsed in the street. As I lay there bleeding, a loud buzz in my head, blurry faces floating above me and voices telling me to relax, the only thing I could think about was: "I'm not gonna miss my appointment in Chester."

An ambulance came. The paramedics ripped open my shirt, stuck electrodes on my chest and then rushed me to the hospital. I was x-rayed and poked and prodded. I was given a tetanus shot. My hands and forearms had an ugly case of "road rash," a lovely euphemism for when macadam turns your flesh to hamburger. A doctor gave me a bottle of painkillers and told me to stay home for a few days. I popped a few pills, got in my car and headed to Chester County. A few miles into my trip, the painkillers kicked in. Whee.

I arrived at the restaurant. My source was waiting. He was aghast at my appearance, torn shirt and pants, bandages on my arms. A four-inch gash on my right thigh was leaking blood through my slacks. I told him what happened. He suggested we meet another time.

No, I've waited too long, I said. Where's the murder file?

I don't have it, he answered.

What?

Look, he said, it's unavailable. Somehow, his commanding officer had found that he was going to show it to me and ordered it locked up. I tried compromising. What if I write a list of questions? You read the file. Then you can answer them based on what you find?

No, he said. The file was not available.

I limped to my car. Sometimes you have days like this.

The following October, as the thirty-second anniversary of Carol's death approached, I spent a couple of days in Hazleton, retracing Marise Chiverella's walking route to school, talking to her parents and to longtime residents about what they remembered. I learned that a man who had been a prime suspect, Harold Rudolph Nicholas, was questioned by police and later was asked to take a lie-detector test. When he didn't show, officers went searching for him. A few hours later, he was found dead beneath the exhaust pipe of his Buick. A suicide. He left no note.

We published the story on October 21, 1994. "2 towns, 2 murders, 2 mysteries."

On February 4, 1995, more than two years after the series first appeared, the Bucks County grand jury let out. There was no indictment in the Carol Dougherty case. The DA and the Bristol police, as usual, wouldn't say a word.

I wrote a story anyway. Through various sources, I pieced together what the DA and state police had found. The hairs in both cases were sent to a laboratory. They didn't match. However, the hairs found in Carol's hand were "consistent" with one of the original suspects questioned in 1962. The man had been seen near St. Mark's the day of the murder. He had a history of molesting children. He was traced to Louisiana, and the DA had sent a couple of detectives to interview him. He wouldn't talk.

They were pretty sure they had their man. But then a blow: though the hairs were "consistent"—police talk for "pretty good match"—further DNA testing showed that it couldn't be determined for sure whether the hairs matched the ones found in Carol's hand. Without witnesses to the crime, they needed a positive match to prosecute.

The state police reexamined Carol's clothes. Using special iodine vapor lighting, they found two fingerprints on her plastic hair band. One print was traced to a state police investigator who handled the evidence in 1966. The other was so badly blurred that positive identification was impossible.

"We're fairly certain who did this," my source confided.

And no, it wasn't Father Sabadish, he added. Sabadish had lied and acted strangely for good reason: his dalliances had been revealed when Carol was killed in his church.

"He liked the ladies, but he wasn't a killer. It wasn't his style," the source said.

I called Frank Dougherty and told him.

Look, Frank, I did the best I could.

"I appreciate that, John," he said sadly. "It's all anyone could expect at this late date."

Afterward, I sat at my desk for awhile. In front of me were several thick files I had accumulated on the Dougherty case. I paged through them, looked at the pictures of Carol. On my way home, I stopped at the Pond Street Grill for a beer.

Readers still call me or send letters on the case. If it's a tip, I check it out. The Vidocq Society would still like to investigate, but at this writing, the murder file is in the custody of the Bucks County DA's office.

Each time I see Detective Morris or Chief Peranteau, I ask: Anything new on Carol?

No, they say.

The Dougherty case still nags, the questions linger.

I've been asked a thousand times, who did it? I always give the same answer: If I knew that, I'd be a hero.

I'm not. I'm a newspaper reporter.

**J. D. Mullane** was born in Philadelphia and grew up in Levittown, Pennsylvania. He attended Bucks County Community College and graduated from Temple University with a B.A. in journalism. He began his career in 1987 as an education writer for his hometown paper, the *Bucks County Courier Times.* He won the Al Nakkula Award for Police Reporting for his series on Carol Dougherty.

# SEVEN

—⟶⟶—

# Roy

## S. K. BARDWELL
### The Houston Post
### and
### The Houston Chronicle

The time I had to spend hours in the emergency room because I walked into a warehouse that firefighters hadn't taped off yet because it wasn't really burning, but which turned out to be full of poisonous gas, an editor at the *Houston Post* asked me, "Why the hell did you get so close?"

"Because I could," I said. "Stupid," I added silently.

No doubt he was thinking the same of me, but in my fifteen years in newspapers, I've decided that attitude— tempered with just enough caution to keep one from being maimed or killed—makes the best police reporters.

The time I pursued a suspected serial killer, coaxing and cajoling until I was spending long, tedious hours listening to him alternately drone and rant, prying to get at the details of his life, trying to find the secret that made him what he was—it was because I could.

Now, I figure I probably know more about Roy Alan
Stuart than anyone, including Roy.

Emergency rooms are not necessarily the worst thing
that can happen to a police reporter who does things because she can.

*"What do you want with me?" was the first thing Roy
asked me, the first time we met over breakfast at a little
cafe in Angleton, about fifty miles due south of Houston.*

*"Just to talk," I said, knowing it wasn't enough to
satisfy the animal-like wariness he had developed over a
criminal career that spanned thirty years of questioning,
arrests, and indictments in ten rapes and four sexually
motivated murders. He'd been convicted in only one rape
and most recently in a drug delivery case. Investigators
familiar with him said the stints in prison had only made
him cagier.*

*"Yeah? About what?" I chewed a mouthful of waffle,
buying a little time and deciding I might as well be
blunt—it's hard to bullshit a career bullshitter.*

*"Cops say you've killed a lot of women." I watched
him over the edge of my coffee cup.*

*"I ain't never killed nobody," he said, loud enough to
make the people at the next table turn and look. "Is that
what this is? They think I'll tell you all the shit they
couldn't get me to say?"*

*"I'm a reporter, Roy. I'm here to see if there's a story.
Why would the cops send me?"*

*"They hate me."*

*"Why?"*

*"Because of who I am." He looked at me, and I noticed
his eyes for the first time: Such a pale blue, they were
almost colorless, like eyes that used to be blue and got
left out in the sun too long.*

*"Who are you?"*
*"Me? Oh, I'm that famous serial killer, Roy Stuart."*
*He made a dry, raspy noise in his throat that I think was*
*meant to be a laugh. "I'm nobody," he added, and I knew*
*I had him—to a nobody, the allure of someone who listens*
*is powerfully seductive.*

I had first learned of Roy in 1987, while I was working
at the *Brazosport Facts,* a 23,000-circulation daily in Brazoria County. It was my second paper, my fourth year in
the business, and although the *Facts* wasn't big enough
to allow any of its twelve reporters to specialize, I had
already discovered that crime was what I was best at and
what I like best.

Even for a small paper, the body found November 5,
1986, wasn't a big story. Tucked between Houston and
the Gulf of Mexico, Brazoria is a huge county, and its
expanses of rice fields and salt marshes made it a con-
venient dumping ground for Houston killers. The humid-
ity that helps preserve the living in South Texas is less
kind to the dead—many of the bodies are never identified.

This one was, finally. Terri Denise McDaniels, a 26-
year-old drug addict–prostitute who worked around the
rundown old LaMonte Hotel in downtown Houston, had
been raped and strangled. She had never been reported
missing. Like all the other whores, addicts and vagrants
in downtown Houston, she was disposable—no one even
knew she was gone until her body was found.

Brazoria County Sheriff's Department Detective John
Barnes made the trip to the LaMonte in February 1987.
He spent the day talking with McDaniels's peers and
learned she had last been seen November 1, getting into
a small, blue or gray station wagon with a thin, sandy-
blond man.

In March 1987, the nude body of a woman was found in shallow water along the Bastrop Bayou, in Brazoria County. When the body was identified as 33-year-old Carolyn Rivera, Barnes thought the name was familiar. It took him a while, but he found it, in the inactive McDaniels file: Rivera was one of the LaMonte-area prostitutes he had interviewed the month before.

Another trip to the LaMonte confirmed investigators' suspicions of a serial killer: Rivera had last been seen getting into a small station wagon, perhaps light green or gray, with a thin, sandy-blond man.

Barnes put out the word and, on April 1, 1987, the Houston police department got a call from someone who said the sandy-blond man in the station wagon was cruising the LaMonte. The car was stopped by Central Patrol in the 1700 block of Congress, behind the old hotel. Its driver, 39-year-old Roy Alan Stuart—a small, thin man with sandy-blond hair—was arrested for driving while intoxicated.

Then there was Stuart's history: It began when he was fourteen, living in Amarillo with his mother and sister. In addition to numerous charges of theft, burglary and forgery, and a slew of misdemeanors, there were arrests in ten rape cases and in the sexually motivated murders of two women.

Stuart had preyed mainly on whores, hitchhikers and other women of dubious moral character, whose disappearances went unnoticed or whose testimony was considered lacking in credibility: As a result, he had been convicted only once, in a 1975 Amarillo aggravated rape case. The jury gave him ninety-nine years, but a judicial error prompted an appeals court to overturn the conviction and send it back to Amarillo for a new trial in 1978: With their witnesses gone, prosecutors allowed Stuart to plead guilty to a lesser charge, in return for fifteen years and a day.

*"I hate a sloppy woman,"* Roy told me on one visit.
*"You mean, a bad housekeeper?"* It was unlikely he would ever see my house, I thought, but I'd hate to die for it if he ever did.
*"I mean sloppy, in everything. Their hair, their clothes, their houses. Ain't nothin' worse'n a damn sloppy woman."*
*"Were all your wives neat?"* When I met him, Roy's third marriage was in the process of falling apart.
*"Not all of 'em. None of 'em like Twila. I mean, there wasn't nothin' dirty about that woman."* Twila's real name was Huey Tysar. She had come to the States in 1980 from Taiwan, after Roy selected her from a mail-order bride catalog. They married while he was still in prison.
*"They's only three kinds of people,"* Stuart told me once: *"Black, White and Chinese."* All Asian people were Chinese to Stuart. He had a penchant for Asian pornography and extolled the virtues of *"Chinese"* women frequently: *"They don't give you no shit. They just do like they're supposed to. And they're real, real clean about everything they do."*

Her citizenship assured by the marriage, Twila wasted no time pursuing her own agenda: She went to school and to work, eventually landing a low-level federal job and bringing her mother and a cousin over from Taiwan. She didn't neglect her wifely duties, either: After his parole, she gave Roy a son and came up with several attempts at providing him with alibis when he was arrested for the murders of McDaniels and Rivera in 1987.
In the end, it wasn't Twila's feeble alibi attempts that

got Roy out of trouble. It was his penchant for targeting women whose very lifestyles thwarted attempts to prosecute their killers: The two cases against Roy were dropped because the witnesses who could put McDaniels and Rivera in his car with him were drunks and dopers and prone to disappearing without notice and because, prosecutors pointed out, Rivera's hair and fingerprints were probably in hundreds of cars.

But by the time they had to release him, Roy's background and demeanor had convinced everyone who dealt with him that he was, in fact, a serial killer.

"He enjoyed it." said Matt Wingo, then a homicide lieutenant with the Brazoria County Sheriff's Department. "He liked the attention he got. He liked feeling like he had the upper hand. And he did."

Perhaps the most frightening thing detectives learned about Stuart was that, after finishing his time in the 1975 rape case, he had been released on parole in 1982 to Brazoria County, where he had lived unnoticed for five years.

Cecil Wingo, Matt's father and the chief investigator for the Harris County Medical Examiner's Office, estimated that since 1982, when Stuart was released, there had been between ninety and one hundred unsolved cases in which women had been murdered and dumped in secluded areas in the area.

Brazoria County, Houston, and several other jurisdictions, all of them with outstanding cases in which the known facts matched Stuart's M.O., pooled their resources and kept Stuart under twenty-four-hour surveillance beginning the moment he was released, when Twila picked him up outside the Brazoria County Courthouse in Angleton.

"Outside the time he spent in prison, those thirty days are about the only time in his life we can say for sure he didn't kill anyone," said Ike Fluellen, a criminal intelligence officer from the Texas Department of Public Safety who helped in the thirty-day surveillance.

The story was finished for the time, but I continued to keep up with Stuart, taking my car to be serviced at the K-Mart where he worked as a mechanic so I could get a good look at him, driving by his place now and then and writing down the license plates of any new cars.

Partly it was just a reporter's curiosity. Mostly it was because Roy lived right down the street from me and had for those five years.

I bore my first son that year, and we moved into Angleton, away from Roy. In 1989, I was hired by the *Houston Post* to cover crime and cops in the fourth largest city in the nation—a dream beat that could turn into a nightmare on any given day, as the city's homicide rate climbed steadily toward a new record, and the *Post* trimmed its staff until it bled.

Although my curiosity about Stuart waned in my frenzied new world, I remained interested in sexually motivated murders and in the ease with which many women can be caught, killed and disposed of without detection. I began keeping track of those I covered and using the paper's archives when I had time to research similar cases back to 1985.

Whenever I had time, I would call the detectives who had worked those old cases and talk with them about the details that were never published. After a few months, a companion list was created: A list of men who, like Roy, are the only suspects in one, two, sometimes several sexually motivated homicides but who have never been charged. In some cases, these men are familiar with the system and use its weaknesses to their benefit—i.e., targeting a victim, committing their crimes and then disposing of their victims in different jurisdictions. In many more cases, the lifestyles of the victims themselves, as with McDaniels and Rivera, thwart prosecution of their killers.

I spent even more time reading about serial sex crimes and serial sex killers. I got permission to attend HPD's in-service classes on those and related subjects. I got to know all the experts. I became something of an expert myself, but I still wondered—what makes them like that? How can they be so normal on the outside and so bent inside?

In June of 1991, Stuart was arrested for delivery of cocaine in a Brazoria County sting. It was more or less a grudge charge, but it got him off the streets for a while, and it gave me an idea. The Texas Department of Corrections's headquarters in Huntsville said Stuart's first parole hearing wouldn't be until July 1992, and his probable release date was February 8, 1996. I squirreled the idea away for future use.

The following June, I wrote to Roy at the Gatesville unit where he was being held.

There was no answer to that letter, nor to the two others I sent. In July 1992, when Stuart was supposed to be up for parole for the first time, I called the warden at Gatesville and learned the Board of Pardons and Paroles had again done that for which it was becoming famous that summer: Stuart had been granted an early release, June 30. He had applied for parole to Tulsa, Oklahoma, and, when Tulsa turned him down, returned to his place in Brazoria. None of the agencies that were supposed to be notified had been notified.

The news elicited a resounding epithet from Matt Wingo, but it meant at least Stuart had not ignored my letters—he had never gotten them. I wrote to Stuart again at his home: "I suspect you have a lot of stories to tell," I wrote him. "Perhaps this is the right time. Perhaps I am the right person."

When the phone rang ten days later, I was in the middle of ten things, as usual, and had forgotten all about the letter. "Susan?" asked the voice on the other end. "This is Roy Stuart. You wrote me a letter." I told him I was glad he called. I told him I'd like to sit down and talk with him. He sounded interested, but wary. "What exactly did you want to talk about?" he asked.

"Your life. Will you meet with me?" Finally he agreed to meet me for breakfast in Angleton. It wasn't until later that day that I realized he had called me by my first name, which I never use in print and had not used in any letters to him.

Before that meeting, Matt called to fill me in on why Roy had wanted to go to Tulsa—something we both had been curious about. That's where Twila had moved with Roy's son. She's gotten a good job and bought a house. Tulsa wouldn't allow Roy to serve his parole there, but the Texas Board of Pardons and Paroles gave him a ten-day pass to go visit her there. Matt had talked with a couple of Tulsa detectives who checked their files and said yeah, as a matter of fact, they did find a couple of dead whores during those ten days—one in a dumpster, one in a field. Both strangled.

Twila ended up coming back to Texas when Roy couldn't go to Tulsa, but she didn't stay long—the marriage dissolved fairly quickly.

The basic facts of Roy Alan Stuart's birth and childhood are fairly pedestrian: He was born March 3, 1948, in Alpine, Texas, to Lena Ruth Davis Stuart and Rennon Roy Stuart. His father left the family when he was fairly young, and Stuart began to exhibit the classic symptoms of the "problem child."

The facts don't explain how Stuart got the way he is, but the details do. It took a long time to get down to details. A long, tedious time.

*"My mama and my sister both,"* he said, pausing to light a cigarette and think of what he wanted to say. *"Well, they both had men, you know, to the house."* There was a long silence.

*"Boyfriends, you mean?"* I asked innocently.

*"No, more than that. A lot of men. You know."* His faded blue eyes looked tired, and I had to administer myself a mental slap to prevent any sympathy from creeping into my feelings about him.

*"I didn't like it, when they came. I'd leave, just go out and not go back until the cars was gone."*

*"What did you do while you were out?"*

*"Nothing good. Got into trouble, mostly."* By the time he was fourteen, Stuart had collected a total of six counts of burglary and theft, but he got probation for all of it because of his tender age.

*"Life wasn't really too great, bein' in the house with two women,"* he told me another day. *"I had to do all the work, and I didn't never do nothin' right, seems like."*

*"You mean the cleaning and stuff?"*

*"Yeah, like the trash and everything—hell, they'd sit around all day with ever' damn trash can in the house full, waitin' for me to get home so's I'd carry it out for 'em."* I was just about to try to lead him to another subject when he continued, with enough vehemence to startle me, *"And nasty? I never seen anyone so goddamn nasty. They'd put their goddamn, you know, their female stuff, in the trash and not cover it or nothin' and I swear to*

*god, it would make me sick to my goddamn stomach car-
ryin' that shit out.''*

*"You mean, their sanitary napkins?''*

*"I can't even talk about that shit, it makes me so god-
damn sick. I don't wanna talk about them no more, any
how.''*

When he was sixteen, Stuart armed himself with a BB
gun, assaulted and tried to rape a woman near his home.
His probation in the earlier cases was transferred to com-
mitment at a children's psychiatric center where he was
diagnosed as violent, with schizophrenic tendencies. Further treatment was suggested, but when the term of his
probation was up, Stuart was gone.

Four months later the still-sixteen-year-old Stuart was
again a suspect in the attempted rape of a woman in Amarillo. He was never arrested, because the victim did not
want to testify. In July, he was picked up and questioned
in another rape, in November, yet another. In December,
he left Amarillo with fifteen-year-old Glenda Joy Welch.
They headed to Arizona, where they got picked up in
Flagstaff trying to cash checks they had stolen from her
parents. They were returned to Amarillo, where charges
of statutory rape, theft and forgery were dropped when
Stuart married the girl.

*"We got along all right, for kids, I guess,'' Stuart said
of the marriage. "We wasn't perfect, by any means, we
had a pretty tough go of it.'' Later in the conversation he
tells me Glenda was "pretty clean.'' I learned that for a
woman, that was apparently Stuart's highest praise.*

*They married in August 1966, and for a few years, Stu-
art was arrested for nothing more serious than passing
hot, worthless or forged checks. Then, in 1969, Glenda*

*and Stuart's infant son were killed in a car crash in Canyon, Texas.*

*"Yeah, I was pretty tore up over it," Stuart told me of the deadly wreck. "That was a real bad time for me. I started thinkin' nothin' was ever gonna work out for me." It was probably a real bad day for Glenda and the baby, too, I thought—I had already grown accustomed to Stuart's supreme self-centeredness.*

*I doubt that his grief drove him to marry Trunell Day less than six months after Glenda and his son were killed. Convenience, maybe. "I love women," he told me once. "I like to be married, especially if they cook and clean and like that. You need a woman for stuff like that."*

Trunell, who has a daughter by Stuart, told investigators her five-year marriage to Stuart was marked by frequent, impromptu changes of address. There was a good reason: In the summer of 1971 the nude body of Linda Kay Simmons was found in an Amarillo pasture. Three weeks later, just as detectives were closing in on Stuart in that case, the nude body of Kay Sands was found in another pasture. Both women had last been seen with Stuart.

Stuart was charged with both murders. Charges in the Simmons case would later be dismissed, because evidence in the Sands case was stronger. In the meantime, though, Stuart posted bond and was freed to await trial. Two weeks later he was charged with two attempted rapes, of a dancer who accepted a ride with him and, on the following night, a nineteen-year-old hitchhiker.

The dancer had the distinction of being a surviving victim of Stuart's. She told a chilling story: She met Stuart at the Cabana Lounge and agreed to have drinks with him between shows. He asked her out, and she declined. "He gave me the creeps,'' she said: During one break, Stuart caught a cricket and sliced it open with his pocketknife. "It bled,'' the dancer recalled. "He held it up for me to see, and he asked me if I ever looked at myself in the mirror while I was having my period, and watched it bleed.''

When Stuart asked her out after work, she declined and said he left. When she went outside, she said one of the tires on her car was flat, and Stuart was waiting. She accepted his offer of a ride.

Stuart drove her first to a blue and white trailer, the dancer said, where Stuart picked up some drugs and had a fight with a woman, striking her in the face before he left. After that, she said, Stuart drove into the canyons of Palo Duro State Park, which made her uneasy. When he turned off his car's lights, she said she began trying to figure out a way to get out of the moving car but couldn't.

Finally he parked, and the dancer said he grabbed her by the throat and forced her to give him head, telling her the whole time that he was going to kill her. When she finished, she said he forced her down in the front seat, with her head between the back of the driver's seat and the steering wheel and began to rape her. It is the same sequence of events and positions other surviving victims had described and the ones that evidence indicates was used in killing Rivera.

The dancer described how Stuart would choke her to the point of unconsciousness, then allow her to revive, as he raped her. Slowly, painstakingly, she worked her knee up toward her chin, wedging her foot against Stuart's body. During one of the periods when she was allowed to breathe, the dancer kicked as hard as she could, sending Stuart through the windshield and knocking him unconscious long enough for her to get out and run.

"I was naked. I didn't know where I was. I couldn't see any lights, anywhere. I knew he was going to wake up and come for me. I knew he would kill me," the woman said. By the time she made her way to the nearest lighted place she could find, she was covered with ant and mosquito bites, and her feet were bloody.

The woman gave police a statement and charges were filed against Stuart, who was arrested again, but not before he picked up and attacked a young hitchhiker who told police she fought and fought and, finally, he let her go, telling her, "See you around."

The young woman told authorities Stuart came over "to talk" and during the visit simply got off her couch, grabbed her by the throat and told her, "I hate to do this, but I'm going to have to kill you now." He was pulling at her clothing with his other hand, and the woman said she was about to black out when she made a strangling noise that appeared to stop Stuart. He left, telling her, "See you around."

Charges in both cases were dropped within a month: The hitchhiker didn't stick around to testify, and the dancer announced she would not testify against Stuart. Much later, the dancer explained her decision: Four days after Stuart's attack on her, the woman from the blue and white trailer—the one she'd seen Stuart strike—came to the dancer's home and told her she would be killed if she didn't drop the charges.

Stuart was acquitted of Kay Sands's murder. One way or another, all the cases against him had disappeared by 1972 and for two years, he would face nothing more serious than traffic violations.

Still, said his second wife, Stuart was hardly well adjusted during that period: "He never could sleep, he was afraid to go to sleep," she said. "He'd have nightmares.

A lot of them were about his mother. He was terrified of his mother.''

*"My mother? Oh, she's OK. You know, just a mother,"* Stuart told me the first time I brought the subject up.

*Much later, during one of his occasional outbursts, he referred to his mother as "a cunt," then stopped himself with nothing short of a gasp and apologized profusely. I don't think he was apologizing to me. He seemed frightened and, on one of our next few meetings, said he hoped I wasn't thinking of trying to talk with his mother. He cited her health and age, and I agreed not to upset her.*

*"Good," he said. "She don't know much anyways. About me, I mean." Right.*

Early in 1974, Stuart was charged with aggravated rape, for an attack on a prostitute. The case was dismissed because the prostitute declined to testify.

At the end of 1974, Stuart attacked and raped his wife's best friend, who was nineteen and pregnant. She told authorities he had come over "to talk" and, without provocation, got off her couch, grabbed her throat and forced her down to the floor. After raping her, she said Stuart told her, "I'm sorry about this, but I'm going to have to kill you now." At some point while he was choking her, she said a strangling noise she made seemed to "bring him out of it," and he apologized to her and left. She refused to file charges.

When Stuart raped a woman in the middle of Amarillo's Rivera Park in the middle of the afternoon in February 1975, police knew they finally had him. He was convicted and given ninety-nine years a few months later. Even then, his legal luck held, and in 1982 he ended up down the street from me.

There are documented occasions—many of them—
when Stuart has picked up whores, done his business with
them and released them unharmed. For years, investigators had wondered what it was that ''set him off,'' causing
him to strangle some of his companions. I had already
guessed when Stuart confirmed my speculation one day
in December 1992. He called to ask me if I'd like to go
fishing with him sometime. Roy was an avid fisherman.
The bodies of McDaniels and Rivera were found near
some of his favorite fishing spots.

*"Sure," I told him anyway, confident that if the time
actually came, I would think of some way to keep safe.
"God, I haven't been fishing since I was a little girl," I
went on. "I used to go with my dad." We talked on a
while, about fishing and childhood and the like, and I
mentioned that while I had enjoyed the time with my father, I had never cared much for the fruits of our labor.
"Fish are kind of nasty," I explained. There was one of
those silences that I had learned often preceded a tirade.
I braced myself.*

*"They ain't half as goddamn nasty as a woman," he
started out.*

*"What?"*

*"Women," he repeated. "You know, when they's
bleedin'. That is the nastiest, filthiest thing there is in the
whole fuckin' world. I know. That time of the month, they
oughtta jus' go away somewheres and stay there 'til it's
over." The only good thing about these tirades was that
I was not required to respond.*

*"I never could see how they could live like that," he
went on. "I couldn't live like that. They fuckin' stink.
Nothin' but a bunch of nasty, stinkin' cunts. Makes me
sick, jus' thinkin' about it. God a'mighty, I'd sooner be*

*dead'n have to put up with a fuckin' filthy, bleedin'
woman." He seemed to have wound down a bit, so I tried
prompting him a little.*

*"You think women should die because they menstru-
ate?" There was silence. I thought he was catching his
breath, getting ready to launch another blast. Instead, he
simply hung up. I didn't hear from him again for a year
and a half. Obviously, Roy decided we had gotten a little
too close to something. I knew what.*

I could have pursued Roy again. I could have written
him, called him. I might have, if it hadn't been for the
lipstick thing.

Houston homicide Sgt. Tom Ladd is one of the officers
whose advice I sought before beginning my meetings with
Roy. The first thing every single one of them told me was,
"Don't get in a car with him."

In the vast majority of the cases against Roy, the attack
had occurred in his car and followed the same pattern:
First, he forced the woman to give him head while he was
in the driver's seat. Next, the rape, in the car's front seat,
with the woman's head between the back of the driver's
seat and the steering wheel. The whole time, the victim
would be choked. When she passed out, he would loosen
his grip and allow her to revive. When she struggled, he
would tighten his grip.

Other advice I'd been given concerned my appearance:
"Don't wear anything short, or low, or tight," Ladd had
told me. "No jewelry. Nothing real feminine."

"Lay off perfume and makeup," Matt Wingo had
agreed. "You want to avoid him thinking of you as a
woman." I had worn jeans, T-shirts and sneakers to most
of my meetings with Roy. No perfume or jewelry and
little makeup. Except for the meeting early in December,

when I'd forgotten to remove the vivid red lipstick I was
fond of at the time.

*Roy seemed uneasy at that meeting. He wouldn't look
at me when I was talking to him, but I'd catch him sneak-
ing looks at me when he thought I wasn't watching him.
I asked, a couple of times, if he was OK. "Just tired,"
he kept saying.*

"They're all just losers," Ladd said quietly. There was
a silence while we both took drinks. "You want to know
what the secret is?" I nodded mutely. "People are real
easy to hurt and kill. It's a lot easier to do that than it is
to be human. People who choose that way? They're just
too weak to be humans like the rest of us."

I didn't realize it until later, but that bit of information,
from someone who has spent the better part of his life
hunting people who hunt people, was the payoff for my
work with Roy. Now I knew.

Before we left the bar, Ladd asked when I had last seen
Roy, and I told him about the lipstick incident. He stopped
what he was doing and looked at me, hard. "Time to back
off," he said when I finished the story. "Right now. Just
walk away."

"Why?"

"Darlin'," Ladd drawled. "If it has even occurred to
Roy Alan Stuart to notice that you have a mouth, you're
too close."

The lipstick thing had only irritated me before, but I
thought about it harder on the five-mile drive home. Lipstick is red, like blood. Roy hates blood, menstrual blood.
Menstrual blood would get on him when he raped a
woman. Lipstick would get on him when—I pulled the

car over and vomited on the shoulder of the South Freeway.

And as I said, I didn't hear from Roy again after the lipstick incident for a year and a half. Didn't think about him much, either. I had, by then, made the move to the *Houston Chronicle,* where the police beat was just as frenzied, but my life was much more pleasant and secure.

Then one day in May 1994, I got a call from Matt: Roy had been arrested again, at the house that used to be near mine, after a whore he'd picked up in Freeport had gotten loose and run naked with her hands still bound into the yard, screaming, and neighbors had come out to find Roy trying to wrestle her back inside. He kept telling everybody she was a little drunk, and everything was OK.

"You think she'll testify?" We both remembered how so many cases against Roy had ended.

"If they can just keep track of her until it comes to trial," he said.

The next day, I got a call from Ken Ramsey, an investigator from the Brazoria County Sheriff's Department. He wanted to know if I knew Roy Alan Stuart. "I'm afraid so," I told him. "Why?"

"He's asking for you," Ramsey said. "Will he talk to you, do you think?"

"Maybe," I said. "Probably not." I felt inexplicably tired all of a sudden, but I went.

Roy's jaw was all wired up, having been broken by a fellow inmate his first night in jail. He told me Ramsey was behind the attack and ranted about suing the county. I talked with the other inmate later; he beat Roy up because Roy was on television that night, and the other inmate decided Roy thought he was "some big shit or something."

I told Roy I was too busy to come to the jail and see

202 • CRIME ON DEADLINE

him anymore but that he could call me once in a while if
he wanted. I told Ramsey, "I hope you're not counting
on a confession."

Roy called every night. He talked and talked. He said
nothing.

Ramsey, a rookie homicide investigator, found the old
charges in the McDaniels and Rivera cases and got a
rookie prosecutor to take them again. The district attorney
was furious when he found out, and they were dismissed
the next day. Those of us familiar with Stuart worried that
Ramsey would screw up the aggravated kidnapping case.

Finally, Roy called one night and told me in a petulant
voice that he knew I had talked with Ramsey about him.
Cursing Ramsey silently, I asked Roy, "So?"

"I thought you was my friend," he said. I couldn't
believe what I was hearing.

"I have told you a million times, Roy: I am not your
friend. I am a reporter."

"I know, I know. And I'm just a story."

"No," I corrected him. "You're not a story. Nobody
cares about your story anymore. Not until you tell all of
it." He didn't answer, so I went on without him. "Don't
call me again, Roy, until you're ready to tell the whole
story." I hung up. And he stopped calling.

Until October 19, 1994. Roy's trial took only two days.
The jury spent forty-five minutes finding him guilty, and
the judge didn't even hesitate before sentencing him to
life in prison, meaning that he cannot even be considered
for parole for thirty years. For a 46-year-old man not in
the best of health, it was a death sentence. I got a call
from Matt minutes after the verdict, another after the sentence was passed.

Half an hour later, I got a call from Ramsey. "He
started asking for you before we even got him back to the

jail from the courtroom,'' the investigator told me. ''He says to tell you he's ready. What's that mean?''

''Means I'm on my way,'' I told him. I made the fifty-mile drive in thirty-eight minutes. Both the interview rooms were occupied. Jail Capt. John Davenport, another friend from the old days, told me that I could use his office so long as I kept an eye on Roy. A guard was posted just outside, in case.

*Roy looked ten years older and a few inches shorter. His back was stooped, and his face was pasty gray. Shuffling because of the leg shackles, he sat in the chair I pointed to and cleared his throat. "Thanks for comin',"* *he told me. "I didn't know if you would or not."*

*"You want a cigarette?" I shook one toward him and lit one for myself, placing a half-empty soda can between us for an ashtray and figuring John could yell at me later. We smoked in silence a minute. "You said you were ready," I reminded him. He nodded, looking down at the floor.*

*"All these years," he started, speaking so softly I had to lean in to hear him. "I been tellin' people all these years, them stories wasn't true." He trailed off.*

*"Things are different now, Roy." Again he nodded but didn't speak. "Thirty years is a long time, Roy," I tried again. Another nod. "That won't change. But concessions can be made. You know that." Nodding, again. I decided to stop helping him and just let him think about it a while.*

*When he finally looked at me, there was so much agony in his face I almost, just for a second, felt sorry for him. Not quite, but almost. I waited, fighting the urge to break the silence or to look away. He cleared his throat again.*

*"I cain't," he whispered. "I cain't do it."*

*I spent a minute putting my cigarette butt into the soda*

*can and swishing it around to make sure it was out. I was fighting the urge to see how hard I could hit him, wondering if the guard, who no doubt thought he was there to protect me, would stop me if I grabbed Roy by the throat . . .*

*"Yes, you can," I told him firmly. "You can, and you should."*

*"No, I—I just cain't. Not right now. I thought I could, but I just cain't." That about did it, I thought. I stood up and jerked my bag onto my shoulder.*

*"This is it, Roy," I told him. He was looking at the floor again. "I'm not a fucking dog. I'm not going to come when you call me, just so you can see if it still works. Give it up now, or just live with it for the rest of your rotten, pathetic life. I don't really give a shit." He shook his head, silently, still looking at the floor. I knew it wasn't going to happen.*

*I turned at the door and told him, "You're fucking up. You think you can hold on to your little secrets and use them to get some attention whenever you start feeling really small and insignificant. But you used me up, and now I don't care anymore. And the cops? The cops already have what they want." I paused, for effect, but he never looked up. "You're going to die in prison, Roy."*

Ramsey and his captain wanted to know every word, but I had that feeling again, like my blood had been drained and I would collapse any minute. I needed to get home. I needed my children. "He just said he couldn't do it," I explained for the umpteenth time. "I don't know why. No one knows except Roy." Finally, I just left. I thought I might cry, and I refuse to cry in front of people.

There's no doubt in my mind that I will hear from Roy again someday. Five years, ten, fifteen—there will be some crisis in his life, and he will call or write and tell me he's ready. And yes, I'll probably go.

Because I can.

**S. K. Bardwell** is currently a police reporter for the *Houston Chronicle*, where she has worked the beat since 1993. Before that, she spent four years covering the cop beat for the *Houston Post* and five years covering cops and criminals for the *Brazosport Facts*. Her first newspaper job was with the *Angleton Times*, "where I did everything but throw it." During her career, Ms. Bardwell has won numerous prestigious awards, including the MHMR Award of Excellence and the Women's Center Media Award.

# EIGHT

—ɯ—

# Old Notes

## NICK EHLI

### The Billings Gazette

On the day he called the newsroom, Brad Kolberg was desperate. He hadn't seen his girlfriend since dropping her off at the bus station in Bozeman, Montana, nearly five months earlier. As an informant for local drug agents, Nancy Kaufman had disappeared for long stretches before, but she'd always checked in, always called her parents to hear how her two kids were doing.

Kolberg had phoned a couple of other times, hoping I could make checks on Nancy's whereabouts with a few trusted cops. He was frustrated, getting the official runaround, he said.

This phone call, though, was different. Now, detectives in Bozeman were asking him questions about Nancy's disappearance. Now, he was a suspect.

He planned to make the two-hour drive to Billings that night to search for Nancy as he had several other times and perhaps talk to her parents or the drug agents she had mentioned. Anything would help. Could he stop by the newsroom later that night?

I didn't know much about Nancy at that point, only that she'd been repeatedly kicked in the head and nearly choked to death with a telephone cord a year earlier by a man who learned she was providing information to local authorities. Court records identified her only as "the victim," but the name got out.

After Kolberg's first call, I'd checked with a friend in the local drug unit. Most drug agents—skittish about seeing their pictures in the paper or their names in print—typically won't say much to a cop reporter, especially about an informant. This one was different.

One of my first assignments on the police beat was to cover the raid of a local drug dealer's house. The cops had expected a big bust, so I was invited along. The house was trashed when we arrived—holes in the walls and garbage strewn everywhere—but not enough drugs to pay for the door the cops broke down getting inside.

The drug dealer's lawyer planned a lawsuit, claiming agents had destroyed his client's home. When the lawyer called, assuming I would be his star witness, I told him exactly what I saw: the house was in the same condition when the cops left as when they arrived. The lawsuit went away, and I had a source in the drug unit.

He would know if Nancy was in town.

Nancy had indeed provided information to drug agents in the past. She'd signed on as an informant when agents arranged to keep her out of jail on a drug charge. Although she wasn't the brightest person and sometimes sold food stamps to support her own drug habit, she was tough, street-smart, and thrived on adventure.

Working as an informant became everything to Nancy. Always striving for acceptance, she had found her niche. For the first time in her life, the high school dropout had a job she was good at.

Still, it wasn't unusual for agents to lose track of her.

Nancy was Nancy. She'd had a tough life. That's all my source knew.

Kolberg wanted to meet with me anyway. Anything, he said, anything would help.

I doubted that our discussion would lead to anything I could print, but I told him to stop by the newsroom when he got to town. It was a slow night on the cop beat, and the newsroom, except for myself and a few editors, would be empty by the time he arrived. He was grateful and said he would be in as soon as he could. Before hanging up, he said he feared for Nancy's life and where her trail might lead him.

Brad Kolberg never showed up that night.

Two weeks later, on September 29, 1993, an off-duty reserve deputy walking his dog found Kolberg's body floating in a calm and muddy stretch of the Yellowstone River just south of Billings. He had been shot in the back of the head with a shotgun.

Homicide is always front-page news in Billings. Although the population of roughly one hundred thousand is by far the largest in Montana, we average less than a dozen murders each year. I write about most of them. I've learned that every victim has a story, usually one far better than any police press release will tell. Brad Kolberg though, was different from most victims. For once, I didn't have to rely on friends or relatives or court records to tell me about the dead person I was writing about. For once, the victim got to tell his own story.

Nancy Kaufman was not so lucky. Her whereabouts to this day are still unknown, and investigators now believe that Kolberg's concerns were valid and that she is dead as well. Certainly, by now, she would have checked in on her two boys. Certainly, at the very least, she would have called.

Those same investigators, though, readily admit they have more theories than answers as to what happened to Brad Kolberg and Nancy Kaufman.

Was Nancy, an attractive 24-year-old redhead, killed for what she told or what she knew? Did Kolberg ask too many questions of the wrong people, or did he murder Nancy himself, hide the body somewhere in the towering mountains of Montana and then construct an elaborate scheme to conceal his own suicide? Just maybe, is Nancy still alive?

Tunnel vision, a detective working the case told me later, was not an option.

It was around Labor Day 1992 when Kolberg and Nancy first met at a Billings hospital. Brad had pneumonia; Nancy was being treated for the injuries she had suffered at the hand of the angry friend of a drug dealer. They had adjacent rooms. They talked briefly, passed each other in the hallways.

A few months later they were both seeking treatment again, this time at a psychiatric hospital.

Kolberg, who suffered a near-fatal head injury in 1983 while working in the oil fields near his hometown in eastern Montana, was now suffering short, periodic blackouts. The former high school homecoming king would get angry and say or do things he would later not remember.

Relatives said his temper grew short, and he became increasingly frustrated by the injury that he didn't understand.

Nancy—who suffered from brain damage caused by a lack of oxygen when she was born at the family home— was a welcome sight. She didn't mind that her new friend talked so slow.

And he didn't care about the learning disability that

she'd struggled to overcome since being tagged "retardo" in high school.

The two became close friends and the following January, rented an apartment together in nearby Bozeman, a small college town that, in recent years, has become a haven for fashionable celebrities and well-to-do Californians willing to pay high prices for nearby mountain property only a 90-mile drive from Yellowstone Park.

Some native Montanans have welcomed the status and prosperity. Most, though, fear that the state is certain to lose its vastness and character, gaining in return only minimalls, expensive rent and a higher crime rate.

I recently saw a bumper sticker on the back of an old pickup truck that I imagine most natives would agree with: "Welcome to Montana. Now leave."

Brad told relatives that he and Nancy were living together only to save money, but it was obvious to others that what had started out as a friendship became a love affair.

It was even obvious to me. In his phone calls to the newspaper, Kolberg didn't sound like a man looking for just a friend. To him, Nancy meant much more than that.

Nancy apparently felt the same way. In hopes of shaking out a few leads, police had asked the *Gazette* to run a Polaroid of the smiling couple, their arms wrapped tightly around each other. On the side of the snapshot, Nancy had scribbled, "brad it [*sic*] my boyfriend. Now. He's good to me."

As they posed for the camera, Brad and Nancy could have never known what the next few months would bring.

The couple lived together until April 1, 1993, when Kolberg said he dropped Nancy off at the only bus station in Bozeman. Kolberg believed his roommate was headed for Billings. Nancy was anxious to see her two kids, who had been living with her parents for the last several months, ever since she and Kolberg overdosed one night on pills and wine.

But did Nancy ever get on that bus?

Record keeping at the bus station is not a priority, especially with people who pay cash, so there is no manifest somewhere listing "Nancy Kaufman headed to Billings" or, for that matter, anywhere else. Brad Kolberg was the only person who could place her walking into the bus station. He said he could see her waving as he drove away.

A week later, Kolberg reported Nancy as a missing person.

Kolberg told me that he made several trips to Billings to look for Nancy in the following months, undaunted by an anonymous note left on his pickup, warning him to stay away and to stop asking questions. He couldn't stop. He had to find his Nancy.

Kolberg checked the strip joints, the sleazy bars frequented by drug users and with the roadies at the weeklong county fair. No Nancy. Although he said he realized that maybe he couldn't find Nancy because Nancy didn't want to be found, he kept looking. Maybe, he said, she would just come one day.

Three days before his last trip to Billings—a Friday—Kolberg walked into the Bozeman Police Department to ask detectives how their search for his roommate was proceeding. He was questioned for the next several hours.

After the interview, Kolberg told friends that he was a suspect in a murder.

Investigators in Bozeman would never tell me what Kolberg said during that lengthy interview, but Nancy's parents, desperately searching for answers from authorities, were told that they should probably stop hoping for their daughter's safe return. What the police apparently didn't realize, though, was that Nancy's parents, as much as they longed for her, hoping she would be on the other end of every phone call, had long ago concluded that they would never see their daughter alive again.

Although Nancy's parents, Leonard and Hilde Kaufman, had custody of their daughter's two sons, Nancy, fiercely loyal to her family, called nearly every evening to talk to the boys, who at the time were two and three years old. Her parents set up a toll-free number. Now, the boy's birthdays had come and gone and not a word.

No, if Nancy were alive, she would have found a way to at least send a card. She might have stolen the stamp, but she would have sent a card.

Before her disappearance, Nancy told her parents about Kolberg's violent streak and that she planned to leave him. They weren't surprised, then, when Kolberg called to let them know he had reported their daughter as a missing person. When Nancy didn't call, though, and when they learned that she had left behind her clothes and makeup and the pictures of her boys, they knew she was gone.

Kolberg didn't confess to killing Nancy under the questioning of the Bozeman police, but there were his blackouts. Dreams, he said, of a pile of fresh dirt by a telephone pole and an old shack in the mountains near Bozeman where he and Nancy had often gone for long walks were all he could remember. If there was a chance he had killed her, that's where the police should look. To my knowledge, they never did.

But looking out at the miles of grassland, mountains and wilderness that surround Bozeman, it's easy to understand why. Where in this vastness would they search for the remains of Nancy Kaufman? Where would they begin? The police would need Kolberg's help. If he had indeed killed Nancy, they needed to know more.

Kolberg was supposed to come to the police station for another interview the following week. Instead, the next Monday afternoon, he stopped by his estranged wife's house to see his own two children. At the time, his stop didn't seem unusual. He, too, loved his kids.

Later that day, a dozen roses from Brad were delivered to the house. Strange, Kim Kolberg thought. She married Brad in 1985 and again in 1988, with a divorce in between. With the paperwork on their second divorce nearly complete, why now was he sending roses?

"Looking back, I feel he feared his life was in danger, and he didn't know how long he would be around," Kim Kolberg told me for an article published in the *Gazette*. "He went down there looking for Nancy, and that's why he's not here today."

Before leaving for Billings, Brad Kolberg called me for the last time.

I brushed off his not showing up that night—it certainly wasn't the first time I had been stood up by someone who had called believing the newspaper could solve their problems. I've since had to tell myself repeatedly that I could have never known what was going to happen that night to Brad Kolberg.

On the rough side of Billings, a bartender at a seedy little tavern later recalled seeing Kolberg just after midnight with two other men he told investigators he couldn't identify. Thinking he might remember more for someone who wasn't carrying a badge, I questioned him as well.

No offense, he said, but remembering faces isn't a healthy habit in his line of work.

As limited as it was, his was the last reported sighting of Brad Kolberg.

Kolberg's abandoned Ford pickup was found early the next morning in a park where Nancy used to enjoy long walks along the banks of the Yellowstone River.

On the truck's dash, investigators found one of their first clues—a disjointed note about drug dealers and pimps who may have known Nancy, and the phrase "Meet John." The note also indicated that Kolberg planned to telephone Nancy's parents and two local drug agents who knew her.

Those contacts were never made either. And investigators have never ascertained who "John" might be. My name was also on Kolberg's list.

During the next two weeks, county sheriff's deputies and Kolberg's family and friends scoured the massive and heavily wooded park for several hours. The newspaper and the city's two television stations were there as well and reported each failed attempt. By the end, people who never even knew Brad Kolberg had joined in the search.

At night, his brothers canvassed the downtown area, asking questions and looking for anybody who may have seen Brad. His sister, having studied his notes looking for clues, found my number at the paper. She phoned the newsroom, wondering why her brother would have wanted to talk to a reporter. I wondered myself.

Detectives had their suspicions that Kolberg was dead, and so did I. The phone calls to the newspaper, the threats, the abandoned pickup, it all added up. But without a body, Brad Kolberg was simply a missing person.

Then, about two weeks later, the searches and the canvassing given up, an off-duty deputy out walking his dog spotted a body floating about twenty feet from the shore. It was discovered less than a quarter-mile downstream from where Kolberg's pickup was parked.

Authorities that afternoon, scrambling to find some sort

of crime scene they would never locate, surmised that Kolberg had been shot to death somewhere else in the park and then dumped in the river. Most likely, the body had been hung up under water on logs or a rock.

Two weeks in the Yellowstone River had not been kind to the corpse of Brad Kolberg. His body was so badly decomposed that local investigators had to wait until the next afternoon for fingerprints to arrive from Bozeman before they could positively identify the body as the man they had been searching for. An autopsy was needed to determine the cause of death—a single shotgun blast to the back of the head.

Covering homicides, I've seen lots of autopsy photos, but nothing like this. The county coroner and I agreed: Brad Kolberg would not have an open casket.

The weapon that was used to kill him has never been found, although I suspect the Yellowstone River may have something to do with that as well. Over the years, the river has washed away the sins of many a robber or murderer who was simply smart enough to roll down the car window and chuck his weapon of choice over the South Bridge.

George Fina, who along with an accomplice stood in the rear of a pickup and pumped at least eighteen rounds into the back of a local hooker two years earlier, was one of those guys. What Fina didn't realize was that as a warm spell was threatening the banks of the Yellowstone, the snow in the bed of the pickup was also melting, leaving behind a passel of spent shell casings. He was convicted of deliberate homicide, and in all likelihood he will spend the rest of his life inside the Montana State Penitentiary.

Detectives, upon learning that Kolberg had been shot in the back of the head, immediately released to the media that they were investigating a homicide, although they refused to speculate that his death was related to Nancy's disappearance. Talking for the record, they still do.

As with most homicides that I have seen investigated in the county, the sheriff's detectives work feverishly until they've checked out every possible lead and then wait for a break. Usually a killer's biggest mistake is bragging about it to someone who could use the reward money, but in this case, that call never came.

Instead, all of the unanswered questions began piling up, and detectives began conducting their own tests to see whether a person could shoot themselves in the back of the head with a shotgun. With Kolberg, not only did they conclude it was possible, they decided it was likely.

Kolberg owned a shotgun identical to the one that killed him, and in his apartment, officers found matching shells. The gun has never been located, and detectives figure it floated downstream.

Still today, every once in a while, I'll run into a detective who says he's been combing the local pawn shops, hoping to find Brad Kolberg's rusty shotgun.

The day that Kolberg disappeared, his father also found a note from his son that directed him to several letters in a safety deposit box in Bozeman. In part, the note read: "Please make sure everyone gets their respective letters. I have named you as executor to my will, I love you, dad. Your son, Brad."

In the letters to family and friends, Kolberg didn't directly say that he planned to kill himself but instead wrote things such as, "If you see this . . . I will not be seeing you again."

He also wrote about Nancy, how much he cared for her. Detectives are quick to point out the names of all the people Kolberg wrote to; Nancy wasn't one of them.

For investigators, that was enough. And while Kolberg's death is still on the books as a homicide, detectives have privately told me they are convinced that he killed himself—and more than likely, Nancy. The case hasn't been actively investigated for more than a year, although I've yet to find anyone who can explain why Kolberg would choose such a bizarre way to end his own life.

Kolberg's family and friends have not been pleased with that theory, either. Why, they ask, would anybody walk into the Yellowstone River with a shotgun to blow his head off? How would Brad have held a shotgun to shoot himself in the back of the head? Why would he put on such a show that he was trying to find Nancy? Why would he keep calling reporters?

None of it makes sense. I've had several similar telephone calls, not all of them pleasant.

His family and friends also stress that while Kolberg may have been upset by his broken marriage, mounting medical bills and Nancy's disappearance, he had reasons to live.

"The love for his children," his sister, Cheryl Kolberg, told me shortly after Brad's body was found. "I just can't see him taking his own life, no matter how bad it might have gotten. He wouldn't have left them."

Cheryl Kolberg says she realizes her family will probably never know what happened. They are left only with speculation and questions that no one so far has been able to answer. The only thing worse, she confided, would be living again through those weeks when the Kolberg family didn't know if Brad was dead or alive.

Nancy's family has not been that fortunate.

"The worst has been never knowing," said her father, Leonard Kaufman. "The grieving can never end. It just never ends."

Raising Nancy's two children as their own, the Kaufmans, too, are frustrated by the investigation into their daughter's death. They've worked with several different officers who they say have told them, "I'll never drop this case" but then move on through a promotion or to a job in some other city.

Just recently, they saw Nancy's picture on television— not as a missing person, but on a community station's segment of *Yellowstone County's Most Wanted* for writing bad checks. Even though authorities believe she is dead, a warrant for her arrest is still open.

Now, the Kaufmans are putting together the money for an aerial search of the mountains where their daughter once walked with the man they believe is responsible for her death, where they believe they will find Nancy buried, perhaps by an old shack and a telephone pole. They tell me they will no longer rely on the police to find their daughter.

"We've learned that today's headlines are tomorrow's back page," her mother, Hilde, told me. "The bitterness has set in, and I don't know if I'll ever overcome it. I mean, how do you explain to four- and five-year-olds each night that you don't know where their mother is?"

The articles I've written have resulted in a few tips for police, including a reported sighting of Nancy in Billings. But so far, none of those leads have panned out. I doubt they ever will.

I've sorted through this case more times now than I can recall, pouring over old notes, hoping I've missed something along the way. Something that would convince me that Brad Kolberg was either a troubled killer or an innocent victim who died what must have been a horrible death.

But the notes haven't changed much. Brad Kolberg is still dead, Nancy Kaufman is still missing, and that's all anyone can say for sure. Those notes, I'm afraid, will never change.

**Nick Ehli** covers cops and the courts for the *Billings Gazette,* the largest newspaper in Montana. He is a graduate of the University of Montana School of Journalism, where he received the President's Award as the school's outstanding graduate. In 1987, he attended the University of London as an exchange student and was named a Sears Congressional Intern in 1988. Ehli has received numerous awards from the Society of Professional Journalists and the Montana Newspaper Association.

# NINE

—◦◦◦—

# The Disappearance

## YOLANDA RODRÍGUEZ

### The Los Angeles Times

On December 16, 1989, Leticia Hernandez was sitting on the front steps of her home in Oceanside, California. She had been playing with friends in front of the house while her mother washed clothes.

Her mom huffed and puffed in and out of the house, washing and then hanging the clothes out to dry. As darkness fell on the dusty driveway, Leticia's friends went home and the seven-year-old-girl sat on the front steps of the house. Her little brother Jorge, 2, sat next to her. The driveway emptied of children. It grew darker.

And then Leticia disappeared.

And so began my introduction to news reporting. I was a participant in the Minority Editorial Training Program at the *Los Angeles Times* and was assigned to the paper's San Diego office. I had only a few months of reporting experience. Leticia's mysterious disappearance was the first tragedy I wrote about.

But that's not why I remember it.

How can you forget the little girl with a missing-tooth-smile and a braid in her hair who disappeared into the night?

There were three of us in the training program, so we took turns "doing cops." That was reporter slang for working the police beat.

In San Diego, the *Los Angeles Times* was the third-most-read paper, after the *San Diego Union* and the *San Diego Tribune*. There were also several local television stations, including one that broadcasted from Tijuana, Mexico. We reported a mix of news in our paper. Crime stories were not what fed the news engine.

Every morning we'd check in with the local police departments to see what was going on. In the news business, murder and mayhem are always the big stories.

San Diego was the police department I called first, because it was the largest. Then came all the others. But I quickly learned that most of the time when you call and ask the desk officer what's going on, the answer is usually "Nothing, nothing much."

That makes for a very insecure feeling—I always feel like something is going on somewhere, and I'm missing it. So I ask the obvious questions: Any murders? Suicides? Anything weird, funny, strange? Most of the time the cops chuckle and you still get nothing. But every now and then it pays off.

For Leticia, though, I didn't have to ask any of those questions.

"We have a little girl missing," said Officer Bob George, the spokesman for the Oceanside Police Department who answered the telephone the morning I dialed.

My heart stopped. I have nieces and godchildren. I know what it's like to worry and pray for their safety.

Leticia's mother, who was also named Leticia, was the one who called the police. But only after she and her family had scoured the neighborhood, shouting for her daughter to return home. Because she had waited, officers did not begin searching the city until well after midnight.

The search was on for several hours before police typed up a press release that Monday morning. It had only the barest of details—what she looked like, where she was last seen.

I wanted to go out to Oceanside and begin interviewing the girl's family, friends and neighbors. My city editor, Mark Saylor, said he wanted to wait a day before reporting anything lengthy on the missing girl—just in case she was found. I didn't agree.

But I phoned the family and spoke briefly with the little girl's mother. She talked about how worried she was.

My first story was a short one. It basically detailed what police had said.

The next day Leticia was still missing.

I was sitting at my computer when I checked with the Oceanside cops.

"She's still missing," I yelled across a few feet to Mark. He got up and strode over to my desk.

"Why don't you go up there and talk to her mother?" he said.

Yeah, a day after everybody else, I thought.

"OK." I grabbed my things and headed for the exit.

Inside, my stomach began churning. This was real. How would I ask her what I needed to know? It was late morning, and as I walked to the parking garage, I tried to calm myself down. When I reached the car—a scratched-up, dusty white Ford Tempo the *Times* had for us—I sat quietly for a moment leafing through my notes from the day before.

"Leticia Hernandez, 7 yrs., from 1300 block Bush Street, 12-16-89, red shorts, red tank top. white socks, white sandals, black hair in pigtail, brown eyes, 4ft/40lbs, missing 2 upper teeth, birth mark on upper left leg, speaks English . . .'' Along the edge I had written ''PD called 10 P.M.''

The San Diego streets were nearly empty, except for the vendors selling coffee from magazine kiosks and mobile carts. Oceanside was to the north of the city, a full hour away.

I drove along, rehearsing the things I would ask, what I needed to remember. And I agonized over how I would ask my questions. Do I knock on someone's door and say, ''Excuse me, ma'am, I know your daughter is missing. Can we talk?'' No, that wouldn't do.

As I raced along, my eyes were drawn to the Orthodox church that edged the highway. Rays of sun shone on its golden dome forming a cross on its spherical surface. I marveled at its beauty and wondered how God could let a little girl just disappear. Where was she? Who was she with?

The Pacific Coast Highway skirts the ocean as it winds into town. I love to be near the water. I like to look at it, listen to it, inhale it. This day, it had a beautiful aqua tone and the sky a pristine blue. Through my car window, I could see surfers on foamy, shimmering waves and people sunning themselves on blankets they had spread on the sand. It all seemed so peaceful.

And still the little girl was missing.

Once again, I went over the details of the case in my head: I knew what police had said. But I would need more than that, much more. I wanted to know her mother. And I needed her to tell me, in her own words, what her daughter was like. What was she doing during the hours before she disappeared? Who were her close friends?

Before reaching little Leticia's home, I detoured to the police station. It's always better to talk to cops face-to-face. That way you are not just an anonymous voice on the phone. Maybe it helps me to communicate with them better. Besides, I needed to know if there were any new leads in the case.

Entering the low-slung building, I picked up one of the flyers that had been distributed throughout the oceanfront city. Leticia smiled at me.

"No clues," said Officer George, the cop who came out from the back room to meet with me. I listened as he detailed the case, and then, as I headed for the doorway, he yelled: "Everybody says she's really sweet."

The interview I dreaded—but desperately wanted—was close at hand. Leticia's house was at the end of a street lined with small, modest homes. It was set back from the street; a driveway of burnt-orange dirt led to the front door. The young girl's family occupied the first floor, and another family lived above them.

A television truck was parked on the street in front of the two-family dwelling, and I watched as a reporter exited the walkway.

"Damn," I cursed under my breath. This could be good. It meant that her mother was talking. But it could be bad. Maybe her mother was tired of talking.

Reaching for my bag, I pulled out my notebook and pen and took a deep breath. I had that sick feeling in my stomach again. Like butterflies gone mad.

At moments like these, street reporters like to console themselves with the expression "Everyone wants to talk; they just don't know it." It may sound lame if you are not a reporter, but my experience has been that most of the time people really do want to talk. Of course, this was my first time interviewing someone who had experienced a tragedy in their life. And I had that vampire feeling—as though I was going to suck this woman's emotions out of her for tomorrow's paper. Maybe my story will help find Leticia, I told myself as I approached the door.

It was open, so I knocked on the doorjamb as I said a couple of prayers: "please, god, let them find her," and "please, god, let her talk to me."

"*Perdone la molestia,*" I said to the short, plump woman who answered the door. It means "I'm sorry to bother you" in Spanish. What else could I say? It was true.

"*Quiero saber un poco mas de lo que ocurrio con Leticia,*" I wanted to know a little about what happened with Leticia.

"*Si, si, si,*" the five-foot woman motioned me inside. "*Entre.*"

Her brown skin was accentuated by the black and white floral dress she wore. Her dark eyes were puffy, her voice tired. The weary woman settled into a thick-cushioned sofa to talk. Her mother, Victoria, and brother, Javier, sat on either side of her.

The living room was cluttered, but clean. Crocheted doilies protected the side tables. Family photos decorated the walls—of Javier, of the family, of little Leticia. In the corner, a Christmas tree stretched to the ceiling.

There was an uncomfortable silence at first. "Tell me where she was," I broke the ice. "What was she doing?" My notes became a scramble of captured words and phrases in both Spanish and English.

"*Ella estaba jugando,*" the mother explained that her daughter had been playing.

She spoke slowly, as if she was seeing the images in

front of her. "Then it started to get dark and the other children went home. Leticia was sitting on the step with her two-year-old brother, Jorge . . . I was inside the house for about ten minutes . . ."

The next time she went outside, her baby was gone.

Leticia's mother spoke slowly, deliberately, as she explained that her daughter never wandered away from the house. Perhaps her little girl had gone somewhere with a few of the older kids in the neighborhood.

But when she did not return home, the family panicked and began knocking on neighbors' doors. No one had seen her. No one knew what could have happened. Hours passed, and friends joined the search, checking the back streets, the bushes. Still no sign of the sweet-natured seven-year-old.

I asked only a few questions. What does she want to be when she grows up? What is she like? I tried to pose my questions in the present tense, not the past. To put them in the past would mean Leticia was no longer alive.

Her uncle Javier told me the family called her Tita. And that she wanted to be model.

Maria, Leticia's sister, described her as sweet and shy, a momma's girl who liked to settle in her mother's lap whenever she got the chance.

As we chatted, Mrs. Hernandez fell into a silence. Her eyes wandered, and then she started to cry quietly. I wanted to comfort her, to tell her that maybe my story would help. But I couldn't say that. I left her to her thoughts and turned to Javier and Leticia's godmother for answers.

There's a stereotype about reporters barging into people's lives and asking, "How do you feel?" when there has been a tragedy. You're not really supposed to ask that.

What kind of answer do you expect to get? "I feel sad" or "I feel mad." Where do you go from there?

No, you ask concrete questions—what does she want for Christmas? Leticia wanted a bicycle. In the days before her disappearance, the little girl had made decorations for the Christmas tree and wrapped red and green pipe cleaners around the candy canes that hung from its branches.

While we sat on the couch talking, there was a knock on the door. Two of Leticia's teachers dropped by the house. They brought brownies and cookies. It was their contribution, a way of helping the family get through their tragedy. I took the opportunity to interview them.

They told me Leticia was the kind of child who mothered her classmates. If a little kid was feeling sad, she would go over and hug them.

A golden sunlight filled the cozy living room, and suddenly I realized how late it had become. It was time to go. There was nothing left to ask. Nothing I could say.

I hugged Leticia's mother and whispered that I would say a prayer for the family. I was glad I had come but was now faced with another dilemma—I had a story to write and a deadline to meet. It was too late to drive back to San Diego, so I went to a bureau office nearby. I barely remember the drive. But when I arrived, I had only one thought on my mind—write. The bureau chief (that's the person in charge of a branch office of a paper) found me a desk, and I called Mark in San Diego.

"I talked to her," I told him, expecting him to jump for joy or something like that.

"Good," was all he said.

"How long do I have?"

"One hour."

I switched on the computer and scrambled through my notes.

"Where do I start?" I said aloud.

Nancy Ray, a veteran reporter, watched me for a while from beneath her black beret. Then she gave me the advice I needed: "Write. Just sit down and write."

"Where do I start?"

"Don't worry, just start writing. Smoke a cigarette and write," she directed. "Don't worry." She gave me one of her cigarettes—a nonmenthol, Viceroys, I think—and searched the office for an ashtray. She lit one with me. I'm sure we were breaking a no-smoking-in-the-building rule. But we were the only ones left in the office. And besides, I was on deadline.

Nancy left me alone with what was left of her cigarettes and I started . . .

This would be what is known as a "second-day" story. The first-day story was the news that Leticia was missing. This one had no news in it—nothing really new. It was what is known as a news feature—a closer look at something. In this case, a talk with the mother and family of the missing girl. Since it was a news feature, the lead— the first paragraph of a story—did not have to be "hard." It did not have to be a recitation of the facts. It could be "soft." It could say something about the person I was writing about.

*Leticia Hernandez wants to be a model when she grows up, I began. She is also a mothering 7-year-old who braided her own hair for the school photograph that has been reproduced and distributed all over Oceanside and neighboring communities.*

\*   \*   \*

230 • Crime on Deadline

Perhaps not the best lead, but under the circumstances, it was the best I could do.

In the months that passed there were other Leticia stories. Her disappearance attracted national attention because of television programs like *America's Most Wanted, Unsolved Mysteries,* and *Crime Stoppers,* all of which aired segments about the young girl. Each time they did, there were hundreds of calls to police and FBI from people who thought they had seen her. The ''sightings'' placed Leticia across the southern part of the United States, from California to Florida. All of them were ''confirmed''—meaning the description given to police matched that of Leticia. The callers said the little girl was in the company of a man and sometimes a man and a woman. The calls continued for the six months I was in California. But they never led anywhere. I wrote more stories, talked to the family again and again, talked to her teachers. I even interviewed a police officer who had written a song about her.

All the while, I wanted to believe that she was alive. The cops wanted to believe it too. When I left the *Los Angeles Times,* Leticia was still missing. There were no fresh clues. The little girl had just disappeared into the night.

About one year after I left California, a hiker trekking the Canyons found a small skeleton. Next to the tiny bones, police investigators found the clothes the person had been wearing.

It was Leticia.

I later learned that cops had suspected someone all along, but they could never gather physical evidence to link him to the crime. The dozens of sightings had misdirected the police. They thought they led somewhere. But they didn't.

I look at my notes and my clips from that time. I think I could have pressed the cops more, could somehow have made them talk about suspects. But back then, they were so reticent, so unwilling to talk.

No one has ever been prosecuted for these crimes of kidnapping and murder. Whoever took Leticia was still out there.

For me Leticia is still out there too. When I go to bed at night, I still think of her—and still pray for her.

During the writing of this book, **Yolanda Rodríguez** experienced what reporters everywhere fear—the closing of a newspaper. She was a Long Island *Newsday* reporter covering crime, the courts and town government, when *New York Newsday* folded. She headed for sunny Florida, where she now reports for the *Sarasota Herald-Tribune*. Before *Newsday,* Rodriguez was a cop reporter for the *Los Angeles Times*. And before that, she was a Spanish interpreter for the New York State Supreme Court. She is a graduate of Hunter College and an alumna of the Hispanic Women's Leadership Institute at Rutgers University. She won two Society of Professional Journalists awards while at *Newsday* and in-house awards at the *Los Angeles Times*, *Newsday* and the *Herald-Tribune*.

# TEN

—⁓—

# Free to Kill

## LYNN BARTELS

### *The Albuquerque Tribune*

One woman's frantic phone call has saved dozens of lives in New Mexico.

Juli Keller called the *Albuquerque Tribune* in 1991 with a rambling and incoherent story about a convicted murderer, her dead son and a series of drunken-driving arrests.

The city editor, Mike Arrieta Walden, tried to make sense of what the woman said. Then, he passed on his notes to me.

I got the tip for two reasons. I was the city columnist for the *Trib* and always looking for a good story. And no other reporter in New Mexico had written as often or probed more deeply into the state's horrendous drunken-driving problem—the worst in the nation.

I drove out to Albuquerque's west side that October to meet Juli Keller. I had interviewed dozens of families who had lost loved ones to drunken drivers. I knew to expect someone who couldn't quite get on with her life, who relived her son's death over and over, who railed at the system.

But Juli Keller was in worse shape than any victim I had ever met.

She lit one cigarette after another and went through an entire box of Kleenex. The stew she was cooking burned on the stove as she told her story.

Jason Keller Chavez, her only child, was killed by a convicted murderer on parole who had gone for a motorcycle ride after a night of drinking. Her seventeen-year-old son's killer would not even be indicted until five months later. He would walk out of jail after posting a low bond and would be free to drink and drive again.

By the time Keller finished telling me her story, I was as outraged as she was overwhelmed. And we didn't even know the whole story. In the months that followed, I would uncover more snafus surrounding her son's murder.

I began investigating Jason's death writing three columns a week, handling breaking news and performing as a backup assistant city editor, I worked on the story.

Progress was slow, and Juli Keller thought I had given up. At one point she angrily demanded her diaries back "since you aren't going to write anything, after all." I didn't argue. I gave them back. Eventually she relented, but for a while I thought the story was going nowhere.

Keller didn't know it, but I was as frustrated with her as she was with me. She had terrible asthma but smoked like a train. Her electricity was always about to be turned off. I frequently lent her gas money for her car. She just could not get her life on track—if it had ever been.

She got pregnant with Jason when she was a teenager. Two marriages ended in divorce, and she and Jason struggled. He worked after-school jobs to help his mother pay the rent and utilities. He often had to wake her to make sure she got to work.

One of her most treasured keepsakes was a letter Jason wrote on May 7, 1990, thanking her for all the work she was doing in planning his high school graduation party that was to take place at the end of the month.

"I love you more than anyone on this earth and without you, I wouldn't want to be here," he wrote.

Despite their bond, the two had their share of parent-child rows. On July 12, a month and a half after Jason's graduation, he and his mother quarreled. Keller came home to find he had again invited his friends over without her permission. She told him if he couldn't live by her rules to move out. Embarrassed at being scolded in front of his friends, Jason said nothing.

"I just say some really awful things when I'm mad and then I apologize," Keller said, breaking down and reaching for another cigarette.

This time, there would be no chance. That night, Jason and a buddy were on their way to play miniature golf when 27-year-old Roger Herrington and one of his brothers ran a red light and crashed into Jason's battered 1978 green Toyota. Jason died on the way to the hospital. His murderer's blood-alcohol level was 0.15.

Herrington had already been convicted of vehicular homicide by the time Jason's mother called the newspaper. But there hadn't been a lot of coverage of her son's death, and she was frustrated not only by the lack of publicity but also because she thought there was a lot she didn't know.

She was right.

I set out to find out all I could about Roger Herrington.

It would not be easy. Nearly every government official who had dealt with him had reason not to talk: screwups surrounded his case.

My biggest obstacle, I knew, would be the New Mexico Department of Corrections. Herrington was paroled to

New Mexico in 1989, after serving less than five years for stabbing a 23-year-old Kentucky man to death. New Mexico was supposed to be watching him.

My relationship with the corrections department was still a little shaky. I had shattered all credibility after a disastrous relationship with a maximum-security inmate I met while covering the infamous Independence Day Breakout in 1987. Only years later can I joke about my relationship with the prisoner, who was paroled several months after the breakout.

After the incident I spent months slowly and painstakingly trying to rebuild a relationship with the corrections folks. But I didn't know if I had come far enough to get the information I needed for the Herrington story. At first I talked to prison spokesman Don Caviness, who would get information from parole officer Erma Sedillo and relay it to me.

Finally, after weeks of calls, I was able to talk to Sedillo directly. It proved to be the big break in the case.

Juli Keller hated Sedillo's guts. She blamed the parole officer for her son's death. But I eventually came to view the soft-spoken woman as another victim. She had an impossible caseload. Every time she had asked the state of Kentucky to come get Herrington, Kentucky had refused. The court never notified her of restrictions placed on the criminal after his arrests in Albuquerque.

One afternoon Sedillo opened her file to me. She met Herrington on May 30, 1989. He and his mother were excited about Herrington's fresh start at the age of twenty-six.

Sedillo figured the last person she would have problems with would be Herrington.

"Instead," she said, "the case will haunt me for the rest of my life."

Only months after that first meeting, Herrington tested positive for cocaine and amphetamines. Albuquerque police arrested him on a drunken-driving charge. A month later, they arrested him on a felony forgery charge.

Sedillo had had it. Just seven months after their first meeting, she wrote Kentucky and recommended that Herrington be returned for a parole revocation hearing. Kentucky wrote back, asking for more information and saying it would wait and see what happened with the forgery charge.

Sedillo didn't answer the letter.

"That was my fault," she said, in an interview in her tiny office at the Parole Office in Albuquerque. "I really thought that when I sent them that memo the first time, they were going to take him back," she said, adding that she was supervising ninety other people at the time. "I didn't push it. I didn't call Kentucky."

Prosecutors eventually dismissed the DWI charge, which might have been enough to send Herrington home. It had been filed in Albuquerque's Metropolitan Court, the busiest court in the state, where cases often must be dismissed because they can't be heard in a timely manner.

"Metro Court is just Trinity Site with a wet fuse," District Attorney Bob Schwartz would later say.

As for the forgery charge, in a surprise move, another of Herrington's brothers took the stand and announced he was the guilty party. Prosecutors didn't believe the other Herrington, but the jury did. Roger Herrington was convicted only of a misdemeanor charge, concealing his identity. Kentucky said the conviction wasn't big enough to warrant parole revocation.

Roger Herrington wasn't indicted in Jason's death until December 1990, nearly five months after the crash. The judge who presided over his arraignment was the same judge who had presided over his forgery trial. Judge Pat Murdoch knew Herrington was a convicted murderer on parole. Still, he set the bond at only $2,500, allowing Herrington to get out of jail by paying $250. The judge also added a new twist to the case. He told Herrington that he was suspending his driving privileges and that he could only drive to and from his day construction job. If he violated that condition, he would be thrown in jail. It meant nothing, words on a court document that only a reporter would read months later.

Juli Keller may have been grieving, but Herrington was having a great time. Three months after his indictment, at 3:30 on a March 1991 morning, an Albuquerque cop found Herrington standing beside his car. The slim and surly man was drunk but insisted he could make it home. The officer took him to jail to sleep it off; no crime had been committed because Herrington wasn't driving.

Police arrested Herrington in April and again in May on drunken-driving charges. He was so drunk during one arrest that he had peed in his pants while swearing at police, the arresting officer told me.

In all three of Herrington's contacts with police, officers had entered his name in their computer. Nothing came up. Nowhere did they learn that he was free on bond for a heinous alcohol offense or that he was out of jail on special restrictions. The same problem occurred at the jail, where Herrington was allowed to walk in April after paying only a $50 bond. No one had any idea that Herrington was a man with a past.

"You're expecting the criminal justice system to work. This is chaos," Deputy Police Chief David Ramirez said, when later interviewed about the amazing chain of events that allow Herrington to roam the streets.

Most incredible of all was how Herrington's drinking-

and-driving days ended: Juli Keller put an end to them that May. She learned from a friend of a friend of a friend who knew that Herrington had been in trouble yet again.

Keller had been too scared to drive after Jason's death, but she got behind the wheel of her car and drove to police headquarters to ask for the arrest reports. The May 12 drunken-driving arrest particularly bothered her. Mother's Day was May 12. She couldn't bear to be in her apartment surrounded by her son's pictures, so she had rented a motel room.

Keller raised hell and an emergency hearing was held. Roger Herrington's bond was raised, and this time his family didn't bail him out. The next month, he pleaded guilty to killing Jason. That surprised—and relieved—prosecutors since Herrington had been trying to pin the death of Jason Keller on his brother, although the evidence showed that he was the one driving the motorcycle that night. In June of 1991, Judge Murdoch sentenced Roger Herrington to eight years in prison, a tough sentence by New Mexico standards.

"Mr. Herrington," he said, "it's a case like this that makes the court sorry that it can't weigh the value of human lives and, in that balance, give Jason back his and take yours away."

"Free to Kill," a special four-page pullout, appeared in the *Trib* in April 1992. It told the story of how a breakdown in the criminal-justice system led to Jason's death.

I rarely read the end of "Free to Kill" without getting the blues. It reminds me of so many New Mexicans whose lives have been destroyed by drunken drivers:

> These days, Juli Keller drives a car with a bumper sticker that reads, "A drunk driver killed my son and I am MADD."

Now and then, she goes to meetings sponsored by Mothers Against Drunken Driving where she cries along with all the others whose lives were shattered by drunken drivers. More often, she finds comfort in family and friends.

One of the entries in her diary simply reads, "I couldn't sleep at all last night. I'm so sad."

What torments Keller is how the system failed over and over and over again and how her son paid for that breakdown.

"What a long, strange trip it's been," Keller said. "That's what I want printed on my tombstone."

Juli Keller could not stop weeping when she read the article. Justice, she said, had come nearly two years after her son's death.

A second person read the story with just as much interest. The *Tribune*'s managing editor, John Temple, called me into his office.

"This is incredible stuff," he said, referring to the numerous glitches I had uncovered in Albuquerque's police, court and parole systems. "I think we should dig deeper."

As a result, the *Tribune* began a six-month probe into the problem of drunken driving. The logo was "DWI: Why Can't We Stop It?"

In our investigation, we uncovered a driver who had at least twenty-five—and possibly forty-one—arrests for driving while intoxicated. We rode with DWI officers and watched as drunken drivers stumbled and vomited and still maintained they had had nothing to drink. We sat in packed courtrooms and watched as inexperienced prosecutors and lousy judges allowed these same people to go scot free. We revealed how liquor interests controlled the legislature. We discovered that drunken drivers killed every thirty-four hours and that 261 people had died in 1991 in New Mexico.

During that summer, I rode with Albuquerque's crack DWI unit at night and went to Metro Court during the day. My roommate had a minimum-wage job, and he once figured he was making 4,000 times an hour what I was earning, but I loved every minute. The only bad thing was I started smoking again after hanging out all the time with cops.

The *Tribune* had hired me in January 1984 after a 3½-year stint at the *Gallup Independent* in Gallup, New Mexico, where I covered cops and city hall. The *Trib* quickly put me to work covering cops, including Metro Court and the jail. After just nine short months I was moved to city hall, but as my editors would say, I never really left the cop beat. When I covered education, when I covered the legislature in Santa Fe, when I was a general assignment reporter, when I was named the city columnist, I still got tons of tips from my cop sources and continued to write about crime.

I had kept my contacts at the police department, Metro Court and the City-County Jail. I did lunches. I went to coffee. I sent congratulation cards when people got promoted or had babies. Unwittingly, I had placed myself in an incredible position when the DWI series was hatched.

At Metro Court, I was allowed behind the counters to search for records. I had unprecedented access to the court, the police and the jail. My request for a charge account to pay for all these court records was instantly approved. At police headquarters, despite an internal battle brewing over the DWI squad's overtime, my ride-along requests got an instant go. Ride when you want, I was told. All officers are available to you.

By that time, I had a partner, reporter Ed Asher, who

also rode with the DWI unit, but not as frequently. Ed's specialty was records reporting, and it was his job to feed volumes of Metro Court and Motor Vehicle Division data into our computer to find out the average fine and the average jail stay of a DWI offender. Are you ready for this? The average fine is $17, and the average sentence is seven and a half days, but 56 percent of those found guilty don't get fined or jailed at all.

The DWI unit was in the midst of an overtime audit when I began riding, and the last thing they wanted was some nosy reporter hanging around. That first night in June 1992 I remember well. When I asked, "Which officer am I riding with?" they looked at each other. "Uh, John, you'll have to take her with you," they said to the newest officer on the ten-officer squad.

That move ultimately ended up giving the *Trib* a blockbuster story that we ran with in August instead of waiting for the series in December. I sat in the passenger seat of Officer John Williams' police cruiser while he cruised for drunks. Trying to get him to loosen him up, I asked the officer to recount for me his most memorable DWI arrest.

"Art Aragon," he said, without hesitation.

He had arrested Aragon on May 9 on a drunken-driving charge. When he entered Aragon's name and birthdate into the computer in his police car he thought the machine had malfunctioned. One DWI arrest after another appeared. Williams arrested the 32-year-old on what he thought was Aragon's forty-first DWI.

"GUY TO CHECK OUT," I wrote in my notebook and later transcribed into my computer. Every day, I faithfully wrote inches of copy about my experience on the street or in court. Project editor J. Lowe Davis had insisted that I keep a computer record, almost a diary, so that when I started writing in November, I could easily pull up names and details. I am ever grateful for that piece of advice. (Davis went to work for the *U.S. Virgin Islands Daily News,* where she was the editor of the 1995 Pulitzer-prize winning series "USVI Crime: Who's to Blame?")

One of my best sources turned out to be the hardest-working assistant district attorney I've ever met. June Stein prosecuted multiple DWI offenders. She was in her office by 6:00 A.M. and rarely left before 8:00 P.M. The first time I called her at work on a Saturday, I had planned to leave her a message on her machine. She answered. It turned out she always worked weekends—without any extra pay, of course. DWI officers called her for advice. Rookie prosecutors relied on her help.

I met June in July while she was doing a ride-along with the DWI unit. "MIGHT BE A GOOD SOURCE," I wrote in my notes. Little did I know.

One day in August I was sitting in her office, and we were talking about repeat offenders—the bane of New Mexico and most states' drunken-driving problems. "I heard about this guy Art Aragon who was arrested in May," I began.

"Arrested twice in May," she corrected.

It turned out that after Aragon's May 9 arrest by Officer Williams, he was taken to a hospital to be treated for a hand injury. He slipped away and went to a home where police arrested him again and brought him back to the hospital. Two days later, he again escaped. And two days later, Aragon was arrested on another drunken-driving charge.

The system again let him go. Aragon got out of jail without anyone knowing about his DWI arrest and escape just two days earlier because the paperwork hadn't been filed.

I left June's office and went to the jail to pore over the

booking sheets for the week. I didn't always do that. This week, for some reason, I did. There it was: Art Aragon. Arrested on a DWI charge. Blood-alcohol level: 0.24.

I called June. She was incredulous that he had been arrested again.

I called my editors. They decided to run with a story that Saturday.

Tracking down Aragon's DWI history was nearly impossible. Ed and I discovered that Motor Vehicle records contradict Metro Court records, which contradict probation records. We tracked twenty-five DWI arrests, but Aragon may have had a dozen more. The headline that Saturday remains one of my favorites. Two-inch letters in red blared from the page: "ONE MAN, 25 DWI ARRESTS, And he is still out there."

TV stations followed the story. We have a fierce rivalry with the *Albuquerque Journal* and, in traditional lameness, it came back with, "We knew it, but we just hadn't printed it." Right. (Later, as we broke even more stories, friends at the *Journal* jokingly told us their slogan, which played off ours, had become, "DWI: How Can We Stop *Them*?")

The Art Aragon story got even wilder.

I was riding with the DWI unit later that month when two men walked out of a convenience store about 3:00 A.M. A DWI officer ran up to me. "Lynn, that's Art Aragon," he said.

I couldn't believe it.

"Cover me," I said, and raced to catch up with Aragon, who was halfway down the block. He had two six-packs in his shopping bag.

"Art," I started, "I'm Lynn Bartels of the *Albuquerque Tribune*, and I am so glad to see you drinking—and walking."

Drink makes some men mean, but Aragon was friendly, even curious. He invited me to go drinking with him and wanted to know why I had made him a household name.

"I didn't kill anybody," he said.

"Yet," I answered.

The next week I was telling all this to District Attorney Bob Schwartz, and he wanted to know why the police hadn't arrested him.

"For what?" I said. "There was no warrant."

I had discovered another loophole in the system. Charges had been filed in his latest three DWI arrests, but no warrant was ever issued. That was immediately corrected after my conversation with Schwartz.

Four days later, my home phone rang early in the morning. It was a jail sergeant I had met during my first stint on the police beat, and he was laughing.

"Lynn, guess who we've got here?" he said.

Art Aragon. And Aragon wanted to make a phone call—to me!

It turns out that a bouncer at a nightclub had read our first story about Aragon and then the story about a warrant being issued. He had called police when he saw Aragon in the parking lot.

Another front-page scoop followed.

During a DWI seminar that fall, a public defender talked about poor Art Aragon and how he would never receive a fair trial and blah, blah, blah.

I couldn't wait to answer her. I told the audience that while reporting the Aragon story, we contacted Aragon's friends and his family. Without fail, I said, they thanked us for trying to do something. The people who loved Art Aragon were frustrated, too, with a system that continued to let him drink and drive. They thought our efforts might save his life and someone else's.

2

"He wanted to stop drinking," one of his friends told the newspaper. "He wanted help."

This was a project in which the public was invited along for the ride. Early on, we told our readers we were investigating drunken driving.

I wrote a column every Monday on a variety of DWI topics. Readers called with great ideas. I interviewed a California vintner who witnessed a horrible DWI crash in New Mexico and vowed never to return to the state until it faced its alcohol problem.

In October, we showed how liquor interests controlled the New Mexico Legislature.

In November, we ran a story about ten of the worst DWI offenders in Albuquerque and how they got that way.

And in December our four-day, four-page series appeared.

We had taken the system apart like a fine watch, explaining to our readers why it didn't run and what was needed to make it tick:

In New Mexico we love our cars and we love our booze. Which would be fine, if we didn't mix them. But we do, with horrifying consequences.

Year after bloody year, New Mexico leads the nation DWI-caused deaths per capita. New Mexico's theme has been "party on," and we had it first, long before Mike Meyers and Dana Carvey made it popular on "Wayne's World."

Every Saturday night is New Year's Eve in New Mexico. New Mexico has such a serious alcohol problem that half of its thirty-three counties rank in the top 2 percent of counties nationwide for alcohol-caused deaths. The rest of the counties rank in the top 20 percent of all counties in the nation.

That would change if New Mexico were willing to make some changes.

Henry Geissler, who for nineteen years has lectured convicted drunken drivers on the danger of DWI, is one of the advocates for change.

"The state of New Mexico for almost as long as I can remember has led the nation in automobile accidents, DWIs and alcohol-related deaths," Geissler said.

"In other states, fewer people die in a flood or a hurricane, and the governor declares the state a disaster area.

"I think the time has come to take extraordinary measures and have the governor declare New Mexico a disaster area."

Just days after the final installment, a family of five drove to the outskirts of Albuquerque on Christmas Eve to see the city lights. A former alcohol counselor driving on the wrong side of the interstate plowed into the family's car. He was traveling more than ninety miles per hour at the time of impact. Five hours after the crash, his blood-alcohol level was 0.10. The mother and three daughters died instantly. The husband was seriously injured.

Upon hearing of the incident, the public exploded. New Mexicans used our series as a blueprint to demand reform.

Only two months earlier, the powerful legislature had dismissed our investigation, calling it "a desperate attempt by an afternoon newspaper to try to hold on to the few newspapers that you do sell." They were the words of a leading lawmaker—with a DWI arrest on his record, of course.

Legislators like this one ate their words.

Drunken-driving measures dominated the 1993 legislative session. Lawmakers passed significant reform, much of which had been recommended by the *Tribune* in its series.

And that spring, journalists gave the project a number of prestigious honors, including the Roy Howard and Sigma Delta Chi awards for public service. Contest judges again and again said they were terrified of ever visiting our state.

But our biggest reward came nearly a year after Juli Keller's first phone call to the paper.

The New Mexico Traffic Safety Bureau reported that drunken-driving deaths had dropped an astounding 20 percent during the first five months of 1993.

Director John Fenner made me cry when he attributed the success to Lynn Bartels and the *Albuquerque Tribune.*

**Lynn Bartels** has covered crime for the *Rocky Mountain News* in Denver, Colorado, since July 1993. Previously, she worked for thirteen years as a police reporter in New Mexico, for the *Albuquerque Tribune,* where she won numerous awards for investigative reporting and column writing. In 1990, she won the National Society of Newspaper Columnists' Award for humor writing. And her work was selected to appear in *Best of the Rest,* a book about the best local columnists. The Vermilion, South Dakota, native is a 1977 graduate of Cottey College and a 1980 graduate of Northern Arizona University.

# ELEVEN

—ᴟᴟ—

# Murder on the 5:33

## LISA BETH PULITZER

### *The New York Times*

The Long Island courthouse lobby was buzzing with reporters, some chatting on cellular phones, others standing
in their usual cliques discussing the upcoming testimony.

Media technicians were running long, black television
cables to the pool camera that had been set up inside the
dimly lit courtroom. It was the same courtroom in which
I had watched auto mechanic Joey Buttafuoco admit to
having sexual relations with underage Amy Fisher. And
across the hall from the one where I witnessed serial killer
Joel Rifkin become ill after court officers served him a
nitrate-filled bologna sandwich—he was allergic!

But the media turnout on this day rivaled anything I'd
ever seen—even the O. J. Simpson case. The folding tables that had been set up along one wall of the expansive
lobby were lined with minitelevision sets—one for each
network affiliate. Reporters wearing bulky, black ear-
phones sat in front of them adjusting their audio boxes in
preparation for the dramatic testimony that would soon
take place.

Court officers were warning that seats inside the galley
would be limited and urged journalists to print their names

on the list posted near the metal detector that had been moved to the entranceway of Judge Donald Belfi's courtroom.

I would just flash my *New York Times* press pass.

Looking around at the mass of people, I realized that many of the faces were unfamiliar. There were camera crews from *Inside Edition,* the *Oprah Winfrey Show,* even a Japanese television station.

Carol Cohen from WBAB radio and Keiran Crowley from the *New York Post* were huddled together behind one of the lobby's marble pillars, probably comparing notes to see who had wrested away the most dazzling quotes from the defense counsel. I always hated that part of the job: a hungry pack of reporters chasing after one person, everyone trying to get him or her to say something that would make their story "exclusive."

Clutching my notebook, I leaned against one the marble support beams and talked quietly with my favorite court buff, Leo Castanza. The feisty 75-year-old had retired from his career as a construction contractor years before and treated the courts like a full-time job, reporting to the hall of justice five days a week to sit in on cases that interested him. It's better than television, he would always tell me.

As we stood chatting, a commotion stirred near the rear entrance door. Dozens of cameramen jumped to attention and scrambled to grab their Beta-cams.

"He's coming. He's coming," somebody shouted into the crowded lobby.

A tall, blond man appeared in the vestibule. He was surrounded by prosecutors and court personnel. His broad shoulders filled a navy blue suit; his thin fingers clutched the gold handle of a cherry-wood cane. This was the first time since the incident that the media had seen the young man. He had been semi-conscious for almost a month before beginning a year of intensive rehabilitation. He looked better than we had imagined.

Court officers pushed a path as the star witness slowly ambulated through the crowd, his doting mother by his side. In a frenzy everyone raced after him. Immediately we were stopped by court officers demanding to search our belongings.

The whistle of a passing train echoed in the distance, creating an eerie backdrop for the proceedings now getting underway in the crowded Mineola courtroom. Newspaper journalists, television reporters, police officers, and curiosity seekers squeezed into the hard-back chairs that lined the gallery. To the left sat the victims, their friends and relatives.

No one spoke.

"Can you state your name for the record?" the prosecutor began, directing his stare at the young man seated on the witness stand.

"Kevin McCarthy," the man answered, his speech slightly garbled. His left vocal cord and left arm remained paralyzed, and doctors had testified that he had lost 10 percent of his brain. A portion of his skull had been replaced with a titanium plate.

"Mr. McCarthy," the prosecutor continued. "Can you tell us what you remember about December 7, 1993?"

For the following twenty minutes, Kevin McCarthy would bring the roomful of spectators to tears with his recollections. Fighting a speech impediment, he recounted for the twelve people seated in the jury box how his father had finally convinced him to come to work with him at Prudential Securities in Manhattan. It was his second week on the job. He met his father, Dennis, at Pennsyl-

vania Station. The two men boarded the 5:33 for Hicksville. They sat side by side, as they usually did, in the
third car of the train.

"I remember leaving Penn Station, then hearing an in-
distinguishable sound, and hearing people talking next to
me about my hand sliding along the bar in front of my
seat," Kevin McCarthy remained composed but stared
straight ahead.

Rays of sunlight peeked through the blinds of the courtroom's towering windows, creating shadows on the wood
table where the defendant sat impassively. In a few
minutes it would be his turn to cross-examine the witness.

"When was the first time you found out about the death
of your father?" the diminutive district attorney prodded,
his short, thick fingers pressed tightly against the wood
podium.

A dead silence fell over the room. Reporters held their
pens and looked up.

Through eyes filled with tears the young man scanned
the rear of the courtroom for his mother, who sat in the
second row totally focused on her son's recollections.
Then he began: "In the hospital when I realized he wasn't
coming to see me."

Kevin struggled as he continued to recount his story,
telling how it wasn't until Christmastime, twenty days
later, that he realized that both he and his father, Dennis,
had been shot in the head as they sat reading the evening
paper.

Dennis McCarthy died slumped over in his son's lap.

It was a day I would never forget . . .

I had been working around the clock for the metro desk
of the *New York Times*, assisting the three full-timers who
staffed the Long Island bureau. A lot was happening on
my beat. Almost every morning, I found myself fighting

for a good spot at the press conferences held on the front steps of police headquarters in Mineola, a bustling residential town that was slowly becoming the hub of Nassau County.

The official-looking brick and glass building was located on Franklin Avenue, just around the corner from the county court complex on Old Country Road and the dozens of newly constructed office buildings and fast-food restaurants that were springing up along the main boulevards.

Since I was one of the shortest reporters working the beat, I was often pushed out of earshot by the television cameramen and the arrogant network news reporters. In spite of my handicap, I always managed to get the inside story.

I liked to think it was because of my careful note taking and slick interviewing tactics, but one police officer confessed that it had more to do with the fact that I looked like a five-foot-tall version of Meg Ryan, with the body of Jayne Mansfield. There was a downside to being short, blond and buxom. No one ever took me seriously. That is, of course, until they saw *The New York Times* press pass hanging from my neck.

But on this day I would forego the press conferences and drive to neighboring Suffolk County to follow up on a story for Metro. Over the weekend, two high school seniors had carried out a suicide pact. The girls had agreed to swallow several hits of acid, wash them down with some booze, and then lay together on the tracks of the Long Island Railroad as an eastbound train plowed in their direction. I was the reporter assigned to ring the doorbells of family members—a job I loathed.

No one was home at the first house. Three women

dressed in traditional silk saris answered the door at the second residence. One was Mili Subudhi's mother. The petite brunette thanked me for stopping by and apologized for not being able to discuss her deceased daughter with me. It was Indian custom, she murmured in a low voice, that prevented her from talking until five days had passed.

By then, I knew, the story would no longer be newsworthy.

I apologized for the intrusion and backed away, retreating to the warmth of my car. Exhausted, I began the forty-five-minute ride back to the cottage I rented with my pug dogs on a sprawling estate on Long Island's Gold Coast. The two-bedroom chalet had been the servants' quarters for the help that once worked on the neatly manicured property. These days, the home was used as a source of income for the mansion's owner—a way to pay for the tremendous cost of upkeep.

I knew I had to bang out a "memo" (a short summary of what I had learned through my reporting) about the suicides to Jon Rabinovitz, the L.I. reporter who would be writing the story for the Sunday edition, but I was tired and decided to pour myself a glass of Pinot Grigio and sprawl out on the couch to catch the tail end of the evening news.

Suddenly the phone rang. It was Jack, my editor, directing me to drop the suicide story and go immediately to the Garden City train station. There had been a mass shooting in one of the commuter cars.

"What about the memo?" I quizzed. I really didn't want to go back out in the sub-freezing weather, but as I listened to Jack detailing the incident, I couldn't help but be intrigued. My bones ached from the dampness and from the hours I had already spent behind the wheel negotiating the curvy roads of the hilly North Shore. But breaking news excited me, and I found it impossible to say no to a big story.

"Forget it," he answered in a firm, deep voice. "This story is for tonight. You'll phone the desk as soon as you get on the scene!"

Grudgingly, I pulled on my coat, grabbed a scarf, and climbed back into my car. The temperature outside had plummeted to fifteen degrees, and the black ice that blanketed the roads made for dangerous driving conditions. And a constant state of frostbite for on-the-spot reporters like me.

As I raced along the windy roadways on my way to Garden City, I realized I had no idea where the train station was and pulled over to consult my Hagstrom, which was ripped in spots and brown with coffee stains.

Great, I shouted aloud as I reviewed the map; there are two train stations. Embarrassed that I didn't know where I was supposed to report, I scoured the streets, looking for police activity. Following the map's directions, I arrived at the first train station. Nothing.

Either I was at the wrong location or whatever was happening had already occurred. It wouldn't be the first time I would be last on the scene. Although the *Times* had a reputation of excellence in Manhattan, on Long Island we were notorious for showing up a day late to even the biggest of crimes.

And then there was my own problem with tardiness. While most arraignments, press conferences and "perp walks" (when the police parade the accused perpetrator before the media on his or her way to the arraignment court) take place before 9:00 A.M., my internal clock is programmed to rise no earlier than 10:15 A.M.

Hail droplets pounded my windshield as I dialed the Public Information Office of the police department from my newly purchased car phone. I installed the cellular service after spending several hours trying to flag somebody down to pull my car out of the three feet of mud I had gotten stuck in at the last crime scene.

"Public Information," a grumpy voice shouted into the receiver.

"This is Lisa Pulitzer from the *New York Times*," I loved saying that. "Can you tell me where the crime scene in Garden City is?"

"Yeah, Merrillon Avenue," the officer barked.

"I'm in Mineola, about a block from police headquarters. How do I get there?" I begged.

"Look it up in a Hagstrom," he hung up.

So much for the clout of *The New York Times*. The mention of the prestigious paper obviously pulled no weight with the police. What a creep, I thought, as I continued to drive the desolate roadways, unaware that the miserable officer was the only one on duty that night and was being bombarded with calls from television stations as far away as Japan.

But he was my last hope.

Although I had used the Hagstrom before and could find the page and even the grid of the place I was supposed to be going to, I could never figure out how it related to my present location.

The car's defroster blew hot air onto the fogged windshield as I motored along on the deserted roads of Mineola, unaware that Garden City and Merillon Avenue where just around the corner. Multicolored Christmas lights flashed from the towering pine trees and from the rooftops of the mansions that lined the streets of the wealthy village. On the lawns were expensive and elaborate holiday decorations: white angels, red-nosed reindeers, even a flashing Santa Claus leading a horse-drawn sleigh.

Christmas was just three weeks away—and so was my deadline for the true-crime book about Long Island serial killer Joel Rifkin I was writing with fellow journalist Joan Swirsky. I had been the *New York Times* reporter to break the story of the landscaper who had supposedly strangled seventeen prostitutes, some of them right at his mother's dining room table. Joan and I had already spent hours in dark alleyways interviewing secret sources about the murderer. Pretrial hearings in the case were under way at the county courthouse. But much of the testimony being given by state police did not coincide with what we had uncovered. I was looking forward to hearing what Joel Rifkin would have to say when he took the stand the following day on his own behalf.

Speeding along in the darkness, I listened to radio reports detailing the Long Island Railroad massacre. Streets began to look familiar to me, and after passing police headquarters for the third time, I realized I was driving in circles. I felt tired and wished I was home in my living room slurping down a bowl of spicy Thai soup. In the distance, I could make out the whirling red and white lights of the police cars that were sealing off the streets to the Merrillon Avenue train station. Great, where am I going to park?

As I neared the scene, I could see emergency personnel setting up giant trucks with portable floodlights and hordes of people running in all directions. I watched in horror as rescue workers and firefighters, bundled in ankle-length rubber rain gear, pulled bodies from the silver commuter train that had stopped along the platform.

Holy shit, I thought, as I abandoned my car in front of an enormous English Tudor. What the hell happened here? Clutching my pen and paper, I moved in closer, trying to listen to the whispers of nearby reporters talking to their editors on portable cell phones. Scanning the chaos, I looked for an official to interview.

Police brass were standing behind the yellow and black crime scene tape that cordoned off much of the station and the neighboring blocks. The night was silent, but the glaring lights made it seem loud. Emergency medical technicians sprinted by, transporting injured passengers on stretchers to awaiting ambulances. The streets were filled with people crying out the names of family members.

I quickly joined the crush of reporters encircling Captain Palmer Tagle, the Nassau County police spokesman in charge of disseminating information to the media. His thin face looked weary; his reddish-brown hair was tousled by the gusty winds that were casting a chill into the night air.

"For reasons still unknown," the captain told us, "an unidentified gunman emptied at least two clips from a 9mm Ruger into commuters on the 5:33. At least five people are known to be dead." My pen was frozen. Pressing hard on my notepad, I tried to get it to write, scratching the pages with the worthless ballpoint. The noise must have been annoying one of the other reporters because a spare came flying at me from an unknown direction.

Captain Tagle could provide us with no other information. All we knew was that dozens of passengers had been shot by a mad gunman while they sat reading their evening newspapers in the train's third car.

All service from Pennsylvania Station had been suspended on the Hicksville line, leaving thousands of commuters stranded in Manhattan—a situation that added to the bedlam. The LIRR was the only means of mass transportation for the hundreds of thousands who commuted to the city daily. And while riders often found themselves standing for most of the rush-hour ride, most agreed that it was better than the alternative of sitting in bumper-to-bumper traffic on the Long Island Expressway—the world's biggest parking lot.

With train service now halted, the wives and husbands who didn't see their loved ones walk through the door at the regular time immediately assumed the worst and flocked to Merrillon Avenue in search of their spouses.

As television reporters went live from the scene—using the frantic rescue effort as a backdrop—I stared blankly at the motionless train. It was ironic that all the lawyers, secretaries and businesspeople who had boarded the railway in Manhattan had probably breathed a sigh of relief knowing—at least subconsciously—that they had made it out of the crime-ridden concrete city and were on their way back to the safety of the suburbs.

Overwhelmed by the pandemonium, I hurried back to my car to phone the night editor. The sidewalk was slippery, and my fingers were frozen inside my gloves. As I ran past the police barricades, I felt as if I was in a dream. In the distance, I could make out the silhouette of my colleague, Peter Marks. Peter had been a staff reporter for *Newsday* before winning a spot on the Long Island desk of the *Times*. His well-written articles often appeared on page A-1 and were the envy of reporters from both newspapers. In a frenzy I shouted to him, but he could not stop to chat. Instead, he waved, smiled, and then dashed off after a group of residents.

As I flew past Captain Tagle, who was still surrounded by a pack of television reporters, something made me stop. "Palmer," I shouted. "Any idea who the gunman is?"

I felt someone grabbing my arm. It was a police officer

I knew from the beat. "They say he's a black man from Brooklyn," he whispered. "He boarded the train in Jamaica. You didn't hear it from me." Getting information from secret sources was always a problem. For one, the *Times* didn't like to print anything that couldn't be attributed to someone. But more important, there was always a fine line between what someone was telling you for publication without attribution and what was meant to be heard and not printed. It was sometimes difficult to differentiate between the two.

Dialing the desk, I turned up the car's heater and collected my thoughts—and my notes, which were scrawled over every inch of my wire-bound notepad. Should I tell the desk the hot tip I just got?

"Lisa, can you hold on a second?" one of the editors queried. The biggest mistake I ever made was giving *The New York Times* my car-phone number. The editors had this annoying habit of ringing up my bill by calling me every few minutes with outlandish questions about the story I just phoned in from the scene. Things like "You said his blazer was blue. Did you mean light blue or navy?" or "You forgot to tell us if the waves were big when they washed away that beach house on Fire Island."

This, coupled with the fact that car-phone pirates, working the Manhattan garage in which I had parked, bootlegged my cellular number to the tune of $900 on calls to drug dealers in New Jersey, prompted me to disconnect the service the following year.

"Lisa, are you still there?" a voice came back on the line. "We'll get back to you!"

I waited in the cold temperatures for the return call—which I would have to pay for at the end of the month. Yes, I would just about break even on this evening's assignment.

The night editor told me that he had sent Peter to police headquarters, where the gunman—and dozens of commuters—would be questioned by detectives. I was to cover Town Hall, the red-brick building where officials would soon release the names of those passengers who had been killed or taken to area hospitals for treatment.

The large clock on the wall of the expansive lobby read 8:15 P.M.

County police in their official blue uniforms milled about as the room began to flood with people desperate to find their loved ones. Everywhere I looked there was someone crying, pleading with police to help them.

My toes tingled inside my furry boots as they thawed from the icy cold conditions outside. People ran past me. They were searching for someone who could direct them.

Folding chairs had been set up around the colonial-style waiting room. Christmas wreaths and strands of garland decorated the cream-colored walls, and encircled the wood banister that led to the building's loft-style second floor. In the far left corner, someone had arranged a table with hot coffee and doughnuts. Behind it was the conference area where police brass were now meeting to determine their course of action.

Glancing around the large lobby at the clusters of people, many still bundled in heavy winter coats, scarves and hats, I tried to pick out the ones who would be least offended at being interviewed. Two middle-aged women stood near the double entrance doors sobbing aloud as a steady stream of people raced frantically past them. A mother and her teenage daughter sat on a sofa holding hands. Neither one spoke they just waited. There was a man in a pinstripe suit looking for his wife, a woman in a wheelchair waiting for her mother, and a short, balding man in a blue ski coat pacing the gray marble floor.

I would never forget him.

Smelling the freshly brewed coffee, I made my way to the rear of the room to pour myself a cup. For a moment I stood frozen, massaging the hot Styrofoam between my fingers. The heat was a welcome relief from the hours of biting cold I had endured at the chaotic crime scene.

Just as I mustered up the courage to approach the two women standing together by the entranceway, a group of officers mounted the staircase. Looking down over the banister at the crush of desperate faces, one of them stepped forward and reeled off instructions.

"We ask that everybody give their name and the name of the person they are looking for to the desk clerk seated at the counter in the back room," the well-dressed detective directed, pointing his long arm toward the back door of the waiting area. "Then, in a few minutes we will begin releasing the names of the victims and the hospitals they have been taken to."

An hour passed. Still no word.

It was difficult sitting in that room with all those people. I fought back tears as I eavesdropped on their conversations, listening as they asked God to help them find their family members. Their stories were heart wrenching, their fears tremendous.

Finally, a group of plainclothes policemen emerged from a rear office. In paramilitary fashion, they climbed the steps, clinging to the festively decorated banister for support. "Can I have your attention, please," one of them shouted over the sobs and cries that had filled the waiting area for the last ninety minutes. "To make this process easier, we will call only the names of those people who have an injured party."

As the detective in the tan suit unraveled a sheet of paper he held in his hand, an eerie silence fell over the room. The plan made no sense. These people wanted information about the whereabouts of their loved ones; good news, like "Your husband is safe and waiting for you at home." Now, instead of wishing that their names be called, they would have to hope they were not.

The officer shouted only one name into the crowd.

Everyone in the room stood frozen and glanced around to see who would step forward. My heart was pounding so fast that I felt as though I would faint. I stared as four police officers grabbed the arm of the balding man in the blue ski coat and escorted him out the back doorway. Was it his wife? His daughter?

My wristwatch read 10:20 P.M. I was twenty minutes past deadline for the third edition. Quickly I ran to my car and dialed the desk. The night reporter manning the phones typed as I read from the notes I had scribbled.

"Can you give me some color?" the desk reporter wanted me to describe the scene.

"Fucking nightmare! Does that sum it up?" I proceeded to tell him of the long, drawn-out wait, of the people desperate for word, and of the middle-aged man in the blue ski coat.

"Are you sure that was his name?" he quizzed. "We have a list of the six people who were killed, and I don't see anyone with that last name."

"Yes, that's what I heard," I shot back, annoyed that once again they were questioning me.

It was 2:00 A.M. when I finally pulled into my snow-covered driveway. I had worked for sixteen hours straight and should have been exhausted. But when I closed my eyes to sleep, visions of bright lights and screaming people—and the guy in the blue ski coat—haunted my mind.

Thank God I didn't have to meet Joan at the courthouse until 11:00 A.M. The sight of my fifty-something writing partner standing outside the building puffing on a cigarette—strands of her brown hair neatly secured on the crown of her head by a rhinestone-studded clip—always made me laugh. Each day she would show up for court decked out in high heels and a bright-colored miniskirt. Her long, shapely legs attracted stares from the court buffs who attended the trial. She loved to hang around and mingle with the other reporters, but hated when I was late—which was just about every day. It was hard to be on time with my crazy schedule.

Brinnnnnngggg . . . Brinnnnggg . . . I jumped up. A ray of sun peeked through the lace curtains of my bedroom window as I fumbled around for the telephone.

"Hello," I answered, clearing my throat.

"Lisa, it's Jack at the Metro desk," his voice sounded uneasy. "I know you worked late last night, but there's been an accident. Jonathan was hit by a bus this morning on his way to the arraignment. You've got to get to Mineola ASAP. Peter is on his way, but he's in Brooklyn. Can you make it?"

"What time is it? Is Jon okay?" I asked, trying to orient myself.

"Yes, his car was totaled, but he's not hurt . . . and it's eight forty-five," Jack answered.

"Eight forty-five!" I started. "What time is the arraignment?"

"It's called for nine thirty."

"I'm leaving now," I hung up.

Parking at the courthouse was impossible. Satellite news trucks lined the sidewalk. Television cameramen from *Hard Copy,* CNN and all the major networks

crowded the cement steps leading to the two-story courthouse. A metal detector had been set up in the lobby, and
court officers were demanding that journalists display
their press credentials on the outside of their coats and
surrender their pocketbooks and briefcases to be searched.
Word was spreading that authorities were fearful that an
angry relative of one of the victims would make an attempt on the alleged gunman's life.

The room on the first floor where Joel Rifkin was
scheduled to testify was dark. Journalists were racing to
the small courtroom in the basement. I quickly descended
the stairwell but was immediately halted by the swarm of
reporters and television cameramen that clogged the cav-
ernous hallway. Not even for Joey Buttafuoco was the
crowd this thick.

Pressing my body along the far wall, I inched my way
around the throng of newspeople who were waving microphones and shouting questions at the prosecutor they
had entrapped. A cadre of court officers in their official
white shirts blocked the doorway to the tiny arraignment
room. There was not an empty chair in the place. Great,
I thought, if I don't find a seat, I'll probably get thrown
out of here.

As I scanned the rows, I noticed Pat Milton from the
Associated Press and Kieran Crowley from the *New York
Post* seated together exchanging notes. I waved to them,
hoping they would offer to let me squeeze in next to them.

"Lisa," Kieran yelled from behind dark sunglasses,
"take that seat in the front row." He was the epitome of
a crime reporter in his long, black trench coat, and black-
framed shades, which he wore even when he was indoors.

There were two seats. And they looked to be reserved.
My heart was pounding from the anxiety of being the only
reporter from the *Times* at such a big news event. I didn't

want to blow it. And I didn't want to sit right in the front row. Reluctantly, I made my way toward the empty chair, taking several deep breaths to relax my nerves.

"Is this seat taken?" I questioned the middle-aged woman in the third chair.

"Just sit down, Pulitzer!" I heard Kieran shout to me.

Opening my notebook to a blank page, I pulled on my gold-framed eyeglasses and waited. Everything looked blurry, and I realized that there was a spot of something horrible caked on my left lens. Scrounging around in the bottom of my purse for a tissue, I tried not to make too much noise.

"All rise," the bailiff shouted as the gray-haired judge entered the chamber and took his seat at the bench. Lawyers in conservative blue suits stood before him exchanging words. One of them sat down in the empty chair next to me.

All of a sudden, I heard banging and clanking coming from the back of the room. I looked up—closing my left eye to avoid the dirty spot on my lens—in time to see the six court officers already stationed around the courtroom reach for their guns. All eyes were on the battalion of people now entering from the rear.

A cortege of officers formed an impenetrable border around a diminutive black man, hardly the demonic brute I had created in my mind. He was shackled and chained. On the outside of his orange jail suit was a bulletproof vest. On his feet, he wore brown leather sandals with no socks.

The sight of the impish-looking suspect with the egg-shaped head and bulging eyes spurred a flurry of whispers in the packed courtroom. This was the mad gunman who had cold calculatingly opened fire on innocent commuters?

Several of the officers appeared nervous as they clutched the thick silver chains that hung from the man's vest and steered him toward the judge's bench. Then, the entourage came to a halt directly next to me. The lawyer to my left stood up, gripping the wooden railing that separated the spectators from the magistrate.

"Your honor," he began . . .

The defendant remained impassive as the bailiff read the charges: six counts of second-degree murder, one count of criminal possession of a weapon. There were more, but they sounded technical and emotionless compared to the real-life carnage this man had inflicted.

The son of a prominent businessman, Colin Ferguson, a native of Jamaica, enjoyed an elite private school education on the Caribbean island. He later immigrated to the United States, where he married and enrolled in college to become a lawyer.

But, things did not run smoothly for the often aggrieved young man. His marriage ended in divorce, efforts to obtain a college degree proved fruitless and a series of jobs terminated with accusations of racism.

In the duffel bag he was carrying the night of the shooting, police found handwritten notes telling of his hatred of whites, Asians, "Uncle Tom" blacks, Adelphi University and Governor Mario Cuomo. They also explained why the gunman had chosen Nassau County for his murderous spree. "NYC was spared because of my respect for Mayor David Dinkins and Comm. Raymond Kelley who officially are still in office," was scrawled on one sheet of paper. "Nassau County is the venue," was scratched on another.

Dozens of eyewitnesses had ID'ed him to police as the one who had boarded the train in Jamaica, Queens. The one who was carrying a duffel bag filled with a 9mm semiautomatic pistol and dozens of Full Metal Jacket and Black Talon armor piercing bullets.

They told detectives the gunman had remained seated as the train unloaded passengers in New Hyde Park. But, as the train began heading toward Merillon Avenue, he stood up and opened fire, first on the man immediately to his right, blasting five rounds into his chest, arm and face.

Over the hysterical screams of passengers, he strode deliberately down the center aisle of the car, swinging his pistol from left to right, as he emptied his clip into open-eyed commuters.

Instinctually, riders sprang from their seats and ran for cover, bottlenecked at the front of the car. Desperate, they attempted to climb over the cowering passengers who lay screaming, their faces pressed against the cold steel floor. They were trying to get to the door that would allow them to move into the next car. But it was blocked by people crouching on the ground pretending to be dead.

For a moment, there was silence as the gunman paused at the first set of doors and reloaded his weapon. Afraid even to breathe, riders peeked through squinted eyes as passengers fell to the floor in a pool of blood. The commuter car had become a prison cell for the nearly one hundred passengers trapped inside.

With nowhere to run, three riders mustered up the courage to take on the crazed shooter as he reloaded for a second time and aimed his gun in their direction. "Let's get him," one of them shouted as the trio raced after the assailant—shielded only by a briefcase—and pinned him to a seat, taking his weapon and holding him until police arrived with handcuffs.

"Don't hurt me," the gunman pleaded. He had killed four people and wounded at least twenty others. Two more would die before the week's end.

In a heavy, Jamaican accent, the defendant, thirty-five-year-old Colin Ferguson, now stood before the court and pleaded "not guilty."

Oooohs and ahhhs erupted from the spectator gallery as a convoy of officers whisked the suspect from the courtroom. They had been instructed to "get Ferguson out of there as fast as possible."

The school of journalists went out of control when the battalion disappeared behind the wood-and-glass door that led to the awaiting sheriff's van. Darting down the bare corridor, they fought, tripping over each other as they tried to grab a quote from the county prosecutor and the court-appointed defense attorney.

Somehow I became sandwiched between several of the radio reporters and had no choice but to run along as the mob enveloped the men and fired questions at them, all at the same time. It was hard to breathe. People were pressed against me so tightly that I felt as if my chest would cave in. In one last attempt, I slid underneath them to get some air.

Upstairs, crews were waiting around to catch the testimony of Joel Rifkin. I dialed Jack from the lone pay phone that hung on the wall.

"It's over," I told him.

"Good, you made it," Jack said. He directed me to "dump" my notes to Jon Rabinovitz, who had found alternate transportation to the Garden City bureau.

"Do you want me to cover Rifkin?" I asked.

"John McQuiston's in there. Go see if he needs relief," my editor instructed.

The serial killer would never take the stand that day—

270 • CRIME ON DEADLINE

or any other day. At the last minute, his defense attorney would change the legal strategy. And by the end of the month, Joel would change his defense attorney.

As for Colin Ferguson, he would become his own lawyer.

"Your honor, I want to go pro-se," Ferguson disclosed to the packed courtroom that he wanted to invoke his legal right to act as his own attorney. The defendant was desperate to shake the two defense lawyers he had retained; he wanted to represent himself. But William Kunstler, the crusading liberal civil rights attorney, and his partner, Ronald Kuby, refused to excuse themselves from the case on the ground that their client was not legally competent to stand trial, and therefore not competent to make a decision on his own behalf.

"This case will be a disaster if he is permitted to represent himself, a travesty of justice," Kuby lectured the reporters that surrounded him in the lobby.

He was right.

Day after day I sat in the front row, next to *Times* reporter John McQuiston and directly behind the defendant. John was the staff reporter assigned to cover the trial, and I was the stringer assigned to work it with him. John and I had worked out an arrangement. He would cover the morning sessions, leaving the courthouse at lunch to write the story for the next day's paper. I would take over in the afternoons, phoning in all the testimony and events that occurred in and out of the courtroom. But it was sometimes unnerving watching the defendant interrogate the very people he had victimized just one year before.

"Sir," Ferguson would question the witness. "Did you see the suspect get on the train?"

"Yeah, I saw *you* get on the train," the witness would answer, pointing his finger at the man who was questioning him.

"Judge," Ferguson would get annoyed. "Direct him to answer the question."

"I am answering it," the witness would interrupt. "*You* were the guy with the gun."

Some of the victims would get violent, threatening to leap from the witness stand and "kick the ass" of Ferguson. Others would bring themselves to tears as they recounted the horrific details.

"Did you see the suspect shoot you?" Ferguson droned in his Caribbean drawl.

"I saw *you* shoot me." The witness would become infuriated.

Throughout the trial, Joyce Gorycki and her 11-year-old daughter, Karyn, sat stoically in the third row, listening as witness after witness recounted the details of James Gorycki's death. He too, was shot at close range by the out-of-control gunman. I had attended the funeral services of the beloved husband and father and was devastated each time I looked over at the mother and daughter clutching each other's hands.

The trial took six weeks. The jury deliberated for ten hours. The twelve men and women found Colin Ferguson guilty as charged.

Now it was Judge Donald Belfi's turn to administer justice. The portly magistrate had already tolerated more than his share, biting his lip when the defendant demanded more time in the law library, a private telephone in his jail cell and extensions on his case.

He had grimaced as the guilty gunman cross-examined his victims and accused them of racism and said nothing when Ferguson tried to pin the six murders on the courageous man who had wrestled him to the ground, calling the whole thing a conspiracy against an innocent man.

Now the judge could have his moment—telling Ferguson of his outrage at his lack of remorse for his crimes before sentencing the mass murderer to the maximum— life in prison with no possibility of parole.

"In my twenty-one years as a judge, I have never presided over a trial with a more selfish and self-centered defendant than you. The vicious crimes you committed on December 7, 1993, were the acts of a coward," Judge Belfi lectured the convicted killer.

Reporters pushed and shoved to grab a good spot in front of the podium where the victims and their families would make their final statements.

Carolyn McCarthy went first. Stepping up to the microphone, the slight, sallow woman thanked members of the media for their support and sensitivity "during the most difficult time of my life." McCarthy had buried her husband and endured a year of doctors visits and extensive rehabilitation for her only son. In the years to follow, the determined mother would lead a battle for gun control, bringing a multi-million dollar lawsuit against the makers of the Black Talon bullet. She would also add her name to the ballot as an Independent contender for a seat in congress. Beside McCarthy stood a man with a familiar face. He was not very tall and appeared to be in his mid to late forties, with a receding hairline and a crooked smile. I scanned my memory trying to recall where I had seen him before, studying him as he stepped forward to take the mike.

It was him, I silently exclaimed, the man in the blue ski coat.

My eyes welled with tears as I listened to him memorialize his brother-in-law, Dennis McCarthy, one of six people to die at the hands of Colin Ferguson. Instantly, my thoughts returned to the lobby of Town Hall—I could see the distraught man whose name had been called by county detectives that snowy, December evening. Now, on the last day of the trial, he stood before me, holding the hand of his sister-in-law.

With the verdict in and the sentence handed down, this case was finally over.

Outside, reporters went live for the evening news. Inside, news technicians packed up their belongings. The scene was reminiscent of the final day on a movie set, with crews dismantling lights, tripods, television monitors and thousands of feet of AV cable. John and I walked side by side in silence, the heels of our shoes clicking on the marble floor.

As we descended the steps of the building, I realized that Colin Ferguson was not the only one who had been sentenced that day. His victims would forever be imprisoned by the haunting events of December 7, 1993. For some it would be a lifetime of painful rehabilitation for their maiming injuries. For others it would be horrific nightmares and sleepless nights recalling the terror of that thirty-minute train ride.

But the sentence would be harshest for those who lost a loved one to the random bullets fired by Colin Ferguson. For them it would be a lifetime of longing to hold the hand of a husband, sit across the table from a daughter, kiss the cheek of a son.

For us, it was over. For them, it never will be.

The next morning I sat at my kitchen table, sipping hot coffee and reading the morning paper. Suddenly, the phone rang.

It was Jack . . .

My first newspaper job was with the Long Island section of *The New York Times,* in July of 1991. One year later, I began the most exciting assignment of my life—working as a correspondent for the paper's Metro desk, covering the crimes of the "idyllic" suburbs. One of the first cases I followed resulted in a book contract. Writing it was no easy task. I spent months holed up in the Great Neck office of fellow journalist Joan Swirsky. Together we laughed, cried and co-authored *Crossing the Line: The True Story of Long Island Serial Killer Joel Rifkin,* released in October of 1994 by Berkley Books.